John J. Stretch
Ellen M. Burkemper
William J. Hutchison
Jan Wilson
Editors

Practicing Social Justice

Practicing Social Justice has been co-published simultaneously as *Social Thought*, Volume 22, Numbers 2/3 2003.

Pre-publication
REVIEWS,
COMMENTARIES,
EVALUATIONS . . .

"**I** HIGHLY RECOMMEND THIS IMPORTANT EDITED WORK to practitioners, academics, and students majoring in the human services and related fields. . . . Fills an important void in the area of social justice and related issues . . . . Offers a detailed analysis of numerous social justice issues."

John T. Pardeck, PhD, LCSW
Editor, Journal of Social Work in Disability and Rehabilitation

More pre-publication
REVIEWS, COMMENTARIES, EVALUATIONS . . .

"An excellent overview of the issues surrounding social justice and tying social work theory into real-world applications. . . . Provides distinct examples of programs that have worked. . . . RECOMMENDED for those just entering into social work as an overview of the many facets of social justice, and to those who have been in the field for a number of years who may be experiencing the frustration of working diligently without seeing much in results, as it demonstrates the potential of connecting justice with service."

Dianna P. Moore, CEcD
Executive Director
Missouri Association
for Social Welfare

"AN ESSENTIAL CONTRIBUTION to our social work knowledge base. . . . The discussions of social and economic justice clarify distinctions, present competing definitions, and describe alternative models and exemplars of practice."

Charles D. Cowger, PhD
Professor and Director
School of Social Work
University of Missouri–Columbia

More pre-publication
REVIEWS, COMMENTARIES, EVALUATIONS . . .

"**A**lthough social justice is a core commitment of social work, there is a continuing dearth of educational materials that help gtraduate and undergraduate sutdents comprehend the myriad aspects of this complex concept. This book discusses the different theories of social justice, exposes the forms, extent and sources of social injustice in our daily lives, and shows the numerous ways in which social work practice can promote social justice, especially for the most deprived and vulnerable of our fellow citizens."

Shanti Khinduka, PhD
*President, Inter-University
Consortium for International
Social Development (IUCISD)
Dean and George Warren Brown
Distinguished University Professsor
George Warren Brown
School of Social Work
Washington University in St. Louis*

The Haworth Press, Inc.

Practicing Social Justice

Practicing Social Justice has been co-published simultaneously as *Social Thought*, Volume 22, Numbers 2/3 2003.

The *Social Thought* Monographic "Separates"

Below is a list of "separates," which in serials librarianship means a special issue simultaneously published as a special journal issue or double-issue *and* as a "separate" hardbound monograph. (This is a format which we also call a "DocuSerial.")

"Separates" are published because specialized libraries or professionals may wish to purchase a specific thematic issue by itself in a format which can be separately cataloged and shelved, as opposed to purchasing the journal on an on-going basis. Faculty members may also more easily consider a "separate" for classroom adoption.

"Separates" are carefully classified separately with the major book jobbers so that the journal tie-in can be noted on new book order slips to avoid duplicate purchasing.

You may wish to visit Haworth's website at . . .

http://www.HaworthPress.com

. . . to search our online catalog for complete tables of contents of these separates and related publications.

You may also call 1-800-HAWORTH (outside US/Canada: 607-722-5857), or Fax 1-800-895-0582 (outside US/Canada: 607-771-0012), or e-mail at:

docdelivery@haworthpress.com

Practicing Social Justice, edited by John J. Stretch, PhD, MBA, ACSW, LCSW, Ellen M. Burkemper, PhD, LCSW, MFT, William J. Hutchison, PhD, and Jan Wilson, ACSW, LCSW (Vol. 22, No. 2/3, 2003). *"I highly recommend this important edited work to practitioners, academics, and students working in the human services and related fields. . . . Fills an important void in the area of social justice and related issues. . . . Offers a detailed analysis of numerous social justice issues." (John T. Pardeck, PhD, LCSW, Editor,* Journal of Social Work in Disability and Rehabilitation*)*

Issues in Global Aging, edited by Frederick L. Ahearn, Jr., DSW (Vol. 20, No. 3/4, 2001). *"Fine scholarship . . . very useful. Ahearn has assembled a fine cohort of experts on aging who address various issues. The first section approaches them from the western industrial model perspective, but also provides an example of an Islamic traditional approach. The second section deals less with formal religiosity than with issues of spiritual transcendence in older persons. A balanced portrait of the aged as people rather than statistics." (Charles Guzzetta, EdD, Professor, Hunter College, City University of New York)*

Transpersonal Perspectives on Spirituality in Social Work, edited by Edward R. Canda, PhD, and Elizabeth D. Smith, DSW (Vol. 20, No. ½, 2001). *"Comprehensive . . . provides theoretical and practice-oriented studies on the emerging field of transpersonal social work. The writing is both scholarly and relevant to practice. Of interest to scholars, practitioners, and students alike." (John R. Graham, PhD, RSW, Associate Professor, Faculty of Social Work, University of Calgary, Alberta, Canada)*

Raising Our Children Out of Poverty, edited by John J. Stretch, PhD, Maria Bartlett, PhD, William J. Hutchison, PhD, Susan A. Taylor, PhD, and Jan Wilson, MSW (Vol. 19, No. 2, 1999). *This book shows what can be done at the national and local community levels to raise children out of poverty by strengthening families, communities, and social services.*

Postmodernism, Religion and the Future of Social Work, edited by Roland G. Meinert, PhD, John T. Pardeck, PhD, and John W. Murphy, PhD (Vol. 18, No. 3, 1998). *"Critically important for social work as it attempts to effectively respond to its increasingly complex roles and demands. . . . A book worth owning and studying." (John M. Herrick, PhD, Acting Director, School of Social Work, Michigan State University, East Lansing, Michigan)*

Spirituality in Social Work: New Directions, edited by Edward R. Canda, PhD (Vol. 18, No. 2, 1998). *"Provides interesting insights and references for those who seek to develop curricula responsive to the spiritual challenges confronting our profession and the populations we serve." (Au-Deane S. Cowley, PhD, Associate Dean, Graduate School of Social Work, University of Utah, Salt Lake City)*

Practicing Social Justice

John J. Stretch
Ellen M. Burkemper
William J. Hutchison
Jan Wilson
Editors

Practicing Social Justice has been co-published simultaneously as *Social Thought*, Volume 22, Numbers 2/3 2003.

The Haworth Press, Inc.
and The Haworth Pastoral Press,
an Imprint of The Haworth Press, Inc.
New York · London · Oxford

Practicing Social Justice has been co-published simultaneously as
Social Thought™, Volume 22, Numbers 2/3 2003.

© 2003 by The Haworth Press, All rights reserved. No part of this work may be reproduced or utilized
in any form or by any means, electronic or mechanical, including photocopying, microfilm and record-
ing, or by any information storage and retrieval system, without permission in writing from the publisher. Printed in the United States of America.

The development, preparation, and publication of this work has been undertaken with great care. However, the publisher, employees, editors, and agents of The Haworth Press and all imprints of The
Haworth Press, Inc., including The Haworth Medical Press® and Pharmaceutical Products Press®, are
not responsible for any errors contained herein or for consequences that may ensue from use of materials or information contained in this work. Opinions expressed by the author(s) are not necessarily those
of The Haworth Press, Inc.

Cover design by Lora Wiggins

Library of Congress Cataloging-in-Publication Data

Practicing social justice / John J. Stretch . . . [et al.], editors.
     p. cm.
     "Co-published simultaneously as Social thought, volume 22, numbers 2/3 2003."
     Includes bibliographical references and index.
     ISBN 0-7890-2106-4 (hard cover : alk. paper) – ISBN 0-7890-2107-2 (soft cover : alk. paper)
     1. Social work with people with social disabilities. 2. Social justice. I. Stretch, John J.
HV41.P655 2003   2003009567
303.3'72–dc21

Indexing, Abstracting & Website/Internet Coverage

This section provides you with a list of major indexing & abstracting services. That is to say, each service began covering this periodical during the year noted in the right column. Most Websites which are listed below have indicated that they will either post, disseminate, compile, archive, cite or alert their own Website users with research-based content from this work. (This list is as current as the copyright date of this publication.)

Abstracting, Website/Indexing Coverage.........Year When Coverage Began

- *Applied Social Sciences Index & Abstracts (ASSIA)*
  (Online: ASSI via Data-Star) (CDRom: ASSIA Plus)
  <www.csa.com>.......................................1998

- *caredata CD: The social and community care database*
  <www.scie.org.uk> 1995

- *Catholic Periodical & Literature Index (CPLI), The*.............2001

- *CINAHL (Cumulative Index to Nursing & Allied Health*
  Literature), in print, EBSCO, and SilverPlatter,
  Data-Star, and PaperChase <www.cinahl.com> 2000

- *CNPIEC Reference Guide: Chinese National Directory*
  of Foreign Periodicals...................................1995

- *EAP Abstracts Plus*.......................................2000

- *Family & Society Studies Worldwide <www.nisc.com>* 2000

- *FRANCIS. INIST/CNRS <www.inist.fr>* 1999

- *Guide to Social Science and Religion in Periodical Literature* 1995

(continued)

*Special Bibliographic Notes related to special journal issues
(separates) and indexing/abstracting:*

- indexing/abstracting services in this list will also cover material in any "separate" that is co-published simultaneously with Haworth's special thematic journal issue or DocuSerial. Indexing/abstracting usually covers material at the article/chapter level.
- monographic co-editions are intended for either non-subscribers or libraries which intend to purchase a second copy for their circulating collections.
- monographic co-editions are reported to all jobbers/wholesalers/approval plans. The source journal is listed as the "series" to assist the prevention of duplicate purchasing in the same manner utilized for books-in-series.
- to facilitate user/access services all indexing/abstracting services are encouraged to utilize the co-indexing entry note indicated at the bottom of the first page of each article/chapter/contribution.
- this is intended to assist a library user of any reference tool (whether print, electronic, online, or CD-ROM) to locate the monographic version if the library has purchased this version but not a subscription to the source journal.
- individual articles/chapters in any Haworth publication are also available through the Haworth Document Delivery Service (HDDS).

Practicing Social Justice

CONTENTS

ALL HAWORTH BOOKS AND JOURNALS
ARE PRINTED ON CERTIFIED
ACID-FREE PAPER

ABOUT THE EDITORS

John J. Stretch, PhD, MBA, ACSW, LCSW, is Professor of Social Work in the School of Social Service at Saint Louis University. He is a charter member of the Academy of Certified Social Workers and a Licensed Clinical Social Worker in the state of Missouri. Dr. Stretch is a nationally recognized social activist in the field of homelessness and housing. He has published extensively in major professional journals and books.

Ellen M. Burkemper, PhD, LCSW, MFT, is Assistant Professor of Social Work in the School of Social Service at Saint Louis University. Her areas of teaching include social work practice theory, values and ethics, marriage and family therapy, and human behavior. She has 20 years of practice experience, including community mental health, private practice, and foster care. Her licenses include Clinical Social Work, Marriage and Family Therapy, and Registered Nurse. Her scholarship is in the area of ethical decision making and sibling shared care.

William J. Hutchison, PhD, is Associate Professor of Social Work in the School of Social Service at Saint Louis University. His area of teaching includes Social Welfare Policy and Spirituality, and Values and Religious Dimensions of Social Work. He serves on the Advisory Board of the Center for Social Justice Education and Research of the School of Social Service. From 1983 to 1993 he served as Dean of the School. He has published articles and book reviews in *Social Work* and *Social Thought: Journal of Religion in the Social Services.*

Jan Wilson, ACSW, LCSW, is Associate Clinical Professor and Field Education liaison in the practicum program at Saint Louis University's School of Social Service, having joined the faculty in 1996. Her 25 years of professional experience includes work as a therapist program administrator and community organizer. She has focused on services for families and children in child welfare, mental health, residential treatment, and school and community settings. Her interests also include consumer movement, inclusive programs for adults and children with developmental disabilities, health promotion for children and youth, and school social work. She serves on the Center for Social Justice Education Committee.

The Right of Justice:
Contributions
of Social Work Practice-Research

Ellen M. Burkemper
John J. Stretch

... to none deny or delay, right or justice.

–Magna Carta, 1215, clause 40

This volume addresses justice. The articles, written by social workers, examine societal structures that present challenges to justice and point to possibilities for change. Social justice has consistently been of importance in the field of social work in its historical efforts to alleviate social problems (Reid, 1977). Brieland (1981) champions justice as a basic human right.

Social justice is difficult to fully conceptualize. The definition of social justice in the *Social Work Dictionary* is an "ideal condition in which all members of a society have the same basic rights, protection, opportunities, obligations, and social benefits" (Barker, 1999, p. 451). The National Association of Social

Ellen M. Burkemper, PhD, is Assistant Professor of Social Work, School of Social Service, Saint Louis University, 3550 Lindell Boulevard, St. Louis, MO 63103 (E-mail: burkemem@slu.edu).

John J. Stretch, PhD, is Professor of Social Work, School of Social Service, Saint Louis University, 3550 Lindell Boulevard, St. Louis, MO 63103 (E-mail: stretchj@slu.edu).

[Haworth co-indexing entry note]: "The Right of Justice: Contributions of Social Work Practice-Research." Burkemper, Ellen M., and John J. Stretch. Co-published simultaneously in *Social Thought* (The Haworth Press, Inc.) Vol. 22, No. 2/3, 2003, pp. 1-6; and: *Practicing Social Justice* (ed: John J. Stretch et al.) The Haworth Press, Inc., 2003, pp. 1-6. Single or multiple copies of this article are available for a fee from The Haworth Document Delivery Service [1-800-HAWORTH, 9:00 a.m. - 5:00 p.m. (EST). E-mail address: docdelivery@haworthpress.com].

© 2003 by The Haworth Press, Inc. All rights reserved.
http://www.haworthpress.com/store/product.asp?sku=J131
10.1300/J131v22n02_01

Workers *Code of Ethics* states that a commitment for social workers to promote social justice is a fundamental mandate of the profession (National Association of Social Workers, 1996). Social justice curriculum content is required by the Council on Social Work Education (CSWE, 1994), the accrediting body for schools of social work.

What research will lead toward promoting social justice in social work practice? Research on social justice practice relies principally on the eradication of social injustice (Longres & Scanlon, 2001). This collection follows that perspective. The articles presented are specifically concerned with practice research projects that challenge the status quo of social injustice.

Fourteen articles are the result of a collaborative social justice practice model composed of faculty, students and community agencies. Founded in 1998, the Emmet and Mary Martha Doerr Center for Social Justice at the Saint Louis University School of Social Service brings together a unique combination of social work education opportunities and a commitment to the practice of social justice. The Center achieves this blend through the application of five educational principles:

1. focusing on the education of the whole person;
2. promoting open inquiry in the pursuit of truth;
3. respecting and valuing the uniqueness of each person;
4. celebrating diversity; and
5. living a commitment to social justice through the practice of social work.

John Paul II in *Redemportis Misso* (1990) calls for reconciliation, a preferential option for the poor and solidarity. Reaffirming a social justice imperative for all Jesuit institutions, the 34th General Congregation set an agenda of social justice as a moral imperative for human rights, life, the environment, and interdependence in a global world. The General Congregation highlighted the special social justice needs of the disenfranchised and the excluded–refugees, the persecuted, indigenous peoples, and the unemployed and underemployed (Institute of Jesuit Sources, 1995).

Saint Louis University, as a Jesuit institution, challenges students not just to *learn* about justice, but also *to do* justice. There is an obligation in the faith community to witness, participate, and practice social justice in the spirit of the Gospel message (O'Brien & Shannon, 1997), a witnessing of a faith that does justice. The School of Social Service fulfills this obligation by providing students the opportunity proposed by Gil (1998) for a social justice-based professional education.

In a recent policy debate on the definition and the practice implications of social justice (Pelton, 2001; Longres & Scanlon, 2001), tension is shown to exist between the social and economic rights of the individual and of the collective. This debate also brings to light the question of how we can best insure equality and equity for disadvantaged groups. Swenson (1998) recognizes social justice as an outcome for clinical social work. For Swenson, social justice is the foundation for empowerment practice and feminist practice.

This volume has articles demonstrating social justice in action. At the core of social justice are the reciprocal rights and obligations due to each human being. In his article "Whose Justice? An Examination of Nine Models of Justice" McCormick examines nine theories of justice. These theories include philosophical, sectarian, and nonsectarian orientations. His own critique, through a perspective of equalities and rights, is provocative and provides a backdrop for other contributions which follow.

The practice of justice should result in social change. Effective practice must be based on empirical evidence (Gambrill, 2001). The Center brings together social work practice, social justice principles and empirical research in the pursuit of societal change. "Practicing Social Justice: Community-Based Research, Education, and Practice" by Gallagher, Cook, Tebb and Berg-Weger details the Center for Social Justice's collaborative research and education mission. Through collaborations, faculty, students, and practitioners receive funding to carry out defined community-based social justice projects, many of which are contained in this publication. The partnered approach combines the talents of university faculty and students and the practice community through the application of the Center's five guiding educational principles.

Birkenmaier in her article, "On Becoming a Social Justice Practitioner," demonstrates the importance for students to actively incorporate social change efforts into their own practice. Practicing justice becomes real when one assists those affected by injustice. This consciousness-raising article brings home the importance of *doing* justice as social work practice.

Societal injustice is manifested in many ways. Race and poverty, historically companion problems, mirror the impact of unjust political and social systems. Hartman's article "The Race/Poverty Intersection: Will We Ever Achieve Liberty and Justice for All?" affirms that the ideal of "liberty and justice for all" cannot be realized until there is substantial recommitment to the democratic principles of a just society. The article is a condensation of an invited plenary address celebrating the 100th anniversary of the Missouri Association for Social Welfare. MASW is a citizen's movement championing social justice for all Missourians.

One approach to address racial polarization at the group dynamic level is presented in Wernet, Follman, Magueja, and Moore-Chambers' study "Building Bridges and Improving Racial Harmony: An Evaluation of the *Bridges Across Racial Polarization Program®*. Racial polarization was reduced through group interactions in a series of interracial dialogues with supportive networks.

A fundamental shift in society's obligation to economically dependent children is presented in Tyuse's "Social Justice and Welfare Reform: A Shift in Policy." The author raises critical questions on how society should justly provide for the economic well-being of our most valuable human asset–our children. Tyuse posits that the Temporary Aid for Needy Families legislation represents a major shift in public policy from child-focused entitlement to a caretaker work-focused requirement. Tyuse questions reform efforts that, as of yet, have not been rigorously investigated from the perspective of their long-term implication and impact on disadvantaged children.

Sherraden, Slosar, Chastain, and Squillace, in their article " 'Human-Sized' Economic Development: Innovations in Missouri," argue for inclusiveness, achieved by a community plan structured to bring about home ownership, macro-enterprises, and the accumulation of capital through savings. This article engages another level of conversation concerning social justice by examining innovative approaches to community economic development, especially for previously neglected poor communities. A distributive justice approach results in sustained neighborhood development. Effective strategies to insure low-income families greater access to the American promise of home ownership and self-sufficiency are developed. Through the authors' concept of "human-sized" development, challenges to community practice are posed.

Stretch and Kreuger, in "The Homeless in Missouri in the '90s: A Continuing Challenge to Social Justice," espouses that all citizens are entitled to safe, sanitary, and affordable housing. They document the rise in homelessness in the state of Missouri during the 1990s, an unprecedented period of economic growth and general prosperity. The article recognizes the plight of thousands who have been left behind. Their work builds on two decades of advocacy to inform just social policy and to support through research effective interventions, which assist individuals and families to escape the permanent status of homelessness. Homelessness in the richest country in the world remains a national disgrace. Political will, bolstered by social justice, would render homelessness entirely preventable.

Injustice is manifest in a lack of understanding by the citizenry and a lack of commitment for basic social service for all citizens. Next presented are social equity issues and the resulting concerns of several other vulnerable populations. Schmitz, Jacobus, Stakeman, Valenzuela, and Sprankel's article "Immigrant and Refugee Communities: Resiliency, Trauma, Policy, and Practice" raises social justice concern for immigrants and refugees entering our country. Their challenge is a need for a greater understanding of the obstacles facing our newest transitioning inhabitants. The article's focus is on providing positive community commitment and response, and employing a holistic framework that will provide for the multiple needs of refugee and immigrant groups.

Vulnerable transitional status also includes women released from prison. Abram and Hoge, in "Doing Justice: Women Ex-Offenders as Group Facilitators, Advocates, and Community Educators," describe a program wherein women ex-offenders are assisted in their efforts to develop community-based support. The program employs an empowering, strength-based approach. The program draws on the innate abilities of former women offenders to build community and solidarity. By the use of mutual social supports, they learn to collectively advocate for their needs.

Linhorst, Eckert, Hamilton, and Young in the article "Practicing Social Justice with Persons with Mental Illness Residing in Psychiatric Hospitals" advocate for innovative inpatient-staff participatory decision making in mental health hospitals. The model offers an approach designed to increase patient control over decisions directly affecting their well-being. Patient self-determination is enhanced when staff and patient interact in joint decision making.

This ongoing debate concerning retribution versus rehabilitation is further developed in a morally challenging article, "Youth Who Murder and Societal Responsibility: An Issue of Social Justice," by Morton and Cook. The authors' concern is society's punitive response to the young who commit homicide. They propose systemic reform with a renewed societal commitment to prevention, intervention, and remediation to restore what has become a blurred line between juvenile and adult criminal justice.

Community change social justice efforts can be woven into community partnering of organizations. Flory and Berg-Weger in the article "Children of High-Conflict Custody Disputes: Striving for Social Justice in Adult-Focused Litigation" are particularly interested in providing a safe environment for supervised visitation of children in high-conflict custody disputes. This program provides security for both parents and children. The approach reduces a conflict environment lessening the potential for violence.

Persons with developmental disabilities are particularly disadvantaged upon entering the criminal justice system according to Linhorst, Bennett, and McCutchen in their article "Practicing Social Justice with Persons with Developmental Disabilities Who Enter the Criminal Justice System." These authors champion the social justice rights of this high-risk population entering a criminal justice system, which is ill prepared to meet their special needs. For example, the developmentally disabled are often disadvantaged by not having sufficient understanding of their Miranda rights. As a result, they often give statements or reveal evidence that proves to be self-incriminating. The authors go on to show that the developmentally disabled spend more time in prison.

They are often not found to be suitable for probation. The article raises a social justice issue of the balance between society's demands for retribution and the vulnerable person's right for compassionate rehabilitation.

Justice is a meta-theoretical construct that is viewed from many perspectives. The contributors to this collection demonstrate how to combine practice intervention and research to ameliorate social-oppressive structures to bring about just social interactions. The Center provides financial support for partnerships of university faculty, students, and community agencies to collaborate on social justice innovative programs so that ". . . none deny or delay, right or justice."

REFERENCES

Barker, R. L. (1999). *The social work dictionary* (4th ed.). Washington, DC: NASW Press.

Brieland, D. (1981). Definition, specialization, and domain in social work. *Social Work, 23*, 79-83.

Council on Social Work Education (1994). *Handbook of accreditation standards and procedures* (4th ed.). Alexandria, VA: Author.

Gambrill, E. (2001). Evaluating the quality of social work education: Options galore. *Journal of Social Work Education, 37*, 418-429.

Gil, D. (1998). *Confronting injustice and oppression: Concepts and strategies for social workers.* New York: Columbia University Press.

Institute of Jesuit Sources (1995). *Documents of the 34th General Assembly of the Society of Jesus.* St. Louis, MO: Author.

John Paul II (1990). Encyclical letter, *Redemptoris Misso,* no. 41, Washington, DC: U. S. Catholic Conference.

Longres, J. & Scanlon, E. (2001). Social justice and the research curriculum. *Journal of Social Work Education, 37*:3: 447-463.

National Association of Social Workers (1996). *Code of ethics.* Washington, DC: Author.

O'Brien, J. & Shannon, T. (Eds.). (1977). *Renewing the earth: Catholic documents on peace, justice, and liberation.* New York: Author.

Pelton. L. (2001). Social justice and social work. *Journal of Social Work Education, 37*:3: 433-444.

Reid, W. (1977). Social work for social problems. *Social Work, 22*, 374-381.

Swenson, C. (1998). Clinical social works' contribution to a social justice perspective. *Social Work, 43*, 527-537.

Whose Justice?
An Examination of Nine Models of Justice

Patrick T. McCormick

SUMMARY. Formal definitions of justice calling us to "render the other their due" are elastic, given shape by our grasp of the moral bonds connecting persons and the relationship between this virtue and other moral habits, affections, or the concrete experience of our lives. This paper, written for a conference on education to justice in Jesuit Universities, examines nine theories of justice (Utilitarianism, Libertarianism, Social Contract, Complex Equality, a Feminist Ethics of Care, Christian Realism, Catholic Social Thought, Liberation Theology, and a Biblical notion of justice) in light of their perspective on the rights and duties persons have to one another and the relationship of justice to compassion and the affections. *[Article copies available for a fee from The Haworth Document Delivery Service: 1-800-HAWORTH. E-mail address: <docdelivery@haworthpress.com> Website: <http://www.HaworthPress.com> © 2003 by The Haworth Press, Inc. All rights reserved.]*

KEYWORDS. Justice, liberty, equality, the common good, solidarity

---

Patrick T. McCormick, STD, is Associate Professor of Christian Ethics in the Religious Studies Department at Gonzaga University, Spokane WA 99258-0001 (E-mail: mccormick@gonzaga.edu).

[Haworth co-indexing entry note]: "Whose Justice? An Examination of Nine Models of Justice." McCormick, Patrick T. Co-published simultaneously in *Social Thought* (The Haworth Press, Inc.) Vol. 22, No. 2/3, 2003, pp. 7-25; and: *Practicing Social Justice* (ed: John J. Stretch et al.) The Haworth Press, Inc., 2003, pp. 7-25. Single or multiple copies of this article are available for a fee from The Haworth Document Delivery Service [1-800-HAWORTH, 9:00 a.m. - 5:00 p.m. (EST). E-mail address: docdelivery@haworthpress.com].

© 2003 by The Haworth Press, Inc. All rights reserved.
http://www.haworthpress.com/store/product.asp?sku=J131
10.1300/J131v22n02_02

7

The notions of right and justice are still far from clear despite the fact that the clearest writers have written about them.

–Leibniz

American readers picking up their first Russian novel often feel like they have wandered off into *terra incognita,* and inevitably a good deal of their initial confusion results from the author's practice of assigning several different names to each of the dozens of characters in these narratives. What the patient and insightful reader soon discovers, however, is that in Russian literature this bounty of appellations and affectionate diminutives is not merely an overkill of synonyms for the individual character, but a way of identifying a host of relationships connecting the ones naming and the one named. And so the confusion resulting from the loss of a single name is eventually replaced by a more complex and nuanced appreciation of characters shaped by a weave of relationships. We come to know who people are by knowing who they are to (many) others.

With justice we seem to have the opposite problem of that encountered in Russian novels, a single term about which we continue to experience a great deal of confusion and disagreement, in spite of the fact that "the clearest writers" have addressed the question tirelessly for centuries. For although nearly all would agree that justice obliges us to render the other their "due," there is no broad consensus about what that "due" is, or even about the specific criteria (need, merit, contribution, talent, or some mixture thereof) we should use in determining the just share or desserts to be apportioned to various persons or communities. Indeed, there is not even agreement about whether liberty, equality, solidarity or the common good is the primary cornerstone on which the edifice of justice is to be constructed.

Still, it is possible that the ultimate source of our confusion about justice lies in deeper disagreements about some fundamental relationships. For justice is not merely about our duty to render the other their due. It is primarily about being in "right relationship" with others. Thus, our understanding of justice is likely to be shaped by what we think "right relationships" between and among persons and communities are, or ought to be, and indeed what rights and/or duties we might have in relation to these others, particularly the poor and oppressed. At the same time, our different judgments about justice are also influenced by how we understand the relationship between this virtue and other moral habits and affections, and whether we see justice as embodied in universal abstract principles or discoverable only in the weave and context of human history.

As members of Jesuit Universities mandated to educate our constituencies for justice, we are often painfully aware of the complexity and ambiguity of the task before us, needing as we do not only to persuade others of the importance of a faith that does justice, but also to determine exactly what the shape and identity of this justice might be. With a number of different and often conflicting theories and approaches competing for the title of legitimate claimant to the throne, which or whose justice are we to choose or espouse? Indeed, does any single theory or approach offer a satisfying answer to the question–"What is justice?"–or should we seek some composite fashioned of the best insights of these various approaches?

In preparing the ground for our common reflections on these questions this essay will follow a two-step process. First, there will be a very brief overview of several differing theories or approaches to justice, identifying some of the critical points of each. (Seven of the theories outlined here are drawn from Lebacqz [1986] and Walzer [1983]. The other two include a feminist ethic of care and the biblical notion of *sedaquah*.) Second, the bulk of the essay will investigate the ways in which these various theories and approaches understand the two sets of relations discussed above. That is, we will examine just how each approach names both the ways persons and communities are related to one another, and the ways in which justice is related to other virtues, to our affections, and to our historical context.

A REVIEW OF NINE VOICES

Utilitarianism

Utilitarians like Jeremy Bentham and John Stuart Mill argue that the right or just choice is that which produces the greatest good. For them and their colleagues utility, which "holds that actions are right in proportion as they tend to promote happiness" (Mill, 1957, p. 10), is the ultimate moral norm, and justice is not a separate or equal principle, but simply a part of utility.

It is not that concerns about justice are unimportant for Utilitarians, or that they do not subscribe to notions of individual rights. Indeed, Mill argues that justice refers to those moral duties of ours, which entitle others to make claims against us. Still, rules about justice, which tend to arise in situations where there are competing claims (usually regarding property) and limited resources, are ultimately valid not if they protect the inherent rights or claims of individuals but if they contribute to increasing overall happiness and security by preserving the good order of society. As Mill argues, "Justice is a name for certain moral requirements, which, regarded collectively, stand higher in the scale of social utility, and are therefore of more paramount obligation than any others" (Mill, 1957, p. 78). As a result, rights will be protected as long as they preserve the greater good, and can be overridden or ignored when they conflict with the principle of utility. Thus, if it creates more happiness, one may break a promise or kill an innocent person.

Libertarianism

The cornerstone principle for the followers of Herbert Spencer and John Locke, on the other hand, is individual liberty. While Spencerian libertarians see liberty as the basic human right from which all other rights are derived and Lockean libertarians contend that liberty (i.e., freedom from constraint) is that necessary condition for the protection of basic rights to life and property, both agree that each person ought to have as much liberty as would be possible without violating the same freedom in others (Sterba, 1998, pp. 41-44).

As a result of this emphasis on the right of individual persons to be as free from constraint as possible, contemporary Libertarians like Robert Nozick (1974) support a minimal (i.e., *laissez faire*) state responsible primarily for protecting the security (usually life, liberty and property) of individuals pursuing their own separate (normally economic) interests. Arguing against a welfare state which redistributes wealth or opportunities to the poor or marginalized, Nozick contends that the needy have no moral claim on the surplus wealth of the rich, and that enforced redistribution is a form of theft, violating the Kantian prohibition of the use of some persons as a means to serve others. He further argues that a right to property is based exclusively on the justice of the original acquisition or subsequent exchanges, which is to measured by the criteria of commutative justice, i.e., the mutual freedom of both parties (Nozick, 1974, pp. 130-170).

Social Contract

Influenced by the social contract theories of Locke and Rousseau, John Rawls has attempted to formulate a theory of "justice as fairness" which takes the rights of individual persons seriously while providing for a minimal protection of the poor and marginalized in society (Rawls, 1971). Rawls begins by imagining a situation in which truly fair and equitable principles of justice might be arrived at, his so-called "original position." Here Rawls envisions a sufficiently large group of intelligent and self-interested (but not envious) individuals assigned the design of guidelines for negotiating conflicts without being told what their own role or status will be once the game begins.

According to Rawls, these intelligent, rational and mutually disinterested parties would agree to two basic principles of justice:

1. the principle of equal liberty, which would assure each person an equal right to the greatest amount of the most basic liberties, and
2. the difference principle, which would allow for social and economic inequalities only when they result in an improved situation for the poor and marginalized.

Complex Equality

Michael Walzer (1983) offers an egalitarian vision of justice, which does not seek to eliminate all differences, but to prevent domination and tyranny. According to Walzer, full equality cannot be achieved without unduly repressing freedom and granting a monopoly of political power to the state. Still, a "complex equality" which respects the diversity of social goods, spheres of human activity, and centers and standards for decision making can effectively prevent the sort of totalitarian monopolies that allow small groups of persons to gain long term dominance over a wide field of human experience.

Arguing that "the principles of justice are themselves pluralistic in form, (and) that different social goods ought to be distributed for different reasons, in accordance with different procedures, (and) by different agents," Walzer (1983, p. 6) contends that a commitment to protect the identity of and boundaries between these various spheres will preserve a complex equality and prevent powerful people from violating standards, usurping goods, and invading spheres. In this way, persons with a social good like wealth will not be able to translate their advantage in the sphere of economics into a similar monopoly in politics, education, or health care. Thus for Walzer, justice is better preserved by a decentralized latticework of autonomous goods, authorities and standards than by any single principle applied universally.

A Feminist Ethic of Care

Carol Gilligan's *In a Different Voice* (1982) claimed to discover an alternate and distinctly feminine ethic of care counterbalancing the Kantian notions of justice informing Kohlberg's model of moral development. And although subsequent feminist reflection has largely rejected either a simple identification of women with an ethic of care or a sharp polarity separating care and justice, feminist critics (Baier, 1995) continue to argue that Gilligan's insights point to some significant deficiencies in traditional Kantian reflections on justice, and raise serious questions about the hegemony of justice as what Rawls has called "the first virtue of social institutions."

In general, feminist criticism has been directed at the individualism, rationalism and abstractness characterizing much of Western philosophical thought on justice (Clement, 1996). Rejecting the notion that justice refers to the duty of independent, equal and largely self-interested parties to respect the rights of other individuals with competing claims, feminists call for a fuller grasp of the relational, social and interdependent character of persons, and for a recognition of the wider obligations of care and compassion for those in need. At the same time, such authors note the epistemological importance of concrete moral experience and an enriched sense of moral passions and affections.

Christian Realism

In the 1930s and '40s theological realists like John Bennett and Reinhold Niebuhr held that love was the highest principle of Christian ethics, but that the pervasive presence of sin in the world made the ideal of sacrificial love embodied in the cross impossible as the basis of a realistic social ethic (Atherton, 1994). Instead, Niebuhr argued that Christians were obliged to work for justice, which took into account the presence of sin and competing self-interests (particularly between groups), and provided the best possible balance of those interests in a sinful world. This it did largely by struggling to increase the power of the victims of injustice and working for a balance of power in both political and economic realms. Indeed, for Niebuhr achieving equal justice often involved struggle and coercion, pressing persons or groups to surrender sinfully unjust advantages, abandon oppressive structures, and share power in a more equitable fashion.

Still, Niebuhr argues that Christians cannot ignore love's siren call, for every manifestation or rule of justice is judged and called to perfection by the self-sacrificing love of Christ. Thus, Niebuhr's justice is always a work in progress, being summoned to that perfect community of friends which is love.

Catholic Social Thought

Recent Catholic teaching has described "action on behalf of justice" as a "constitutive dimension" of the church's mission in the world. It has also called Christians and others of goodwill to uncover, confront and transform oppressive, impoverishing, and decidedly sinful economic, political and social structures by standing in solidarity with and making a preferential option for the poor and marginalized everywhere (Hollenbach, 1977).

Affirming both the inviolable dignity and the social character of human persons, as well as the social end of all created goods, Catholic Social Thought has been increasingly critical of political and economic systems that tolerate a growing gap between the rich and poor and the resulting oppression and marginalization of the latter. Arguing that real justice and the common good calls for the full and integral development of persons and communities everywhere, recent teachings note that such justice depends upon the recognition and protection of an expansive network of rights and responsibilities. These include not merely those civil and political liberties traditionally defended in Libertarian and Kantian theories, but also a broad range of the social, cultural and economic goods needed for a full and fair participation in every social, political, economic and cultural structure. On top of this, there is a profound commitment to address present injustices by making a preferential option for the poor.

Liberation Theology

Calling not just for a preferential option for the poor, but for an epistemological privilege for those living in the margins, theologians like Gustavo Gutierrez and Jose Porfirio Miranda argue that justice requires the ongoing liberation of the poor from all forms of economic, cultural and political oppression. This process begins with "praxis," with the poor (and those in solidarity with them) making a commitment to liberation, engaging and reflecting upon their lived experience of poverty and marginalization, and analyzing that experience in a critical dialogue that uncovers both the structural oppression and injustice causing that poverty and a God who calls them to liberation (Atherton, 1994, pp. 35-39).

Emphasizing more strongly than Catholic Social Thought the need for a confrontational struggle against sinful (largely capitalist) social structures, Miranda and other liberation theologians decry the present maldistribution of wealth and the resulting gap between rich and poor as a systemic injustice and a form of institutional theft and violence. Furthermore, turning to Scripture they find a liberating God who sides with the oppressed and can only be known through entering into the poor's struggle for justice, a struggle which is seen as an integral part of the history of salvation (Lebacqz, 1986, pp. 103-109).

Biblical Justice

Contemporary biblical scholarship offers a number of insights regarding the notion of justice found in Scripture (Donahue, 1987; Gardner, 1995; Lebacqz, 1987). Throughout the Old Testament justice is seen as a covenantal virtue calling the Hebrews to imitate God's liberating and merciful justice by being faithful in their relationships to Yahweh and their neighbor, by exercising responsible stewardship of the shared inheritance of the land, and in particular by showing concern for those "little ones" in the margins. Indeed, the measure of the Hebrews' justice or righteousness before God was primarily to be found in their compassionate remembrance and protection of the widow, orphan and alien. Thus in practices like gleaning and almsgiving, and in the economic readjustments of the sabbatical and jubilee year covenantal justice not only ensured that the poor were not permanently overwhelmed or disenfranchised by their ill fortune, but also that the Hebrew community was holy and righteous in God's eyes.

So too in the New Testament Jesus proclaims liberation to those in the margins, stands in solidarity with the poor and victimized of every sort, and confronts economic, political and religious structures oppressing and alienating the poor and powerless. Likewise, his life and word challenge the community of his disciples to practice a compassionate justice which sides with the poor and seeks liberation from every form of oppression (Kammer, 1991, pp. 41-59).

Right Relations Among Persons and Communities

Mill and other Utilitarians presume a basic equality between persons, noting that utility is to be applied with complete impartiality, and that "one person's happiness . . . is (to be) counted for exactly as much as another's" (Mill, 1957, p. 76). At the same time, they recognize a certain amount of connection between persons, noting that individuals may make justice claims on others to act or refrain from acting in different ways.

The problem, however, for most critics is that utility seems to allow an increased aggregate happiness of the many to override any individual rights or concerns, rendering the person completely secondary to the greater good of the community.

Both Libertarians like Nozick and Social Contract theorists like Rawls seek to defend persons against being swallowed up in a concern for the greater good by giving a lexical priority to individuals and certain basic liberties ascribed to them. For each of these authors the starting point is not the community or the state, but a Kantian notion of equal, independent, rational and largely self-interested individuals needing to find a just manner of negotiating competing claims for a limited set of goods and resources.

Committed to defending the freedom of the individual and articulating a set of objective and universally applicable justice claims, Nozick, Rawls and others offer a minimalist anthropology in which persons are abstracted from the contextual, historical and affective ties, which connect them to a variety of spheres. The result is an intrinsicist vision of the individual focussing on freedom and rationality, and (many would argue) presuming a degree of equality and voluntariness, which is not always characteristic of human relationships (Baier, 1995, pp. 54-56).

On the other hand, Feminists, Catholic Social Thought, and contemporary biblical scholarship regarding justice all tend to stress the social character of persons. By emphasizing the moral obligations of care, solidarity and covenant these three voices argue for a more relational understanding of persons as beings who are born into, develop within, and to a large degree are constituted by a dynamic and interdependent fabric of interpersonal and social relations (Donahue, 1987, pp. 68-78).

As a result, Feminist authors are deeply critical of Kantian notions of autonomy, which fail to take seriously the role of care in shaping the moral development of persons or in defining what it means to be a person within the myriad of (often unequal) relationships of one's life (Clement, 1996, pp. 110-114). At the same time Catholic Social Thought, while affirming the inviolable dignity of the human person and the priority of persons and smaller natural communities over larger and later groups like the state, argues that this dignity is only realizable within community and that all persons are called to acknowledge and be faithful to the solidarity they share as fellow children of God (U.S. Catholic Bishops, 1986, pp. 574-575; John Paul II, 1987, pp. 421-424).

When examining the web of relationships shaping human experience Feminists, Liberation Theologians and Christian Realists are alike in underscoring the distorted, oppressive and/or sinful shape of these ties, and in calling for a liberating struggle confronting and undoing various forms of domination and marginalization. For these groups the "original position," or at least the context out of which one formulates notions and principles of justice is one in which the moral bonds connecting persons and communities have been twisted by injustice, alienation, dependence, and tyranny (Lebacqz, 1986, pp. 101-103; Lebacqz, 1987, pp. 10-37).

As a result of this embedded and sinful disorder, these three voices tend to recognize the need not simply to negotiate the competing claims of equals, but to be engaged in an ongoing struggle to establish and protect the rights of victims of systemic injustice and oppression. At least for Liberation Theologians and Feminists persons are in relationships and called to wholeness through these moral bonds, but both these persons and their relationships are so profoundly misshapen by sin and injustice that it is necessary not merely to contain the unjust claims of those who oppress, but to fundamentally reform and redress structures and relations.

OF RIGHTS AND DUTIES

Not surprisingly, diverse understandings of what constitutes right relations among various persons and between persons and communities will naturally result in differing grasps of the moral claims that such parties can make on one another. Thus, while each approach to justice makes room for some recognition of human rights, the specific content and shape of these rights is quite varied.

In contending that justice refers to those strict moral obligations which persons have to one another, Mill acknowledges the presence of individual rights, but refuses to give them equal status with utility and, at least in the eyes of most critics of Utilitarianism, fails to provide for their sufficient protection (Lebacqz, 1986, pp. 20-22).

Generally, Libertarians and Social Contract theorists have supported a liberal notion of human rights, focussing primarily or exclusively on those civil and political liberties protecting individual persons from constraint, interference or harm. Thus, the basic rights to life, liberty and property defended by Locke are not seen as claims entitling persons to receive the basic goods or services which would be necessary to sustain life, or to be given a sufficient amount or fair share of property. Nor would such rights entitle persons to equal access to goods and services, or even to an equal opportunity to positions, resources or wealth. Instead, what is guaranteed is that persons have a right to be protected from others who would attack their lives, liberty or the property they already possess—presupposing that it has been fairly acquired (Sterba, 1998, pp. 41-44). Indeed, characteristic of a liberal understanding of human rights is an elevation of private property (which might well be seen as a social or economic good and not a fundamental liberty) to the status of a basic right (Sterba, 1998, pp. 53-55).

Particularly in Pope John XXIII's *Peace on Earth* and the 1971 Synod Bishops' *Justice in the World* Catholic Social Thought defends an expansive understanding of human rights, one embracing both civil and political liberties as well as a broad spectrum of social and economic goods (John XXIII, 1963, pp. 132-137; World Synod of Bishops, 1971, pp. 290-291). Arguing that human rights are "the minimum conditions for life in community," and the chief guarantee for the preservation of the common good, contemporary Catholic teachings affirm that all persons and peoples have a right to

1. what is needed to live,
2. what is required for their full and fair participation in every social structure, and
3. all that is requisite for their authentic and integral development (Thompson, 1997, pp. 94-97).

Further, as members of local, national and global societies, all persons and communities should recognize and respect a full range of human rights and actively contribute to the building up a common good which "embraces the sum total of those conditions of social living whereby (persons) are enabled to achieve their own integral perfection more fully and more easily" (John XXIII, 1963, p. 140).

Also, while earlier Catholic Social Thought seemed to support a liberal defense of private property as a fundamental human right, and portrayed the obligation of the wealthy to provide for the basic needs of the poor as an unenforceable duty of charity only, more recent teachings have consistently pointed to the priority of the social end or universal purpose of all created goods, and been deeply critical of economic arrangements which deprive large numbers of persons to access to basic goods and/or prevent their full participation and development (Leo XIII, 1891, pp. 22-23; Paul VI, 1967, p. 245).

Liberation theologians go further to argue that in a world deformed by systemic oppression a right to development is insufficient, and that there is a duty for both the oppressed and their oppressors to work actively for the liberation of all the poor and marginalized from every type of alienation and marginalization. They are also profoundly critical of liberal assumptions about the rights of private property, and in direct refutation of thinkers like Nozick describe the present maldistribution as a systemic injustice and a form of theft. Further, they see the obligations of the oppressed as distinct from their oppressors. The first are to "resist and repudiate" the structural injustices in which they are imprisoned, while the latter need to "recognize, repent, and make reparation for" their participation in structural injustices (Lebacqz, 1987, pp. 86-120).

Finally, a Feminist ethic of care rejects an unbalanced stress on personal autonomy, and argues that within the lifelong network of relationships in which persons find themselves bound and committed to others, often to those in great need, it makes little sense to describe the moral bonds tying us to others primarily in terms of rights and liberties (Smith, 1987). Such moral minimalism ignores the frailty and needs of large segments of the community (and indeed of all persons at some point), allows those who take on caretaker roles to shoulder an unfair burden of the full costs of social life, and fails to provide sufficient capital for a rich common life (Baier, 1995, pp. 52-57; Clement, 1996, pp. 110-114).

DUTIES TO THE POOR

Given the minimalist assumptions Libertarians make about the social ties and duties binding individuals to others, as well as their notion that property rights are grounded in claims flowing from commutative and not distributive justice, it should come as no surprise that Nozick and others deny that the poor or needy have any intrinsic justice claims on the well off (though poverty resulting from an unjust acquisition or exchange would cry out for restitution). Accepting that it might be charitable or meritorious to share one's bounty with those suffering from chronic want, Libertarians see such generosity as completely voluntary, and reject the notion that justice demands this behavior (Sterba, 1998, pp. 42-43).

Rawls, on the other hand, provides for a minimal protection of society's weakest members through his "difference principle," which demands that "social and economic inequalities are to be arranged so that they are both: (a) to the greatest benefit to the least advantaged . . . and (b) attached to offices and positions open to all under conditions of fair equality of opportunity" (Rawls, 1971, p. 302). The grounds for this duty to the poor, however, is not found in a moral bond to those in the margins, but in Rawls' argument that rational self-interested individuals in his "original position" would want some insurance against being harmed or permanently disenfranchised by any gap between rich and poor (Lebacqz, 1986, p. 75).

As we have already seen, Catholic Social Teaching has repeatedly called for a "preferential option for the poor." Based on a recognition of (1) the solidarity all persons are called to by virtue of their shared humanity and common dignity as fellow children of God, (2) the desperate need of millions upon millions of the world's poor, oppressed and marginalized as they are by sinful social structures, and (3) the Bible's covenantal mandate to show concern for the *anawim* (God's little ones), Catholic Social Thought acknowledges a moral obligation to stand in solidarity with and become advocates for the poor (U.S. Catholic Bishops, 1986, pp. 599-601; Dorr, 1992, pp. 1-11). In the concrete this "option for the poor" demands not simply a sharing of one's abundance, but also whatever changes in personal lifestyles and social and economic priorities would be consistent with a commitment to ensure the full participation and development of poor peoples everywhere.

Liberation Theologians go on to argue that the poor themselves have a special knowledge about justice (an epistemological privilege), gleaned from their immediate and chronic experience of structural injustices of every sort, and that it is a committed immersion in and reflection on this experience of oppression and marginalization–and not some abstract notion of a just community of equals–which is to be the starting point for any real grasp of justice. They further contend that in the struggle for justice the poor are not merely to be seen as the objects of solidarity or charity, but as active agents in the processes of constructing a just society (Hennelly, 1994, pp. 16-34).

A moral duty to attend to those in need is a critical element of a Feminist ethic of care, which rejects a paradigm understanding justice primarily as concerning the obligations of substantially independent, self-interested and equal parties who have voluntarily entered into mutual relationships. By attending to the shape of so many of the intimate and familial relationships in which parents and other guardians are called to care for the weak and sick, a number of Feminist writers suggest that the duty to care for others, to come to their aid and attend to them, is a constitutive element of what it means to be moral (or just, in a wider sense), and that this duty to care applies to both the private and public realms (Clement, 1996; Tronto, 1995).

JUSTICE AND OTHER VIRTUES

Plato (*The Republic*, IV, p. 433) argues that justice is supreme among all other virtues, Aristotle (*Ethics*, V, p. 11306) describes it as the single virtue directed to the other, and–as we have already noted–Rawls (1971, p. 3) notes that it is "the first virtue of social institutions." Nonetheless, there is some significant disagreement about whether justice is indeed the *only* social virtue, or whether the moral duties generated by this virtue adequately describe the full range of obligations persons and communities have to one another. Specifically, it is the relationship between justice and compassion (or care, love, mercy, or benevolence), which concerns us. Is compassion a secondary, voluntary virtue reserved to the domestic and religious realms, or does it represent a constitutive element of true justice? Indeed, can there be authentic justice without some form of caring?

Both Mill and Nozick make a rather sharp delineation between justice and charity, seeing the first as concerned with those issues where persons can make actual moral claims on others, where parties have defined rights that are not to be violated. As previously noted, individuals may choose of their own volition to do more than is required by justice, and for Nozick that more would include acts of charity and benevolence in response to the needs and sufferings of others. However, such deeds are beyond the realm of justice.

Reinhold Niebuhr's grasp of the relation between love and justice is a good deal more complex, even somewhat ambiguous. As noted above, Niebuhr (1964, pp. 73, 244) believed that the supreme command and highest principle of Christian morality was love, particularly as it was embodied in the self-sacrificing identification with others found in the cross. At the same time he and Bennett argued that human sinfulness had so tainted persons and communities that Christian love could not be achieved in the public realm, and that justice–which took into account sinful self interest–was to be the guide there. Still, every concrete form of justice was seen as falling short of the ideal of genuine human community, and Niebuhr himself argued that "justice that is only justice is less than justice" (Robertson, 1976, p. 32). Thus, while sin made love untenable as a social norm, every principle or manifestation of justice needed to be critiqued in light of love's command.

In both Scripture and Catholic Social Teaching authentic justice is not seen as being in polar opposition to love, but as shot through and through with compassion. Contemporary biblical scholarship affirms that for the ancient Hebrews the justice of God was not sharply contrasted with other divine virtues like loving mercy and covenantal fidelity, but revealed in saving acts of mercy and compassion (Donahue, 1987, pp. 69, 71-78). At the same time, while early documents like Leo XIII's *The Condition of Labor* reflect a sharp delineation between the duties of justice and charity regarding property, contemporary Catholic Social Thought increasingly argues that "Christian love of neighbor and justice cannot be separated" (Leo XIII, 1891; Henriot, DeBerri & Schultheis, 1989, pp. 19-21). "For love implies an absolute demand of justice, namely recognition of the dignity and rights of one's neighbor. (And) justice attains its inner fullness only in love" (World Synod of Bishops, 1971, p. 293).

Although some early Feminist reflections on care echoed Gilligan's initial polarization of justice and care as representing two separate moral voices, most later authors have tended to reject this approach. Instead, a number of Feminist critics have suggested that any fully adequate description of moral experience will need to incorporate concerns for both justice and care (giving lexical priority to neither). Indeed, a vision of justice that fails to attend to care offers a truncated vision of human persons and the network of moral ties that bind them to each other and larger communities. At the same time an ethic of care which fails to attend to justice concerns like mutuality runs the risk of allowing all sorts of harm in the name of love, or of failing to respect the legitimate needs of those beyond the spheres of family and friendship (Friedman, 1995; Clement, 1996, pp. 110-122; Gudorf, 1987).

JUSTICE AND AFFECTIONS

Traditionally, liberal and Kantian notions of justice have underscored not merely the autonomy of persons, but also their rationality, and sought to describe justice as that "cold virtue" which does not depend on (or become clouded by) the affections and attachments of our ties to friends, family or compatriots, but is instead based on rational choice. For Rawls, the principles of justice "are the principles that free and *rational* (italics added) persons concerned to further their own interests would accept" (Rawls, 1971, p. 11).

In general moral theorists as diverse as Mill, Nozick and Rawls have focussed on rationality as the basis for their theories of justice out of a concern that the emotions tend to impede attempts to arrive at an objective, universal and therefore accurate description of the moral duties and rights of persons and communities. Rational thought, stripped of the biases and prejudices of sentiment, is the only way of human knowing that can be trusted to arrive at an adequate understanding of reality (Callahan, 1991, pp. 95-99).

While natural moral law reasoning tended to be the cornerstone of earlier Catholic Social Teachings on justice, "in recent decades this teaching has been increasingly shaped by the primacy of love." This shift has meant not only a growing recognition that love is a constitutive element of authentic justice, but also that compassion provides both an insight into and a resource for meeting the demands of justice (Henriot et al., 1989, pp. 18-19). As the U.S. Bishops note in their economic pastoral, "unlike the other wayfarers who look on the (dying) man and pass by," the Samaritan in Luke's parable "was moved by compassion at the sight" and came to this stranger's aid (U.S. Catholic Bishops, 1986, p. 589).

The strongest criticism of reason's hegemony, however, comes from Feminist authors, who, while admitting that errant and negative feelings can sometimes impede the processes of discovering and/or doing what is just, note that a reason sterilized of feelings has its own dangers (O'Connor, 1987, pp. 277-281; Callahan, 1991, pp. 127-134). For reason unschooled by affections of compassion, empathy and mercy not only fails to provide the motivation for just actions, but also dismisses an important way of knowing about the world, one well grounded in the rich fabric of concrete experience. As a result, such a narrow rationalism often pays too scant attention to the actual suffering and needs of others, and ends up overlooking or undervaluing the claims of those in need. A rationality, which seeks to step back from the maelstrom of emotions, needs to be careful of becoming indifferent to the cries of injustice.

At the same time certain Feminist (and other) authors are quick to point out that the very capacity of persons to fulfill the duties of critical roles as parents, friends, or spouses, or indeed to grow into morally mature adults depends ultimately on their ability to give and receive love. Unlike Kant, these authors argue that the richness and health of people's emotive life is an essential element of their capacity to be just. Mary Shelley, it would seem, is not alone in warning that persons become monsters without love (Held, 1995; O'Connell, 1998, pp. 65-86).

JUSTICE AND HISTORY

The Utilitarians, Libertarians and Social Contract theorists we have examined are alike in that each has attempted to develop a comprehensive, coherent, consistent and relatively simple theory of justice or moral rightness, one seeking to abstract from the inconsistencies and varieties of human experience to some compact set of universal and objectively verifiable principles. Still, while the advantages and desirability of such an approach seems self-evident, not all are in agreement that a theory consisting of "universal moral formulae and the theoretical justification of these" provides an adequate understanding of either the rich texture of moral experience or the varied demands of justice.

Niebuhr, who argues that reason itself is not immune to the distortion of sin, warns that human understanding is always impeded by bias, and that real objectivity is unobtainable. Indeed, he notes that the presumption of such objectivity, or claim to be in the possession of the real or true perspective, is itself a form of sinful idolatry against which persons and communities need to be eternally vigilant (and repentant). At the same time, given humanity's immersion in a history shaped by sin, Niebuhr (1964, p. 284) contends that each form and principle of justice is itself also a kind of injustice, and thus in constant need of reform. There can, then, be no absolute or universal standards of justice (Robertson, 1976, p. 32).

As noted previously, Michael Walzer's brand of egalitarianism rejects the possibility of a single criterion for distributive justice, arguing "the principles of justice are themselves pluralistic in form." According to Walzer, justice is relative to social meanings, and persons are not able to discover what others are due outside the larger social context and matrix of social meanings. Thus, Walzer (1983, pp. 312-316) argues that an adequate understanding of the demands of justice must be grounded in an understanding of the history, social context and sphere in which persons find themselves.

Feminist authors critique the abstractness and universality of Kantian theories of justice for providing insufficient attention to the shape of concrete experience, and in particular for ignoring or overlooking the specific and distinctive moral experience of women and others in the margins. Arguing for a more inductive approach to moral analysis, Feminist authors have tended to pay closer attention to the contextual and historical shape of human experience, and to the diverse spheres and relationships in which persons are called to be just. Thus, the moral duties and claims of parents, spouses, family members, loved ones, friends and other intimates, as well as the specific shape of these relationships inform and balance more abstract and theoretical notions of justice (Urban Walker, 1995).

Liberation Theologians have also tended to stress an inductive approach to justice, one which begins by engaging and reflecting on the concrete experience of injustice, not from a neutral or objective viewpoint, but from the perspective of

1. those suffering from and committed to overcoming its effects and
2. a biblical narrative and Christian symbols revealing a God committed to come to the aid of the oppressed.

Liberation theologies, then, tend not so much to formulate theories of justice as theories of injustice, or better yet praxis in response to injustice (Lebacqz, 1987, pp. 10-37; Hennelly, 1995, pp. 8-38).

CLOSING

Formal definitions of justice which summon us to "render the other their due," or distribute resources "to each according to their . . ." are elastic, and the content we pour into them will depend largely on what we think the "right relations" between persons ought to be, or how we envision the ties between this virtue and other moral habits, affections, or the concrete experience of our lives. If justice is to describe what we owe others, we must first determine who we are to one another. In addition, if justice is to be the measure of moral communities, we must decide how rich and full these communities need to be.

REFERENCES

Aristotle. *Ethics*. V, 11306.

Atherton, J. (1994). Christian social ethics in context. In J. Artherton (Ed.), *Christian social ethics: A reader*. Cleveland, OH: The Pilgrim Press, 10-49.

Baier, A. C. (1995). The need for more than justice. In V. Held (Ed.), *Justice and care: Essential readings in feminist ethics*. Boulder, CO: Westview Press, 47-58.

Callahan, S. (1991). *In good conscience: Reason and emotion in moral decision making*. San Francisco: Harper Collins.

Clement, G. (1996). *Care, autonomy, and justice: Feminism and the ethic of care*. Boulder, CO: Westview Press.

Donahue, J. (1987). Biblical perspectives on justice. In J. Haughey (Ed.), *The faith that does justice*. New York: Paulist Press, 68-112.

Dorr, D. (1992). *Option for the poor: A hundred years of Catholic social teaching*. Maryknoll, NY: Orbis.

Friedman, M. (1995). Beyond caring: The de-moralization of gender. In V. Held (Ed.), *Justice and care: Essential readings in feminist ethics*. Boulder, CO: Westview Press, 61-77.

Gardner, E. C. (1995). *Justice and Christian ethics*. Cambridge University Press.

Gilligan, C. (1982). *In a different voice: Psychological theory and women's development*. Cambridge, MA: Harvard University Press.

Gudorf, C. (1987). Parenting, mutual love, and sacrifice. In B. Hilkert Andolsen, C. Gudorf, & M. Pellauer (Eds.), *Women's consciousness, women's conscience: A reader in feminist ethics*. San Francisco: Harper and Row, 175-191.

Held, V. (1995). Feminist moral inquiry and the feminist future. In V. Held (Ed.), *Justice and care: Essential readings in feminist ethics.* Boulder, CO: Westview Press, 156-157.

Hennelly, A. (1995). *Liberation theologies: The global pursuit of justice.* Mystic, CT: Twenty-Third Publications.

Henriot, P., DeBerri, E., & Schultheis, M. (1989). *Catholic social teaching: Our best kept secret.* Maryknoll, NY: Orbis.

Hollenbach, D. (1977). Modern Catholic teachings concerning justice. In J. Haughey (Ed.), *The faith that does justice.* New York: Paulist Press, 207-231.

John XXIII. (1963). Peace on earth. In D. O'Brien & T. Shannon (Eds.), *Catholic social thought: The documentary heritage.* Maryknoll, NY: Orbis, 129-162.

John Paul II. (1987). On social concern. In D. O'Brien & T. Shannon (Eds.), *Catholic social thought: The documentary heritage.* Maryknoll, NY: Orbis, 393-436.

Kammer, F. (1991). *Doing faith justice: An introduction to Catholic social thought.* New York: Paulist Press.

Lebacqz, K. (1986). *Six theories of justice: Perspectives from philosophical and theological ethics.* Minneapolis: Augsburg.

Lebacqz, K. (1987). *Justice in an unjust world: Foundations for a Christian approach to justice.* Minneapolis: Augsburg.

Leo XIII. (1891). The condition of labor. In D. O'Brien & T. Shannon (Eds.), *Catholic social thought: The documentary heritage.* Maryknoll, NY: Orbis, 12-39.

Mill, J. S. (1957). *Utilitarianism.* New York: Bobbs-Merrill.

Niebuhr, R. (1964). *Human destiny.* New York: Scribner.

Nozick, R. (1974). *Anarchy, state and utopia.* New York: Basic Books.

O'Connell, T. (1998). *Making disciples: A handbook of Christian moral formation.* New York: Crossroad.

O'Connor, J. (1987). On doing religious ethics. In B. Hilkert Andolsen, C. Gudorf, & M. Pellauer, (Eds.), *Women's consciousness, women's conscience: A reader in feminist ethics.* San Francisco: Harper and Row, 277-281.

Paul VI. (1967). On the development of peoples. In D. O'Brien & T. Shannon (Eds.), *Catholic social thought: The documentary heritage.* Maryknoll, NY: Orbis, 238-262.

Plato. (2000). *The Republic.* Cambridge and New York: Cambridge University Press, IV, 433.

Rawls, J. (1971). *A theory of justice.* Cambridge, MA: Harvard University Press.

Robertson, D.B. (Ed.). (1976). *Love and justice: Selections from the shorter writings of Reinhold Niebuhr.* Gloucester, MA: Peter Smith.

Smith, R. (1987). Feminism and the moral subject. In B. Hilkert Andolsen, C. Gudorf, & M. Pellauer (Eds.), *Women's consciousness, women's conscience: A reader in feminist ethics.* San Francisco: Harper and Row, 235-250.

Sterba, J. (1998). *Justice for here and now.* Cambridge University Press.

Thompson, J. M. (1997). *Justice and peace: A Christian primer.* Maryknoll, NY: Orbis.

Tronto, J. (1995). Women and caring: What can feminists learn about morality from caring? In V. Held (Ed.), *Justice and care: Essential readings in feminist ethics.* Boulder, CO: Westview Press, 101-115.

Urban Walker, M. (1995). Moral understanding: Alternative epistemologies for a feminist ethics. In V. Held (Ed.), *Justice and care: Essential readings in feminist ethics.* Boulder, CO: Westview Press, 139-152.

U.S. Catholic Bishops. (1986). Economic justice for all. In D. O'Brien & T. Shannon (Eds.), *Catholic social thought: The documentary heritage.* Maryknoll, NY: Orbis, 572-680.

Walzer, M. (1983). *Spheres of justice: A defense of pluralism and equality.* New York: Basic Books, Inc.

World Synod of Bishops. (1971). Justice in the world. In D. O'Brien & T. Shannon (Eds.), *Catholic social thought: The documentary heritage.* Maryknoll, NY: Orbis, 287-300.

Practicing Social Justice: Community-Based Research, Education, and Practice

Mary Beth Gallagher
Cynthia A. Loveland Cook
Susan Tebb
Marla Berg-Weger

SUMMARY. The Center for Social Justice Research and Education at Saint Louis University has implemented a model of collaborative research and education among social work practitioners, university faculty and students. The partnerships promote creative practice of social justice in the community.

Social workers in community agencies articulate the relevant practice problems for students and faculty; faculty offer methodological and re-

Mary Beth Gallagher, PhD, is Director of the VOICES Project at Saint Louis University (E-mail: GallagME@SLU.edu).

Cynthia A. Loveland Cook, PhD, ACSW, is Associate Professor in the School of Social Service at Saint Louis University (E-mail: CookCA@SLU.edu).

Susan Tebb, MSW, PhD, is Professor and Dean of the School of Social Service at Saint Louis University (E-mail: TebbSC@SLU.edu).

Marla Berg-Weger, LCSW, PhD, is Associate Professor and Director of Field Education in the School of Social Service at Saint Louis University (E-mail: BergWM@SLU.edu).

Address correspondence to the authors at the School of Social Service at Saint Louis University, 3550 Lindell Boulevard, St. Louis, MO 63103.

[Haworth co-indexing entry note]: "Practicing Social Justice: Community-Based Research, Education, and Practice." Gallagher, Mary Beth et al. Co-published simultaneously in *Social Thought* (The Haworth Press, Inc.) Vol. 22, No. 2/3, 2003, pp. 27-39; and: *Practicing Social Justice* (ed: John J. Stretch et al.) The Haworth Press, Inc., 2003, pp. 27-39. Single or multiple copies of this article are available for a fee from The Haworth Document Delivery Service [1-800-HAWORTH, 9:00 a.m. - 5:00 p.m. (EST). E-mail address: docdelivery@haworthpress.com].

© 2003 by The Haworth Press, Inc. All rights reserved.
http://www.haworthpress.com/store/product.asp?sku=J131
10.1300/J131v22n02_03

source assistance to practitioners; students learn social justice best at the intersection of the perspectives of university and community. Steps in the implementation of the model and examples of the collaboration are described. *[Article copies available for a fee from The Haworth Document Delivery Service: 1-800-HAWORTH. E-mail address: <docdelivery@haworthpress.com> Website: <http://www.HaworthPress.com> © 2003 by The Haworth Press, Inc. All rights reserved.]*

KEYWORDS. Research, collaborative practice, social justice, social work practice, social work education

INTRODUCTION

When Emmett J. and Mary Martha Doerr endowed the Center for Social Justice Education and Research (Center) in the School of Social Service at Saint Louis University in 1997, they imagined the Center contributing to social justice through three essential activities:

- Education of future social work practitioners in the centrality of justice for all marginalized people;
- Scholarly research that would serve practitioners, agencies, communities and populations seeking social justice;
- Strengthening social work practice through the ongoing infusion of social justice education and research.

Faculty and alumni of the school developed ways to carry out activities that would deepen and strengthen the resolve for social justice within the school and in the larger environment of the university.

Implementing these activities demanded a renewed commitment to integrating social justice into the educational and institutional fiber of the school. Further, promoting a partnership between research and practice, parallel to a more personal partnership between the university and the community, would be needed. All these activities would require new and fertile forms of collaboration among students, faculty and practitioners with the common goal of practicing justice.

Currently, the School of Social Service at Saint Louis University attracts significant numbers of students because of its commitment to and emphasis on social justice. Faculty members of the School and its Center for Social Justice Education and Research strive to nourish students' hunger for reflection on justice, and for social justice activities, by incorporating social justice into the lifeblood of the school. How is social justice infused into the policies and practices of a school? Ignacio Ellacuria (1982), slain rector of the University of Central America, expressed this well:

> [I]t does not mean that the university should abdicate its mission of academic excellence–excellence needed in order to solve complex social problems. It does mean that the university should be present intellectually where it is needed: to provide science for those who have no science; to provide skills for the unskilled; to be a voice for those who do not possess the academic qualifications to promote and legitimate their rights. (Kolvenbach, 2000)

Maintaining scholarly excellence while building relationships with vulnerable populations has borne fruit at Saint Louis University and around the country (Hollander & Saltmarsh, 2000). Students and faculty experience how the social justice focus of the Center and the school as a whole enriches student learning and channels energy into a host of meaningful, exciting projects. The Center amplifies the school's concern with *who* our students become, promoting in them a "well-educated solidarity" (Kolvenbach, 2000, p. 9) with marginalized people, learned through contact as well as concepts.

The Center, nested in the school, dedicates itself, first of all, to promoting opportunities for students to address community-based issues of social justice. Opportunities to apply knowledge in real practice settings complement the focus on social justice issues in theoretical classroom-based discussions and debates. The Center also contributes to social work's view of social justice as an essential activity of the profession, as endorsed by the National Association of Social Workers (NASW) (Flynn, 1995; National Association of Social Workers, 1996; Van Soest, 1995).

This article describes the unfolding of this dream of social justice in education, research and practice, as well as the place of such collaborations in the profession of social work. Research and education will be examined separately in their links to social work practice; a description of the current implementation of the integrated model will follow.

RESEARCH AND PRACTICE

Founders of the Center hoped to promote stronger links between research and practice in social work. The gap between academia and the community, as well as between social work research and practice, has been well documented (Gambrill, 1997; Kanfer, 1990; Thyer, Isaac, & Larkin, 1997). Tsang (2000) points out that research too often deals with questions that do not relate to the world of practitioners. For the Center to collaborate effectively with community agencies, faculty and staff knew that they must speak to the community in the language of the community. The Center recognized the need to move from the conceptual interests of researchers to themes designed to answer relevant practice questions. To accomplish this, the Center began the research process with questions that trouble the community and set up strong research partnerships with community agencies. Examples of community-identified research issues include:

- How can society protect people with mental retardation from rearrest and from abuse of their rights in the criminal justice system?
- If nurse aides (often living in poverty, largely women of color and poorly paid) develop a higher sense of empowerment and control in their work lives, might they become better caregivers to another vulnerable population, patients with Alzheimer's Disease?
- What happens to state economic development funds? Is economic development sparked by use of this public resource?

Practice research must inform social work practice. Social work as a profession is moving toward more evidence-based practice (Lovett & Wellendorf, 1991; Thyer, 1989). Research utilization, as a principle of standard social work practice, has even trickled down to social work practice textbooks (Gibbs & Gambrill, 1997; Kirst-Ashman & Hull, 1995; Shulman, 1999; Zastrow, 2000). Despite these forward strides, the integration of research into practice does not appear to be standard practice in the field. The Center for Social Justice was originally organized to facilitate an academic culture that integrates research and practice through the funding of clinically relevant research. The Center simultaneously offers students practical community-based research experience and skills to carry into the field after graduation.

Turnbull, Saltz, and Gwyther (1988) report that, while community agencies may value research, practitioners are usually lacking "opportunities, expectations [and] rewards for engaging in research" (p. 97). When practitioners are asked about barriers to research in practice, they name access to resources (e.g., technical information and assistance) and the absence of funding to be key obstacles (Cook, Freedman, Evans, Rodell, & Taylor, 1992). The Center for Social Justice serves to bridge gaps in needed resources by offering technical information and assistance, as well as modest funding that allow practicing social workers in the community to engage in research that is timely and useful to their practice. For the community agency, receiving the needed support to conduct research assists them in measuring program outcomes, gaining public policy change, and leveraging additional funding.

UNIVERSITY AND COMMUNITY: EDUCATING FOR JUSTICE

A recent survey of Saint Louis University faculty and staff reveals that they contribute hundreds of thousands of community service hours in building homes, donating blood and serving on community agency boards (Delicath & Schaeffer, 2000). The University endorses and promotes the spirit of volunteerism and even institutionalizes its commitment to service through tenure requirements for faculty. Handlin (1986) aptly summarized the need for service contributions by universities:

> . . . a troubled universe can no longer afford the luxury of pursuits confined to an ivory tower, so that [now] scholarship has to prove its worth not on its own terms but by service to the nation and to the world. (p.131)

Despite the world's needs, Boyer (1990) emphasizes, "One is struck by the gap between values in the academy and the needs of the larger world. Service is routinely praised, but accorded little attention" (p. 22). Maloney (2000) observed that, at universities and colleges across the country, "tenure and promotion committees often fail to recognize community-based inquiry as 'real' research" (p. 40).

The Center and the social work profession as a whole aspire to participate in service that includes the direct engagement of people with each other and the development of enduring professional partnerships. When faculty and students bring their scholarly skills as well as their time to the table, they provide service through a sustained collaborative partnership between the university (with its ferment of ideas) and the community (with its crucible of practice). As Boyer (1990) further emphasizes:

> To be considered scholarship, service activities must be tied directly to one's special field of knowledge and relate to, and flow directly out of, this professional activity. Such service is serious, demanding work, requiring the rigor–and the accountability–traditionally associated with research activities. (p. 22)

The Center's vision calls for linking the faculty and students with community practitioners in service to one another. This type of collaborative enterprise benefits all partners, as well as the profession. Tebb, Cook, Berg-Weger, Gallagher, and Flory (2001) describe the barriers faced by agencies and schools in conducting practice-based research. In partnership, they can "build on their respective strengths, specifically the agency's ability to be on the cutting edge of social work practice and the school's expertise in research methods" (Tebb et al., 2001, p. 3). This vision of placing university expertise and resources at the service of the community enjoys deep resonance among the faculty and students at this school. Even with such resonance, the vision must be implemented in practical ways that usually involve getting one's hands dirty with the complications and contradictions of research in real life settings. Little precedent exists for this model. Bok (1990, p. 105) demonstrates that many of the intellectuals at the vortex of social change worked independently of universities (e.g., Rachel Carson, Ralph Nader, Betty Friedan, and Michael Harrington).

How can research designed to advance the body of social work knowledge and inform contemporary social work practice also directly challenge injustice experienced by real people? The Center for Social Justice addresses this issue by inviting community practitioners to undertake the role of principal investigator in the research. Research projects funded by the Center are fashioned by community agencies and serve their immediate research needs. Some agencies wish to conduct needs assessments, to eschew services that are easy to provide in favor of those that most effectively contribute to vulnerable populations, such as homeless adolescents now apart from their homeless families. Other agencies want to explore the effectiveness of a specific intervention (e.g., Will this intervention reduce the domestic violence perpetrated by convicted men against their female partners? Can interracial dialogue groups change racial attitudes?). Still others conduct program evaluations, examining the extent to which their agency mission is attained and exploring strategies for higher levels of achievement. In this way, community agencies draw their research design from the specific challenges and needs they face.

In this nexus of research and practice, faculty collaborators provide the community agency with their own expertise and resources. The faculty collaborator's training fosters the development of a research design that can answer with scholarly integrity the questions posed by the agency. The level of discourse moves from the practice question (e.g., "What prevents adults with chronic mental illness from seeking employment?") to its operationalization as a research question (e.g., "How many individuals must be in our sample to obtain a meaningful result?" Or "How can we protect the confidentiality of our subjects while obtaining medical or court records?"). The faculty member also bears a key responsibility in the protection of human subjects and the negotiation of approval from the Institutional Review Board (IRB). The IRB approval process reveals to the community the commitment of the university to protecting the human rights of all research subjects, especially vulnerable populations.

THE MODEL

The model of practice for the Center is not new (Rapp, Camberlain, & Freeman, 1989; Seidman & Rapport, 1974); it calls for a three-way partnership of community, faculty and students, with each element of the partnership essential to its success. The community group needs the expertise and resources of the faculty and the service of the student. The student benefits from the scholarly instruction provided by faculty and the application of instruction in an agency setting with the community group. The faculty member seeks opportunities to test ideas in an environment where the ideas can most benefit vulnerable populations. Many of these theories are then presented, too, in the court of publication, where critical appraisal by colleagues and peers provides additional refining of those ideas.

IMPLEMENTATION OF THE MODEL IN RESEARCH

The founders of the Center for Social Justice recognize the importance of supporting and encouraging faculty scholarship and want to sustain and enhance scholarly development. What types of support do faculty need in conducting research? The Center's experience shows that two obstacles appear to block faculty research progress more than others do:

1. developing solid research methods and
2. navigating through the IRB process.

In addition to providing support services in these two key areas, the Center pairs students with projects, and pairs community groups with faculty collaborators. The fact that research projects are funded on an ongoing basis, with more faculty and students involved each year, means that the Center, too, contributes to the development of a community of scholars in the school. This community is an intangible asset that reinvigorates the academic life of the school.

The types of help the Center gives to community groups, faculty and students in developing and funding research projects is comprehensive. The Research Committee of the Center plays a vital mentoring role, responding to requests for guidance on designing and funding research. Committee members include a blend of community agency and faculty volunteers who meet as needed, refining the research operation and selecting proposals for funding. The process begins with the long-range development of relationships between the School of Social Service and the community. The terms "agencies" and "community groups" are used here interchangeably, to refer to entities in the community that work with vulnerable populations. Many of these sites serve, too, as practicum placement sites for social work students. Center staff seeks out relationships with agencies that practice the goals of the Center, including the alleviation of unjust social and economic barriers, the education of students as practitioners of social justice, and the support of faculty-community partnerships for social justice research.

The community group may be incorporated as a nonprofit organization with a large staff, even a development department, or may be a grassroots collection of committed but poorly paid staff and volunteers. As the Center builds relationships with community groups, practitioners dialogue with faculty about submitting a proposal. The faculty hear the practice issues that interest community groups; the agencies have the chance to consider which faculty and students might join them to work on a project related to social justice. The Center serves first as matchmaker and maintains contact with the evolving interests of faculty. To help the faculty find research assistants, Center staff maintains a file of students seeking research experience.

The funding cycle begins in the fall with a request for proposals (RFP). Approximately 500 community agencies, organizations and citizens receive the RFP. Agencies can then respond with a Letter of Intent that proposes a research project. Letters of Intent (LOIs) are only three pages long, so that a community organization does not invest a great amount of time in proposing a study that has little likelihood of being funded. The Center's Research Committee reviews the Letters of Intent and rates each using a set of weighted criteria (e.g., relevance to Center goals, methodological quality, value to student research education, feasibility). The Committee typically approves twice the number of LOIs that are expected to be funded.

Once a Letter of Intent is approved, a Proposal Development Workshop follows, helping community agencies to craft successful proposals. Issues addressed in this workshop include:

- What is the best research design to use?
- How should the budget be developed?
- What can reasonably be expected of a student research assistant?
- Who can help to develop the public policy implications of the research?

Principal investigators are the primary audience for the workshop, but all faculty and interested students from the school are invited to attend. Individual research consultation is also offered to community practitioners and faculty before the spring deadline for full proposal submission.

Not all proposals can be funded. However, agencies that are not selected for funding receive specific feedback on alternative sources of funding or alternative approaches to the proposed study. Successfully funded proposals may have changes mandated by the committee. Otherwise, investigators are free to begin their funded research, after IRB approval for protection of human subjects.

Securing IRB approval has become more complex and time-consuming. Recent university-wide research shutdowns by the federal government, in concern for unethical practices, has led to more rigorous IRB requirements and consequent delays in processing requests. The Center encourages the faculty collaborator to assume the responsibility for the interface with the IRB, while the community agency usually shoulders the responsibility for data collection. Eager students help with all tasks, including the IRB submission, subject recruitment, data collection, analyses and dissemination of findings.

The duration of most projects is one to two years. Projects from the Center have already resulted in a number of publications and paper presentations, as well as revitalized community agency priorities and practice (Abram, Anderson, Baker, Palacios, & Stevenson, 2000; Birkenmaier, in press; Chastain & Slosar, 2000; Coleman, 1999; Cook, Morton, & DiTraglia, 2000; Flory & Dunn, 2000; Krehmeyer, Salsich, & Schmitz, 1999; Linhorst, Bennett, & McCutchen, in press; Linhorst & Eckert, 1999 and 2001; Linhorst, Eckert, Hamilton, & Young, 1999 and in press; Linhorst, Hamilton, Young, & Eckert, in press; Maguire, Linhorst, McCutchen, & Bennett, 1999; Palmer, 1999; Rome & Slaght, 1999; Schmitz, 1999; Sherraden, Slosar, & Chastain, 2001; Stretch, Bartlett, Hutchison, Taylor, & Wilson, 1999; Wernet, 2000; as well as other articles in this volume).

Implementation of the Model in Education

An alumnus of the Saint Louis University School of Social Service recently likened the role of social worker to that of a gardener, who provides water, compost, and access to light to nurture the growth of the plants (Shipp, 2000). Like the gardener, the Center for Social Justice nurtures students' unique interests in practicing justice in community settings, providing a range of experiences to meet student needs. Some students have a desire to rectify community injustices, but do not know where to begin. Others lack knowledge of settings that provide direct contact with vulnerable populations and opportunities to make an institutional or systemic difference. For still other students, the Center offers a wake-up call: social justice is the vocation of social workers. To address all of these needs, the Center decided to fund relevant student practice experiences besides the research projects (Birkenmaier, 2003). Bachelor and master's level students in the program complete one to four practica in the course of their studies. The Center offers stipends for such practica if students meet the following requirements:

- The student is serving a vulnerable population.
- The experience supports social justice.
- The student creates a "sustainable benefit" from the practice, such as public presentations on policy needs and strategies, production of a manual or information tool to leave in the community agency for community use, a letter to the editor or newspaper commentary to highlight a social problem or policy need, etc.

These competitive education stipends become an incentive for students to deepen their education in social justice. The Education Committee of the Center for Social Justice has designed a structure and created a set of priorities to reinforce social work's role as agent of social change. Besides funding practica, the Center supports immersion-style education experiences in Cuernavaca, Mexico, where students interact with community organizers in very low-income areas. In fifteen days, students discover the international context of poverty, the implications of multinational corporations, globalization, world trade agreements and solidarity. Students subsidized in this college credit experience commit in advance to service within the university when they return. Even without this commitment, there is no restraining students' zealous work to spread their knowledge of international poverty and its policy implications for the U.S. The stories told to students by the people they encounter move hearts deeply. Because of the success of this educational experience, the school is currently creating a similar educational expedition to Ghana.

CONCLUSION

Of the many paths to social justice, the Center has chosen to integrate research, practice and education. This path relies on the complementary talents and working collaboration of social work students, practitioners and faculty. These collaborations require a willingness to consider openly others' perspectives in order to create an approach to social work practice that is more comprehensive, fulfilling and effective in bringing about social justice. What all three collaborative entities attain together is a more powerful force to create justice for and with vulnerable populations.

These three essential collaborative entities do not blend to become one; instead, each offers its unique contribution within the context of the others. The products of this collaboration include the informing of practice with scholarship; the focus of research on community concerns; and the scholarly and practical education of students in the amelioration of social injustice. Together the chemistry of the collaboration infuses the Center's projects and members with energy and purpose. Practitioners, students and faculty fix their eyes on the horizon of social justice, with different, yet complementary perspectives. The partnership model proposed here, a model that continues to be fine-tuned and modified through experience and mutual feedback, offers an important contribution to the profession of social work.

REFERENCES

Abram, F.Y., Anderson, D., Baker, B., Palacios, P. & Stevenson, C. (2000, December). *Advocating for female offenders: Changing views of blame.* Paper presented at the 100th Annual Conference of Missouri Association for Social Welfare, St. Louis.

Birkenmaier, J. (2003). On becoming a social justice practitioner. *Social Thought, 22*(2/3), 41-54.

Bok, D. (1990). *Universities and the future of America.* Durham, NC: Duke University Press.

Boyer, E. (1990). *Scholarship reconsidered: Priorities of the professoriate.* New York: The Carnegie Foundation for the Advancement of Teaching.

Chastain, N. & Slosar, B. (2000, December). *"Human sized" economic development in Missouri: Challenges and opportunities.* Paper presented at the 100th Annual Conference of Missouri Association for Social Welfare, St. Louis.

Coleman S. J., J.A. (1999). Compassion, solidarity and empowerment: The ethical contribution of religion to society. In J.J. Stretch, M. Bartlett, W. Hutchison, S. A. Taylor, & J. Wilson (Eds.), *Raising our children out of poverty.* New York: Haworth Press.

Cook, C. A. L., Freedman, J. A., Evans, R., Rodell, D. & Taylor, R. M. (1992). Research in social work practice: Benefits of and obstacles to implementation in the Department of Veterans Affairs. *Health and Social Work, 17*(3), 214-222.

Cook, C.A.L., Morton, L. & DiTraglia, C. (2000, December). *Juvenile offenders and the revolving door syndrome.* Paper presented at the 100th Annual Conference of Missouri Association for Social Welfare, St. Louis.

Delicath, T. & Schaeffer, B. (2000). *Beyond the classroom: Service for others.* St. Louis: Saint Louis University Office of Enrollment and Academic Research & Community Outreach Center.

Ellacuria, I. (1982, June). *The task of the Christian university.* Paper presented at the University of Santa Clara for the International Convocation, Santa Clara, CA.

Flory, B. & Dunn, J. (2000, December). *Investigating children's well-being in a supervised access setting.* Paper presented at the 100th Annual Conference of Missouri Association for Social Welfare, St. Louis.

Flynn, J.P. (1995). Social justice in social agencies. In R.L. Edwards, (Editor in Chief), *Encyclopedia of social work* (19th Edition). Washington, DC: NASW Press, 2173-2179.

Gambrill, E. (1997). Social work education: Current concerns and possible futures. In M. Reisch & E. Gambrill (Eds.), *Social work in the 21st century.* Thousand Oaks, CA: Pine Forge Press, 317-327.

Gibbs, L. & Gambrill, E. (1997). *Critical thinking for social workers.* Thousand Oaks, CA: Pine Forge Press.

Handlin, O. (1986). Epilogue-Continuities. In B. Bailyn, D. Fleming, O. Handlin, & S. Thernstrom (Eds.), *Glimpses of the Harvard past.* Cambridge, MA: Harvard University Press, 129-131.

Hollander, E. L. & Saltmarsh, J. (2000). The engaged university. *Academe, 86*(4), 29-32.

Kanfer, F. H. (1990). The scientist-practitioner connection: A bridge in need of constant attention. *Professional Psychology: Research and Practice, 21,* 264-270.

Kirst-Ashman, K. K. & Hull, G. H., Jr. (1995). *Understanding generalist practice.* Chicago: Nelson-Hall.

Kolvenbach, P. H. (2000). The service of faith and the promotion of justice in American Jesuit higher education. *Commitment to Justice in Jesuit Higher Education.* Retrieved March 1, 2001, from the World Wide Web: *http://www.scu.edu/news/releases/1000/kolvenbach_speech.html.*

Krehmeyer, C., Salsich, Jr., P. W., & Schmitz, C. L. (1999). Ecumenical housing: Providing housing and services. In J.J. Stretch, M. Bartlett, W. Hutchison, S. A.Taylor, & J. Wilson (Eds.), *Raising our children out of poverty.* New York: Haworth Press, 89-102.

Linhorst, D.M., Bennett, L. & McCutchen, T. (in press). The development and implementation of a program for offenders with developmental disabilities. *Mental Retardation.*

Linhorst, D.M. & Eckert, A. (2001, April). *Involving forensic clients in program evaluation.* Paper presented at the Annual Missouri Forensic Conference, Lake Ozark, MO.

Linhorst, D. M. & Eckert, A. (1999, April). *Empowering forensic clients residing in long-term psychiatric hospitals: Opportunities and limitations.* Presented at the Annual Missouri Forensic Conference, Lake Ozark, MO.

Linhorst, D. M., Eckert, A., Hamilton, G. & Young, E. (in press). The involvement of a consumer council in organizational decision making in a public psychiatric hospital. *Journal of Behavioral Health Services and Research.*

Linhorst, D. M., Eckert, A., Hamilton, G. & Young, E. (1999, September). *Empowering persons with mental illnesses: Limitations and opportunities.* Presented at the Annual Missouri Association for Social Welfare Conference, Columbia, MO.

Linhorst, D.M., Hamilton, G., Eckert, A. & Young, E. *Promoting client participation in organizational decision making.* Manuscript submitted for publication.

Linhorst, D. M., Hamilton, G., Young, E. & Eckert, A. (in press). Opportunities and limitations to empowering persons with severe mental illness through treatment planning. *Social Work.*

Linhorst, D. M., McCutchen, T. & Bennett, L. *Recidivism among offenders with developmental disabilities participating in a case management program.* Manuscript submitted for publication.

Lovett, M. K. & Wellendorf, S. A. (1991). *Research utilization: A study guide.* Ida Grove, IA: Horn Video Productions.

Maguire, M., Linhorst, D.M., McCutchen, T. & Bennett, L. (1999, September). *Developmentally disabled offenders: An evaluation of services.* Presented at the Annual Missouri Association for Social Welfare Conference, Columbia, MO.

Maloney, W. A. (2000). The community as a classroom. *Academe, 86*(4), pp. 38-42.

National Association of Social Workers (1996). *Code of Ethics,* revised by NASW Delegate Assembly. Silver Spring, MD.

Palmer, N. (1999). Fostering resiliency in children: Lessons learned in transcending adversity. In J.J. Stretch, M. Bartlett, W. Hutchison, S. A. Taylor, & J. Wilson (Eds.), *Raising our children out of poverty.* New York: Haworth Press, 69-87.

Rapp, C.A., Camberlain, R. & Freeman, E. (1989). Practicum: New opportunities for training, research and service delivery. *Journal of Teaching in Social Work, 3*(1), 3-16.

Rome, S. H. & Slaght, E. F. (1999). Welfare reform and the future of foster care. In J.J. Stretch, M. Bartlett, W. Hutchison, S. A. Taylor, & J. Wilson (Eds.), *Raising our children out of poverty.* New York: Haworth Press, 21-36.

Schmitz, C. L. (1999). Collaborative practice in low income communities: University, agency, public school partnerships. In J.J. Stretch, M. Bartlett, W. Hutchison, S. A. Taylor, & J. Wilson (Eds.), *Raising our children out of poverty.* New York: Haworth Press, 53-67.

Seidman, E. & Rappaport, J. (1974). The educational pyramid: A paradigm for training, research, and manpower utilization in community psychology. *American Journal of Community Psychology, 2*(2), 119-130.

Sherraden, M. S., Slosar, B. & Chastain, A. (March 9, 2001). *"Human-sized" economic development: Giving communities in state policy.* A paper presented at the 47th Annual Program Meeting Council on Social Work Education, Dallas, TX.

Shipp, D. (2000, September). *Building bridges to social justice.* Keynote presentation for Social Justice Night to School of Social Service at Saint Louis University.

Shulman, L. (1999). *The skills of helping individuals, families, groups and communities.* Itasca, IL: Peacock.

Stretch, J. J., Bartlett, M., Hutchison, W. J., Taylor, S. A. & Wilson, J., Eds. (1999). *Raising our children out of poverty.* Co-published simultaneously as *Social Thought (Vol. 19, number 2, 1999).*

Tebb, S. S., Cook, C. A. L., Berg-Weger, M., Gallagher, M.B., & Flory, B. (2001). *The research education partnership model: Community, faculty and student partnerships in practice evaluation.* Manuscript submitted for publication.

Thyer, B. A. (1989). First principles of practice research. *British Journal of Social Work, 29*, 353-359.

Thyer, B.A., Isaac, A. & Larkin, R. (1997). Integrating research and practice. In M. Reisch & E. Gambrill (Eds.), *Social work in the 21st century.* Thousand Oaks, CA: Pine Forge Press, 311-316.

Tsang, A. K. T. (2000). Bridging the gap between clinical practice and research: An integrated practice-oriented model. *Journal of Social Service Research, 26*(4), 69-85.

Turnbull, J. E., Saltz, C. C. & Gwyther, L. P. (1988). A prescription for promoting social work research in a university hospital. *Health and Social Work, 13*, 97-105.

Van Soest, D. (1995). Peace and social justice. In R. L. Edwards (Editor in Chief), *Encyclopedia of social work* (19th Edition). Washington, DC: NASW Press, 1810-1818.

Wernet, S. (2000, December). *Program evaluation of bridges across racial polarization.* Paper presented at the 100th Annual Conference of Missouri Association for Social Welfare, St. Louis.

Zastrow, C. (2000). *Introduction to social work and social welfare.* Belmont, CA: Brooks/Cole Wadsworth Publishing.

On Becoming a Social Justice Practitioner

Julie Birkenmaier

SUMMARY. Working toward social justice has always been a part of the social work profession. However, many social workers experience difficulty incorporating social change activities within their professional practice. Practitioners must both learn to practice social change while students and be supported in such activities in their professional practice. An example of a resource within a social work program that explicitly ties practice and social justice is described. Suggestions for integrating justice into practice are included. *[Article copies available for a fee from The Haworth Document Delivery Service: 1-800-HAWORTH. E-mail address: <docdelivery@haworthpress.com> Website: <http://www.HaworthPress.com> © 2003 by The Haworth Press, Inc. All rights reserved.]*

KEYWORDS. Social justice, social work, practice, education

INTRODUCTION

The social work profession has deep, historical and contemporary roots into the struggle for social justice in the culture and society of the United States. The core values of social work emphasize working to promote human devel-

Julie Birkenmaier, MSW, LCSW, is Associate Clinical Professor at Saint Louis University School of Social Service.

Address correspondence to: Julie Birkenmaier, MSW, LCSW, 3550 Lindell Blvd., St. Louis, MO 63103 (E-mail: Birkenjm@slu.edu).

The author would like to thank Dr. Marla Berg-Weger, Saint Louis University School of Social Service, for her invaluable assistance in preparing this manuscript.

[Haworth co-indexing entry note]: "On Becoming a Social Justice Practitioner." Birkenmaier, Julie. Co-published simultaneously in *Social Thought* (The Haworth Press, Inc.) Vol. 22, No. 2/3, 2003, pp. 41-54; and: *Practicing Social Justice* (ed: John J. Stretch et al.) The Haworth Press, Inc., 2003, pp. 41-54. Single or multiple copies of this article are available for a fee from The Haworth Document Delivery Service [1-800-HAWORTH, 9:00 a.m. - 5:00 p.m. (EST). E-mail address: docdelivery@haworthpress.com].

© 2003 by The Haworth Press, Inc. All rights reserved.
http://www.haworthpress.com/store/product.asp?sku=J131
10.1300/J131v22n02_04

opment and the improvement of social conditions. Starting with Jane Addams, social work has a long history of working to improve the lives of individual clients and alter the social structures that create and sustain social inequities. However, since the beginning of the profession tension has existed between the roles of social work advocacy and direct service (Barker, 1999; Witkin, 1998). As the profession has evolved, this tension has persisted. How much should the profession stress a social worker's responsibility to help individuals and families adjust to inequalities, domination and exploitation rather than the responsibility to work toward social reform (Gil, 1998)? Is it possible to work toward structural reform through direct work with individuals, families and groups?

By virtue of membership in the profession, social workers embrace the idea of social justice. The difficulties involved in working toward justice in practice are manifold, to include: lack of knowledge and training in incorporating a social justice perspective and social change activities in practice; lack of administrative support for such activities; and the increasing focus on the agency bottom-line and efficiency. As many social workers seek to gain legitimacy and acceptance as mental health practitioners, social change activities may be viewed as distinct from professional activities. While the profession has become increasingly professional and legitimated, the commitment to pursuing social justice has been inconsistent and seen by some as faltering (Jacobson, 2001; Sachs & Newdom, 1999). Further, the increase in private practice and decrease in advocacy taking place in the profession has raised the alarm of those who take the pulse of the social work profession (Brill, 1989). Individualizing problems in direct clinical practice can also serve to maintain unjust social and institutional forces that directly relate to personal problems (Sachs & Newdom, 1999).

While the service delivery and activist roles can be viewed as competing, another view of the roles is as complementary and intertwined. As a profession, social workers feel a strong loyalty to their clients. This loyalty generally plays out through the provision of resources and services to assist clients in the short term. Social workers are uniquely suited to assist clients with immediate human needs and work to change institutions to be responsive to the needs of all. Since the beginning, social workers are one of the few professions that work with the oppressed and act to ameliorate misery and work to create structures that are more just and humane (Sachs & Newdom, 1999). Through both advocacy and direct service, social workers have sought better conditions in institutions, the workplace, the home and the community (Prigoff, 2000).

This article will discuss the social justice mandate in the NASW *Code of Ethics* (NASW, 1996) and the implementation in social work practice. Further, an educational model that supports practice infused with social change activities is described. Primary emphasis will be given to discussion of ways in which social workers can develop a social justice perspective on practice as well as to discussion of mechanisms to engage in social change activities within practice.

Social Justice and the NASW **Code of Ethics**

Social work has a demonstrated commitment to social justice through the NASW *Code of Ethics* (NASW, 1996). The topic of social justice appears prominently in the *Code*, to include discussion in the preamble, ethical principles and the final section. Social justice is also included in the set of core values at the foundation of social work's unique purpose and perspective. Further, most social workers are knowledgeable about the inclusion of social justice and are supportive of this content in the *Code* (Brill, 1989).

Social justice is generally discussed as both a process and a product. Social workers are charged, by the *Code*, with ". . . pursuing social change, particularly with and on behalf of vulnerable and oppressed individuals and groups of people." While the *Code* does not specify the exact meaning of social justice, Van Soest (1992) defined the vision of social justice in society to include economic, social and political equality, between and among individuals and groups, as well as within and between institutions. The concept typically involves discussion of fairness, equity and equality (Flynn, 1995). Those concerned with peace often cite social justice as a necessary factor in attaining a lasting peace (Van Soest, 1992). The definition of social justice inevitably involves a vision of a socially just society in which, among other elements, the basic needs of all individuals are met (e.g., material, social-psychological, productive-creative, security, self-actualization and spiritual), essential institutions are held in public trust and administered for the good of all in society, work and production reengineered such that individuals are able to integrate their mental, physical and emotional faculties in their work experience, equality of social, civil, cultural and political rights, responsibilities and opportunities exist, and work and products are in harmony with nature. Further, decision-making at all levels would be truly democratic, nonhierarchical, and decentralized (Gil, 1998; Reeser & Leighninger, 1990; Wakefield, 1998).

Three contemporary views of social justice are:

1. legal justice (i.e., one's obligations to society);
2. commutative justice (i.e., obligations between individuals); and
3. distributive justice (i.e., society's obligation to individuals) (Van Soest, 1995).

Although commutative justice is a part of clinical practice and organizational social work practice, distributive justice has been the focus of social workers' social change activities through seeking responsiveness to the client's needs at the structural or institutional level (Birkenmaier, 1999; Wakefield, 1998). The *Code* defines the preeminent issues of social work and social justice as poverty, unemployment and discrimination. It further discusses the need to provide ". . . needed information, services and resources, equality of opportunity and meaningful participation in decision making for all people." In contrast, social injustices are those conditions or situations that oppress, withhold information, limit full and meaningful participation, establish and/or maintain inequalities, structure the unequal distribution of resources, inhibit development and, in other ways, deny equal opportunities for all (Gil, 1998; Van Soest, 1992).

Social Justice and Social Work Practice

Where do social work practice and social justice interface? Social work literature has viewed the topic of social justice and social work practice in the context of a plethora of societal issues, to include juvenile and criminal justice (Ross & Shireman, 1972), all forms of violence, poverty, drug abuse, trauma and international development (Gil, 1998; Van Soest, 1992; Van Soest & Crosby, 1997), diversity, oppression and the various "isms" (e.g., racism, sexism, ageism and homophobia) (Arnold & Roberts, 1979; Brill, 1989; Chestang, 1993; Gil, 1998; Longres, 1993; Norton, 1993; Rothman, 1971; Van Soest, 1992), and income equality and public assistance (Ozawa, 1993). Social justice has also been considered relative to the context of service delivery within an agency (Flynn, 1995).

Social workers work toward social justice in a variety of professional activities. Such activities include advocating for clients with public and private human service professionals and agencies, supporting the disadvantaged in their collective efforts to improve their social and economic well-being, conducting research to identify inadequacies of the social welfare system and striving to influence political decision-makers through professional organizations about the needs of vulnerable populations. Others seek to shape value preferences in society by working with the media or lobbying legislators (Allen, 1997). Other practice-based examples include: teaching nonviolent conflict resolution in schools, working with families to decrease violence within their families and neighborhoods, evaluating programs to inform policy initiatives toward better service delivery and providing economic literacy training to women to enhance their empowerment (Van Soest, 1992). Social workers that are clinically-focused work toward social justice on a one-to-one basis by engaging clients in reflection and dialogue concerning the consequences of the current social, economic, political, cultural and community realities on their everyday lives. These dialogues are efforts toward expanding clients' critical consciousness about the structures that create and maintain their issues and seek to empower clients to become involved in the community efforts toward institutional change and reform (Gil, 1998; Markowitz, 1997; Swenson, 1994).

Little literature exists that describes the extent to which social workers incorporate working toward social justice in their personal or professional lives. In one of the most comprehensive empirical research on the topic to date, Brill (1989) surveyed 800 members of the Massachusetts chapter of the National Association of Social Workers (NASW). With a response rate of 73%, 585 responses were received. Brill reports that the majority of social workers are not acting on the social injustice mandates of the NASW *Code*. Of those who were active, advocacy for individual clients occurred more frequently than social policy or political action. The most frequently cited obstacles to taking action were limitations imposed by agency funding, lack of time and lack of support. Of particular interest is the finding that social workers who come from groups that are deprived or discriminated against are more likely to care about and act on social injustices. Lastly, social workers reported taking more action on issues of social injustice as private citizens than in professional practice. Brill concludes that, although social workers support taking action on social injustices and do take action in a limited fashion in their personal lives, difficulties exist in incorporating social justice values into their professional practice, to include agency administration sanction and support, as well as time. Clearly, more effort must be made to educate social workers and administrators about the importance and ethical mandate to work toward social justice in their professional practice.

EDUCATION ACTIVITIES OF THE CENTER FOR SOCIAL JUSTICE EDUCATION AND RESEARCH

In an effort to highlight justice-infused practice with students, Saint Louis University School of Social Service's Emmett and Mary Martha Doerr Center for Social Justice Education and Research (CSJER) includes a student education component. The purpose of the CSJER's educational activities is to instill a commitment to social justice and inspire students to take action in their personal and professional lives to work toward social justice as students, in their professional careers and in their personal lives. A committee composed of faculty and community members guide and monitor all sponsored educational efforts. The educational components of the CSJER include stipends for practica, international coursework, and school-sponsored social action activities (i.e., trips to national social action demonstrations). Other funded activities include sponsored educational events at the school (e.g., a "Social Justice Night") and involvement in university-sponsored events related to social justice (e.g., conferences, workshops and speakers). Students are invited to and do participate in all these events. Students may also participate as research assistants and practicum students on CSJER-funded research projects.

The practicum stipend program is an explicit mechanism to encourage justice-based student practice. Practicum is a vital portion of a student's practice training and has a strong influence on the future effectiveness of the student as a practitioner. Concepts and theory are applied in the practicum under supervision. The practicum offers a unique opportunity to learn direct service skills and to build a commitment to social change (Birkenmaier, 1999). The CSJER views the practicum stipend program as an opportunity to assist students to incorporate social justice work as an integral part of practice.

Unlike other CSJER opportunities, the application process is a student-generated process. Students make application by completing an application form. Completing the form entails writing a summary of their planned practicum activities, connecting the planned activities to social justice and describing how the activities will contribute toward efforts to ameliorate a social injustice. Further, students must include a personal statement that describes how the experience will contribute to their personal and professional growth and submit a letter of reference from a former supervisor. In the first four years of operation, the CSJER has provided a stipend to more than nineteen students for their practicum (local, domestic and international practica). Students are encouraged and assisted to apply to the CSJER during the planning process with the faculty liaison, who may also assist them in completing the application. The stipends are not tied to specific agencies, activities or locale; rather, students make application based on the desired agency arrangements and activities. Stipend levels are predetermined: $1,500 for local, $2,000 for national and $2,500 for international experiences. These stipends are at levels large enough to be an incentive for students to apply and allow for sufficient support for travel and housing expenses for national and international practica. These stipends can be applied toward tuition or living expenses during the practicum.

Social Justice Activities

Many types of practice activities incorporate a social justice perspective and represent an effort to achieve social justice on an individual basis and/or in the short-term (Van Soest, 1992). While working toward social justice can include a broad array of activities, the practicum stipend program has focused on the inclusion of efforts to promote systemic change toward social justice and/or development of educational programs that lessen discrimination. The requirements for the stipend include inclusion of a contribution toward an effort to change one or more systemic causes of social injustice. The most straightforward examples of this type of effort include the funding of practica that solely involve state and/or national-level policy research, advocacy and lobbying with nonprofit advocacy organizations and legislators. However, students are also encouraged to combine direct service with a systemic change and/or educational efforts. In this respect, students have worked with many different populations to provide direct services and make efforts to change a system for a group of affected clients. The mixture of direct services, social action and education to lessen discrimination have included the following practicum activities:

- Providing casework for mentally ill homeless and assisting them in their advocacy efforts with state officials for additional state funding for mental health services;
- Providing case management for foster children and assisting a local elected official to research needed policy changes in the foster care system with the intent to submit for state legislation;
- Facilitating leadership development in an after school program for teens, providing "Know Your Rights" training to minority teens regarding police abuses and facilitating advocacy between the youth and the police department;
- Educating municipal officials on alternative sentencing programs that involve community service in lieu of incarceration for low-income clients who have been convicted of a misdemeanor and advocating for the adoption of the program in other municipalities; and
- Educating public school officials and teachers on the educational needs of children affected by sickle-cell anemia and encouraging policy changes to better accommodate such children in the school system.

These efforts all include, in a diversity of forums, an effort to lessen discrimination and oppression of a vulnerable population and/or systemic change to benefit a vulnerable population. The funding criteria are broad enough to include and encourage all social work students at every level and in every area of concentration in the program. In this way, students at virtually every level and in any specialization of the program can experience the connection between practice and social justice in their practicum.

Other educational efforts seek to assist students in learning about the connection between practice and social justice, the importance of working for justice as well as providing tools to work toward social change. Stipends for international coursework that are aimed at promoting global awareness include a provision that students must engage in several social justice activities upon the completion of the course. Activities must include a combination of activities from several categories:

1. education about a social justice topic related to the course experience;
2. advocacy on a social justice issue related to the course;
3. fundraising for populations related to those studied in the course; and/or
4. a service project.

This post-course requirement enhances the students' ability to relate their learning throughout an experiential course abroad to local and international social justice issues as well as mechanisms for their involvement in working toward social justice.

School and university-wide educational activities sponsored by CSJER have sought to impact the social work student body at large. For example, the CSJER launched the educational efforts in 1998 by hosting a national conference with the theme of "Raising Our Children Out of Poverty." The proceedings of this conference were published in a scholarly journal and in book form. Further, a "Social Justice Night" event was held at the school for social work students that entailed a keynote address discussing the interface of social justice and practice, breakout sessions that highlighted practicum and volunteer opportunities to work toward social justice as well as networking with organizations. The CSJER also co-hosted a statewide conference with a statewide advocacy organization and has co-hosted events focusing on issues of international social justice (e.g., the U.S/U.N. sanctions in Iraq), highlighting the interface of global social justice issues.

Successes of the Education Program

Although still in the evolutionary stage, the CSJER has enjoyed several areas of "success" with the practicum stipends. First, the application process mandates a critical examination of social work practice in the framework of social justice, and prompts students to consider systemic change as a part of practice. This perspective is one that the CSJER stipend program would like the students to carry with them into their future professional practice. Anecdotal feedback from currently funded and formerly funded students indicates that, in fact, students do make these connections in a more explicit manner through the application process. Further, the funded experiences have overall been very positive learning experiences. Sponsored events, such as "Social Justice Night" and the conferences, have also received positive evaluations, and efforts have been made to incorporate these events into the curriculum of the school. Instructors are incorporating discussion of sponsored events and funded practica into classroom discussions with more frequency as a result of the education program. As approximately 75% of graduates practice in the local area of the university, these alumni have great potential to impact the service delivery system in the area relative to social change activities.

Challenges of the Education Program

With the success comes ongoing challenges of the stipend program. A common misconception among students is that activities to promote systemic change only apply to those students who are interested in macro practice. On the contrary, the CSJER would like to encourage those students who will be doing direct practice with families in family service agencies and in health care systems to connect direct practice and social justice activities. To address this challenge, the CSJER has employed promotion strategies through the school (i.e., in student orientations and marketing materials) to encourage students from every concentration to consider applying. The Practicum Liaisons have been briefed about the stipends and actively encourage students from all concentrations to apply.

Another challenge involves clarifying those activities that address systemic causes of social injustices. Because no single required course is responsible for directly teaching about social justice and systemic change, students often lack an understanding of social justice and applicability to all practice areas. The Practicum Liaisons assist students in understanding the concept and brainstorm eligible activities with the student that is tailored to the agency opportunities. More efforts must be made to assist students to incorporate social justice into their practice during the practicum.

STRATEGIES FOR INCORPORATING SOCIAL JUSTICE INTO PRACTICE

Becoming a justice practitioner requires both a broad perspective on issues and action to address problems at the systemic level. The following are suggestions and ideas to aid social workers in developing both a justice perspective on practice and the mechanisms to take actions on social injustices.

Develop a Justice Perspective

- Become a critical thinker. Become aware of the way in which social welfare policies, cultural practices and societal norms create and maintain vulnerable and oppressed populations (Dietz, 2000).

- Utilize alternative print, radio, Internet and television media sources that reflect different political and ideological perspectives.
- Learn about vulnerable populations in your community (e.g., immigrants, gays and lesbians and minority populations).
- Dialogue with colleagues at work and agency administrators about the social justice content in the NASW *Code*. Discuss mechanism for staff involvement in seeking social change and addressing social injustices.
- Dialogue with colleagues (both within and outside of the profession) who posses a global perspective on social welfare issues. Seek to understand local social welfare issues from a global viewpoint.
- Become a member of organizations that work on macro-level social welfare issues. Seek to understand individual and family issues of clients in the context of societal, political and economic trends.
- At the global level, learn about developing countries and the relationship between the U.S. and the countries. Educate yourself about U.S. foreign aid and support foreign assistance that will promote sustainable human development.

Work Toward Social Justice

1. As a direct clinical social worker:

- Develop a model of practice that integrates clinical work with social change. Consider individual psychological issues (e.g., depression, self-esteem, anger and communication) in the framework of political, social and economic forces impinging on the individual. View family issues in the context of political and economic issues affecting the local community (Sachs & Newdom, 1999).
- Address basic unmet needs of people, listen and help clients define own needs, empower people to make own decisions, promote leadership skills, encourage democratic participation (Van Soest & Crosby, 1997).
- Become knowledgeable about existing community resources to combat and prevent poverty and exploitation. Become involved and encourage clients to become involved.
- Work to decrease all forms of violence and discrimination.
- Work to increase the use of nonviolent conflict resolution techniques and decrease the usage of weapons (Van Soest, 1995).
- Encourage clients to demonstrate respect for people from other countries and cultures.
- Develop ways to work together with other social work practitioners (i.e., a support group, social action caucuses, e-mail listserv and speakers bu-

reau) to influence the behavior of colleagues, administrators, social work organizations and schools of social work.

- Engage in some aspects of policy practice that effects your clients, such as legislative advocacy, litigation and/or social action (Figueira-McDonough, 1993).

2. As an agency administrator:

- Educate social work staff on the social justice mandates of the *Code.* Provide mechanisms, support and opportunities to discuss topics and integrate action on issues of social injustice into the professional practice of staff (Brill, 1989).
- Become familiar with elected officials. Educate them about agencies, programs and clients. Provide information to them about the needs of clients in the community and systemic causes of oppression, as well as possible ways in which to better address needs through policy changes.

3. As a social work educator:

- Incorporate the topic of social justice into teaching. Engage in dialogue with students about the place social justice values have held historically in the profession and the contributions social work has made to social justice (e.g., the creation of settlement houses, juvenile court services and in the Great Society period of the 1960s) (Fauri, 1988). Discuss the inclusion of social justice in the *Code* and the ways in which social work practitioners include working toward social justice in individual professional practice, as part of institutional practices and as administrators (Brill, 1989). Integrate information, activities and assignments about political campaigns, the political process and candidates into courses (Council on Social Work Education, 2001).
- Advocate for more integration of social justice into the curriculum. Support other faculty who seek to integrate content on social justice into their course content.

Preparation Work

Social workers who have not worked from a justice perspective in the past may find the need to prepare agencies and administrators for a change in their practice. Practitioners who would like to make changes may want to consider the following elements in preparing colleagues and supervisors for such a change. Social workers may need to legitimize the following:

- *A systemic perspective.* Social workers may need to explain the contribution a system makes to the individual and family problems facing clients;

- *Social change activities within direct, clinical practice.* Social workers need to be prepared to explain the role of social workers in assisting to create a better "fit" between clients and the systems with which they interact;
- *Social change activities.* Social workers may need to explain that systemic change is long-term change, and social change activities have been instrumental in large-scale changes in the past; and
- *The risk of retribution involved in social change.* Working toward social justice entails making value judgments on agency and social policy, and taking a stand on issues. Engaging in such activities entails running a risk of incurring negative reactions. However, such a risk is inherent in justice-based practice and is a risk worth taking (Garvin & Seabury, 1997).

Further Research Needed

The topic of justice-based practice is ripe for future research and scholarly publication. Research is needed to explore the extent to which social workers are working toward social change in their practice. To complement Brill's statewide study (1989), a large-scale study on a national level is needed to assess the extent to which social workers are incorporating aspects of the *Code* that deal with social justice. Such a study that stratified subjects into sub-fields of social work (e.g., community organization and health practice), demographics (e.g., age, race and ethnicity) and membership or lack of membership in NASW could yield rich data that could further inform justice efforts and social work educational reforms. An empirical evaluation of the impact of the practicum stipend experience, such as with the CSJER, on post-degree practice would also assist in assessing the impact of such experiences on professional practice. Lastly, a study that examines the motivation for and factors that sustain social workers who are activists could enhance the knowledge base of the profession.

CONCLUSION

The experiences of social work students working with the CSJER is one model of a professional plan on the part of the profession to implement the social justice content in our professional *Code*. Educational opportunities available to students explicitly interweave practice and social justice. This interweaving occurs within practice and assists to mold and shape the view of practice of future practitioners. Working for justice in practice necessitates the integration of direct practice and policy (Witkin, 1998). All social workers, regardless of setting, client population or type of services delivered, are called by the NASW *Code* to advance social justice in our society. This call harkens back to the beginning of the profession, and calls social workers forward into the future of the profession. Practitioners must be trained while they are students to make the connections and be assisted in their justice-based practice. While it is impossible to achieve social justice in the United States without some redistribution of power and economic resources (Brill, 1989), our profession can play a central role in the effort to address social injustices. Social workers who do not become client advocates, who do not work toward helping all who need services receive them and work for social justice in our society must ask themselves whether they are truly abiding by the standard of professional conduct espoused by our professional organization through the NASW *Code*. Our professional networks and resources, including colleagues and professional associations, must continue to bridge the dichotomy between practice and social change (Sachs & Newdom, 1999), strengthen their assistance in framing the justice-practice connection and provide resources to act on the connection for practitioners.

REFERENCES

Allen, J.A. (1997). Social justice, social change and baccalaureate degree generalist social work practice. *The Journal of Baccalaureate Social Work, 3*(1), 14-16.

Arnold, L. & Roberts, W. (Eds.) (1979). *Diversity and social justice: The role of social work and social work education.* Proceedings of a seminar held in Melbourne, August, 1979.

Barker, R.L. (1999). *Milestones in the Development of Social Work and Social Welfare.* Washington, DC: NASW Press.

Birkenmaier, J.M. (1999). Promoting social justice within the practicum. *The New Social Worker, 6*(2), 13-15.

Brill, C.M.K. (1989). *The impact on social work practice of the social injustice content in the NASW Code of Ethics.* Unpublished doctoral dissertation, Brandeis University.

Chestang, L. W. (1993). Infusion of minority content in the curriculum. In D.M. Pearson (Ed.), *Perspectives on Equity and Justice in Social Work* (pp. 1-14). Alexandria, Virginia: Council on Social Work Education.

Council on Social Work Education. (2001). Content winners show social work's role in social justice advocacy. *Social Work Education Reporter, 49*(1), 10.

Dietz, C.A. (2000). Reshaping clinical practice for the new millennium. *Journal of Social Work Education, 36*(3), 503-520.

Fauri, E.P. (1988). Applying historical themes of the profession in the foundation curriculum. *Journal of Teaching in Social Work, 2*(1), 17-31.

Figueira-McDonough, J. (1993). Policy-practice: The neglected side of social work intervention. *Social Work, 38*(2), 179-188.

Flynn, J.P. (1995). Social justice in social agencies. In National Association of Social Work *Encyclopedia of Social Work* (19th edition) (pp. 2174-2179). Washington, DC: NASW Press.

Garvin, C.D. & Seabury, B.A. (1997). *Interpersonal Practice in Social Work: Promoting Competence and Social Justice* (2nd ed.). Boston: Allyn & Bacon.

Gil, D.G. (1998). *Confronting Injustice and Oppression: Concepts and Strategies for Social Workers.* New York: Columbia University Press.

Jacobson, W.B. (2001). Beyond therapy: Bringing social work back to human services reform. *Social Work, 46*(1), 51-61.

Longres. J.F. (1993). Toward a status model of ethnic sensitive practice. In D.M. Pearson (Ed.), *Perspectives on Equity and Justice in Social Work* (pp. 35-48). Alexandria, Virginia: Council on Social Work Education.

Markowitz, L. (1997, November/December). Ramon Rojano won't take it. *Networker.* 25-35.

National Association of Social Workers. (1996). *Code of Ethics.* Washington, DC: Author.

Norton, D.G. (1993). Diversity, early socialization, and temporal development: The dual perspective revisited. In D.M. Pearson (Ed.), *Perspectives on Equity and Justice in Social Work* (pp. 1-14). Alexandria, Virginia: Council on Social Work Education.

Ozawa, M.N. (1993). Inequity in income support for children. In D.M. Pearson (Ed.), *Perspectives on Equity and Justice in Social Work* (pp. 67-88). Alexandria, Virginia: Council on Social Work Education.

Prigoff, A. (2000). *Economics for Social Workers: Social Outcomes of Economic Globalization with Strategies for Community Action.* Stanford, CT: Wadsworth/Thomson.

Reeser, L.C. & Leighninger, L. (1990). Back to our roots: Towards a specialization in social justice. *Journal of Sociology & Social Welfare, 17*(2), 69-87.

Ross, B. & Shireman, C. (1972). *Social Work Practice and Social Justice.* Washington, DC: National Association of Social Workers.

Rothman, J. (1971). *Promoting Social Justice in the Multigroup Society.* New York: Association Press.

Sachs, J. & Newdom, F. (1999). *Clinical Work and Social Action: An Integrative Approach.* New York: The Haworth Press.

Swenson, C.R. (1994). Clinical practice and the decline of community. *Journal of Teaching in Social Work, 10*(1-2), 195-212.

Van Soest, D. (1992). *Incorporating Peace and Social Justice into the Social Work Curriculum.* Washington, DC: National Association of Social Workers.

Van Soest, D. (1995). Peace and social justice. In National Association of Social Workers *Encyclopedia of Social Work* (19th edition) (pp. 1810-1817). Washington, DC: NASW Press.

Van Soest, D. & Crosby, J. (1997). *Challenges of Violence Worldwide: A Curriculum Module.* Washington, DC: National Association of Social Workers.

Wakefield, J.C. (1998). Psychotherapy, distributive justice and social work revisited. *Smith College Studies in Social Work, 69*(1), 25-57.

Witkin, S.L. (1998). Is social work an adjective? *Social Work, 43*(6), 483-486.

The Race/Poverty Intersection: Will We Ever Achieve Liberty and Justice for All?

Chester Hartman

SUMMARY. The intersection of race and poverty presents the two most seemingly intractable social problems in the United States today. Despite gains in the recent decades, unacceptable levels of institutional racism and poverty persist. Increasing income and wealth gaps, resegregation of schools, absence of minorities in the highest levels of government and the private sector, and the racialization of space all are indicators of this failure of democracy. The white majority prefers to imagine a colorblind society, not just as a goal but also as a current reality. The Bush administration's negative attitudes toward affirmative action, as well as former President Clinton's failed Race Initiative, are evidence that "liberty and justice for all" are not to be achieved in the near future. *[Article copies available for a fee from The Haworth Document Delivery Service: 1-800-HAWORTH. E-mail address: <docdelivery@haworthpress.com> Website: <http://www.HaworthPress.com> © 2003 by The Haworth Press, Inc. All rights reserved.]*

KEYWORDS. Race, racism, poverty, housing, education

Chester Hartman is President/Executive Director of the Poverty and Race Research Action Council, Washington, DC.

Address correspondence to: Chester Hartman, PRRAC, 3000 Connecticut Avenue NW, #200, Washington, DC 20008 (E-mail: chartman@prrac.org).

[Haworth co-indexing entry note]: "The Race/Poverty Intersection: Will We Ever Achieve Liberty and Justice for All?" Hartman, Chester. Co-published simultaneously in *Social Thought* (The Haworth Press, Inc.) Vol. 22, No. 2/3, 2003, pp. 55-62; and: *Practicing Social Justice* (ed: John J. Stretch et al.) The Haworth Press, Inc., 2003, pp. 55-62. Single or multiple copies of this article are available for a fee from The Haworth Document Delivery Service [1-800-HAWORTH, 9:00 a.m. - 5:00 p.m. (EST). E-mail address: docdelivery@haworthpress.com].

© 2003 by The Haworth Press, Inc. All rights reserved.
http://www.haworthpress.com/store/product.asp?sku=J131
10.1300/J131v22n02_05

The two most seemingly intractable social problems we have in the United States are racism and poverty, particularly the impact when those two problems intersect. Over the last decade, I've been the executive director of a national organization that deals with these issues, the Poverty and Race Research Action Council, located in Washington, DC. Unfortunately, those years have left me with some rather pessimistic views about these issues. But we have to face things honestly and tell it like it is, if we are ever going to see any serious change.

One would have to be a fool or a willful liar not to recognize that there have been enormous positive changes in the areas of race and poverty over the last few decades. Those of us who are old enough to remember what *de jure* segregation was like in the South as well as the *de facto* kind in the rest of the country clearly understand that there has been a lot of improvement. Just read any good history, such as Taylor Branch's *America in the King Years* (the first two volumes, third one still to come out), to be reminded what life was like for racial minorities before the civil rights movement. There is now a large middle class among Blacks, among Latinos, and among Asian Americans. There is tremendous representation by Blacks and Latinos in government as elected officials. But they are not at the highest level. It's extraordinary that as a country with roughly a 25% population of Blacks and Latinos, we have not a single U.S. Senator, not a single governor representing those two population groups. Think what it would be like if the Senate had 25 Blacks and Latinos, in terms of what issues would be considered, relationships, committee work, etc. And it's not just the Senate and governors' chairs. It's everything, from CEOs, to newspaper editors, to tenured faculty. There's still an enormous underrepresentation of minority groups, at the same time that there's been positive change. Beyond that, there's still a lot of terror around, not only extraordinary examples like James Byrd being dragged behind that truck in Jasper, Texas, but hate crimes and immigrant bashing all over the country. It's important to keep that perspective in mind: lots of change, but still enormous problems.

One of the biggest problems I see is our growing income and wealth gap. Millions of Americans work full time and still live below the poverty line. That's just unacceptable. The extent of child poverty is obscene. Thirty-seven percent of Black children in this country are living in families under the poverty line. Carol Bellamy, who heads UNICEF, recently was interviewed and noted that there are two members of the United Nations who haven't signed the International Convention on the Rights of the Child. One is Somalia, the other is the United States. Sometimes I'm ashamed to be American when I hear things like that. Extreme poverty exists among other groups, such as Native Americans on reservations. We also know how inadequate the poverty line is: $14,000-15,000 for a median-sized family; one can't really live on that. The minimum wage is far too low, has not been raised for far too long, and constantly lags behind consumer price increases. The "Living Wage" movement in dozens of cities around the country has succeeded in substantially raising hourly wages, at least for workers on city contracts and those employed by companies enjoying local government subsidies, such as tax breaks, loans and grants. But that's a tiny portion of the workforce, and the vast majority of cities have not enacted such provisions. Diana Pearce of the University of Washington has developed a new poverty level measure which she calls the Self-sufficiency Standard: what it takes to live decently without public or private assistance or subsidies, to be truly economically independent. In San Francisco, the Self-sufficiency Standard for a family of three–a single parent and 2 kids–is $54,000 a year, roughly four times the official poverty level for a family that size.

The wealth gap is even more important than the income gap, and there have been some very good writings on this issue in recent years. One is *Black Wealth, White Wealth*, by Melvin Oliver and Thomas Shapiro (1997); second is Dalton's Conley's *Being Black, Living in Red: Race, Wealth and Social Policy in America* (1999). These studies show not only that the racial wealth gap is much larger than the income gap, but also that it is of greater importance. Whites and Blacks at the same income level have vastly different wealth positions. And with assets, with wealth, you can pass things to your children, you can weather adversity.

This country lacks the kinds of safety nets that exist in other advanced capitalist countries. We're way, way behind, in health care (44 million Americans uninsured), family supports of all types, job training, and education resources. Welfare reform is an issue on which there has been surprisingly little research done with the respect to its racial impact. Multi-million dollar studies are being done by the Urban Institute, the Manpower Research Demonstration Corporation and others, with few available race data. The small amount that we do have shows that minorities are doing worse; that Whites are leaving the caseloads far more rapidly than are minorities (particularly Blacks); that higher proportions of Blacks return to caseloads after one year. A study of rural counties in Northern Virginia documented the racially disparate treatment by welfare caseworkers in everything from providing information about job possibilities to making transportation options available. About half the Blacks and even one out of five Whites in the study said that Blacks are not treated fairly by the Department of Social Service workers. That's a really damning thing to say about professionals who are undertaking this kind of work. Lack of childcare, lack of transportation, lack of good jobs with training and benefits clearly are going to make our national experiment in ending welfare as we know it something that is going to impact Blacks and other minority Americans much worse than whites.

Housing is another critical area. An article in the *New York Times Magazine* not too long ago was titled "The Year Housing Died." Virtually nothing appeared in the 2000 presidential campaigns about housing. But housing is so central to people's lives. Back in 1937, during his second inaugural address, President Roosevelt voiced his famous lament about "one-third of a nation ill-housed." At that time, the primary issue was slums–rural as well as urban– and severe overcrowding. Those problems still exist to an unacceptable degree, but the principal housing problem now is affordability. And if one adds up the number of people paying more for housing than they should, plus those living in substandard and overcrowded quarters, roughly one-third of the nation still is ill-housed, over 60 years later.

My colleague Michael Stone of the University of Massachusetts-Boston has developed a concept he labels "shelter poverty." Traditionally, social policy has dealt with housing affordability as a percentage of income–20%, 25%, 30%–changing (always rising) in different eras. Right now, tenants living in public housing or receiving Section 8 certificates or vouchers are required to pay 30% of their income, with federal subsidies making up the difference between actual costs and market rents. What Professor Stone has done is start with the minimum detailed budgets the federal government publishes (actually, "published"–the Bureau of Labor Statistics stopped doing this right after Ronald Reagan took office, but Stone uses government Consumer Price Index data to update those numbers) and divided those budget amounts into shelter costs and the cost of non-shelter basics–food, clothing, health care, transportation, etc. He then looked at data on actual incomes and arrived at this astounding conclusion: If households were to allocate their funds to non-shelter basics at the minimum level the government asserts is needed (and if one examines the details, those really are minimal levels), 15 million U.S. households do not have any money left over for housing. They can't (shouldn't) spend 30%, 25%, 20%–they can't even afford a penny for rent or mortgage costs. But of course these people do, have to, pay rent or mortgage costs. And so what suffers is diet, medical care, all the other basic necessities.

Housing, then, is an extraordinarily key issue, and yet as a society we are pretty much ignoring it. In my view, this is due in large part to how costly it would be to guarantee everyone a right to decent, affordable housing, given the gap between what people earn and what housing costs. (And, for the record, one should note that as far back as 1949, in its Preamble to the major postwar housing act, Congress promulgated the National Housing Goal of "a decent home and suitable living environment for every American family.") What's needed are basic changes in how housing is financed, developed, owned and managed, in order to create a large nonprofit social sector for housing, of the kind that exists in many other advanced capitalist countries. That would at least lower the costs of trying to cover the income: cost gap, so social goals would not be constantly fighting market forces that lead to huge inflation in rents and housing prices. But beyond cost considerations, another major reason housing is neglected is rooted in issues of race–what is implied for residential and school integration if government were to act seriously to meet the National Housing Goal. Let me delve a bit into that thorny area.

There is a new racism around that we all need to recognize. One form it takes is hostility towards affirmative action, even though affirmative action has been a very successful program, especially in the areas of higher education and employment. The courts have turned their backs on desegregation of schools, which are resegregating at a rapid rate. We are bombarded with the fatuous notion that we should be a colorblind society and just stop paying so much attention to race. People quote Martin Luther King's famous 1963 March on Washington speech about judging people by the content of their character and not the color of their skin. They ignored the Martin Luther King who four years later said, "A society that has done something special *against* the Negro for hundreds of years must now do something special *for* him."

The issue of reparations for slavery has come into prominence lately, in particularly around Randall Robinson's book, *Debt: What America Owes to Blacks* (2000). I very much favor reparations, although it's a real tough sell. People immediately ask: Who pays? Who benefits? What form does it take? Are they individual payments? Are they collective payments? How do you make parallels with issues like the Japanese Americans forced into concentration camps during World War II, victims who still are alive, whereas there are no slaves alive today, nor are any slaveholders alive. But what should be obvious to everyone–although it may need to be spelled out more persuasively and in greater specificity–are the ways in which the legacy of 250 years of slavery, followed by a century of *de jure* segregation and oppression in the South, have left their mark on large segments of the Black population today, and the ways in which Whites, of all classes, have benefited and continue to benefit from what has accurately been labeled "white skin privilege." Comprehending the impact of that history is critical, but we are a society that tends to ignore the meaning and lessons of history ("that's history" in fact is a common putdown). Reparations are very much in order, justified and needed, although the form they take needs to be carefully crafted: not payments to individuals, but community-building, resource-creating expenditures, for education, job training, housing, health care institutions, and economic development.

Ensuring racial justice in light of historical wrongs raises a major issue about targeted versus universal solutions. Is it better to have solutions specifically targeted to the most disadvantaged, as opposed to programs that are universal: Social Security is a good example of the latter. The reason Social Security got lots of support was because virtually everyone would benefit (although it is interesting to note that farmworkers and domestic workers were originally excluded from Social Security, a somewhat racist feature, defects that were cured later on). The program still has racial disparities: Minorities earn less, therefore, they get lower payments; minorities also don't live as long as whites, due to a host of interrelated factors, and so get fewer payments. Nonetheless, a program that has universal benefits, which at the same time benefits the most disadvantaged, may be the better way to go politically as opposed to specifically targeting the most disadvantaged groups.

A further important dimension of the country's racial patterns is what john powell of the University of Minnesota Institute on Race and Poverty terms "the racialization of space": the increasing segregation of metropolitan areas, whereby the central city is overwhelmingly disproportionately minority and poor while the suburbs are White and middle-class. That's been true for many decades. Urban renewal helped that along, the interstate highway program helped that along, FHA helped that along. But what we are increasingly seeing is that with a huge number of local jurisdictions in any metropolitan area, land use, zoning, and school location decisions made by these local governments exacerbate the racial division of space. Professor powell has pointed out that while Supreme Court decisions have been on the right side in banning racial discrimination within a jurisdiction, that same Court has been unwilling to deal with metropolitan patterns and the relationship between the decisions and actions of individual local governments. One outstanding example of this was the Detroit school segregation case *Milliken v. Bradley*, which did not allow metropolitan solutions to Detroit's school segregation patterns. St. Louis has the largest voluntary school integration program in the nation, one that by and large has been very successful, with a recent quite positive court settlement. But that is the exception: More and more, small local jurisdictions are acting in a way that produces enormous metropolitan disparities.

A very interesting book came out in 1999 called *By the Color of Our Skin: The Illusion of Integration and the Reality of Race* (1999). The authors are both professors at American University: Leonard Steinhorn, a White male, and Barbara Diggs-Brown, an African-American female. While both would love to believe that integration (as opposed to desegregation) is possible, the evidence they pile on in their book–what has happened and is happening in schools, suburban White flight, attitude differences, the differences in what Blacks and Whites find acceptable and need in terms of an integrated environment–compels a much more pessimistic conclusion. For example, most Black families, when asked what they need or what would make them feel comfortable in terms of an integrated residential setting, say 50:50, so that they don't really feel like a minority; most Whites, however, will say 10-15%, and if it gets any higher than that, they move away–demonstrating a wide gap in attitudes and desires that makes true residential (as well as school) integration very difficult to achieve.

There's no question regarding the extent to which the United States is a multicultural society, not just a Black-White society. And so, it's very important to look at parallels and differences between Blacks and other racial groups. At one level, the situation of Blacks is unique because of their history; Asian Americans and Latino Americans are voluntary immigrants to this country; Blacks were forced to come here and endured centuries of slavery and Jim Crow laws. While other ethnic groups–the Irish, Jews, Italians–had a tough time when they arrived and were treated unjustly and despised by the majority groups, they all assimilated: in fact, there's a wonderful book titled *How the Irish Became White* (1995). While the new question might be framed as, "Can Blacks also become White?", serious questions have to be raised as to whether assimilation is or ought to be the goal. How can groups maintain solidarity and valuable cultural patterns without at the same time being subjugated to the dominant culture? The *New York Times Magazine* (1998) a while back had an article called the "Beige-ing of America," pointing out that Latinos and Asian Americans are probably going to assimilate. Intermarriage rates provides some evidence for that trend. That article, by Michael Lind, suggests that this "beige-ing" process may wind up leaving Blacks outside the mainstream, as the one racial group that will remain unassimilated, as well as oppressed–a very frightening prospect. Professors Steinhorn and Diggs-Brown offer this interesting observation:

> Racial integration [not desegregation] depends on social engineering, constant vigilance, government authority, official attention to racial behavior, and willingness by citizens to relinquish at least some personal choice for the greater good. And so, we arrive at a fundamental dilemma of racial integration in America. The same factors that appear essential to successful integration run directly counter to some of our deepest beliefs about self-determination, authority and individual rights.

As noted above, a big question for social policy is, what do we mean by integration? Integration is not the same as assimilation. Integration in the U.S. context cannot mean and should not mean that everyone has to become White. People need to retain and want to retain their own cultures, their own identities; White should not be the standard. That raises policy questions about so-called in-place versus dispersion remedies. One school of thought that says the answer is to deghetto-ize, to move minorities out of central city ghettos, the hypersegregated places that now exist, and get them into white communities.

But while some Black families may prefer move to largely white areas, others may well wonder, why do I have to move out of my neighborhood in order to improve my lot? Why must I leave my community and move to live with whites in order to be able to have better living conditions, better schools? Why not focus on improving the community I now live in, for the benefit of those living there now? Likely the most sensible approach is not either/or social policy, but both/and: integrated communities for those want it, serious in-place remedies for those who want to stay where they are.

An honest look at where our society is right now offers little optimism. The new administration in Washington seems to treat racial justice largely in terms of photo-ops and symbolic appointments. Most discouraging was the Race Initiative undertaken by Bill Clinton, a man with decent instincts on matters having to do with race. When as President, in the spring of 1997, he announced his Initiative, and shortly thereafter appointed historian John Hope Franklin to chair its Advisory Board, we had real hope that at last the country was going to face up to the racism that still pervades our society, and do something serious about it. But it turned out to be a major disappointment. In the end, not a thing happened or changed. The Advisory Board issued a weak report. Bill Clinton, on the way out the door, just five days before leaving office, sent a message to Congress, "The Unfinished Work of Building One America," a cafeteria list of recommendations that, of course, were toothless, giving its timing. One problem was the approach of the Initiative: stressing conversation, personal relations—issues that, while not unimportant, evade the big issues of institutional racism and the legacy of history.

Most Whites don't want to face those issues, would prefer to ignore race, pretend we're a colorblind society. Where this all will lead is unpredictable. Oppressed minorities may rebel, forcing some changes, as has happened in the past. But this is certain: unless and until we face the way racism affects every aspect of our lives, and really do something to extirpate racism, the promise of liberty and justice will remain a mockery.

REFERENCES

Conley, D. (1999). *Being Black, living in the red: Race, wealth, and social policy in America.* Berkeley, CA: University of California Press.

Ignatiev, N. (1995). *How the Irish became white.* New York: Routledge.

Lind, M. (August 16, 1998). "The Beige and the Black" in the *New York Times Magazine.* New York: New York Times.

Oliver, M. L. and Shapiro, T. M. (1997). *Black wealth, white wealth.* New York. Routledge.

Robinson, R. (2000). *Debt: What America owes to Blacks.* New York: Dutton.

Steinhorn, L., and Diggs-Brown, B. (1999). *By the color of our skin: The illusion of integration and the reality of race.* New York: Dutton.

Building Bridges
and Improving Racial Harmony:
An Evaluation of the *Bridges*
Across Racial Polarization Program®

Stephen P. Wernet
Cindy Follman
Cherie Magueja
Robin Moore-Chambers

SUMMARY. Racial polarization is endemic in American society. It reduces the quality of life in our communities. Numerous solutions have been proposed for redressing racism, including racial dialogues. These programs are predicated on the contact hypothesis, i.e., through equal status contact, prejudice will be reduced. The question is whether the contact hypothesis as implemented through a racial dialogue program

---

Stephen P. Wernet, PhD, is Professor, School of Social Service and Department of Public Policy Studies, Saint Louis University, 3550 Lindell Blvd., Saint Louis, MO 63103.

Cindy Follman, MA, is Director of Community Policy and BRIDGES Program, FOCUS Saint Louis, 1910 Pine Street, Saint Louis, MO 63103.

Cherie Magueja, MSW, was a research assistant in the School of Social Service, Saint Louis University.

Robin Moore-Chambers, MSW, was a research assistant in the School of Social Service, Saint Louis University.

Address correspondence to: Stephen P. Wernet, PhD, Professor, School of Social Service, 3550 Lindell Blvd., Saint Louis, MO 63103 (E-mail: wernetsp@slu.edu).

[Haworth co-indexing entry note]: "Building Bridges and Improving Racial Harmony: An Evaluation of the *Bridges Across Racial Polarization Program*®." Wernet, Stephen P. et al. Co-published simultaneously in *Social Thought* (The Haworth Press, Inc.) Vol. 22, No. 2/3, 2003, pp. 63-79; and: *Practicing Social Justice* (ed: John J. Stretch et al.) The Haworth Press, Inc., 2003, pp. 63-79. Single or multiple copies of this article are available for a fee from The Haworth Document Delivery Service [1-800-HAWORTH, 9:00 a.m. - 5:00 p.m. (EST). E-mail address: docdelivery@haworthpress.com].

© 2003 by The Haworth Press, Inc. All rights reserved.
http://www.haworthpress.com/store/product.asp?sku=J131
10.1300/J131v22n02_06

holds and racial networks can be improved among program participants. Through a combination of forced choice and open-ended questions, 72 participants were surveyed to evaluate the impact and success of the *Bridges Across Racial Polarization Program®.* All individuals changed racial networks. The key to program success was the group dynamic. Positive group dynamics developed through positive interpersonal connections, frequent interactions and varied activities. Racial networks and interracial interactions can be enhanced through dialogue-type programs, thereby supporting the contact hypothesis. *[Article copies available for a fee from The Haworth Document Delivery Service: 1-800-HAWORTH. E-mail address: <docdelivery@haworthpress.com> Website: <http://www.HaworthPress.com> © 2003 by The Haworth Press, Inc. All rights reserved.]*

KEYWORDS. Racial polarization, contact hypothesis, group dynamics, racial dialogue, racial networks, program evaluation

INTRODUCTION

Racial polarization is one of the core problems facing the St. Louis region. It keeps the St. Louis region and its citizens from reaching its potential as race cuts through the heart of regional issues such as urban sprawl, light rail expansion, political campaigns, and equal educational opportunity. Based on 1990 census data, Reynolds Farley of the University of Michigan concluded that St. Louis is the eleventh most segregated city in the United States (Associated Press, January 29, 1997). According to the 1995 study, "Discovering Common Ground: Creating the Spirit of Community," St. Louisans perceive the quality of race relations in the St. Louis metropolitan area to be on the decline. Respondents reported that interracial contact is limited, with most contact occurring in public arenas, such as shopping malls and workplaces. More than 80% of all participants in the study said good race relations are very important to a community's quality of life. Respondents perceived race relations within their neighborhoods to be better than they are in the larger St. Louis area. It is important to note, however, that the majority of the St. Louis area neighborhoods are racially segregated. The majority of study participants did not know how they as individuals could begin working toward improved race relations (Metropolitan Diversity Coalition and Confluence St. Louis, 1995).

One means of improving race relations and combating racism is a forum approach known as racial dialogues (Miller and Donner, 2000). Racial dialogues are ". . . structured conversations that encourage expressing one's self and listening to others talk about race and racism" (Miller and Donner, 2000, p. 34). The intent is to provide people a setting within which they can explore their identity and group membership while learning how others address these issues. The goal of racial dialogues is to promote greater understanding by fostering trust, lessening ethnocentrism and confronting negative stereotypes. Sometimes, there is the added benefit of concrete action to confront racism. Nationally, interracial dialogue programs have experienced resurgence. President Clinton's Initiative on Race highlighted and promoted them as do other organizations dedicated to dismantling racism including the National Conference for Community and Justice and the Center for Living Democracy.

The mechanism being invoked by racial dialogues and other such interracial interactions is the Contact Hypothesis (Winborne and Cohen, 1998). The Contact Hypothesis, posited by social psychologist Gordon Allport, asserts "prejudice may be reduced by equal status contact between majority and minority groups in the pursuit of common goals" (Winborne and Cohen, 1998, p. 28). Contact forces individuals to confront their thoughts, beliefs, feelings, and actions towards people who differ from them. Through increased interaction and contact, social distance is decreased, suspicions are reduced, stereotypes are challenged, and difficulties in communicating are also confronted (Brown and Mistry, 1994; Miller and Donner, 2000; Thomas, 1999).

One of the settings within which the contact hypothesis is frequently tested is the group. Groups are ". . . social microcosm(s) of wider society . . . (Brown and Mistry, 1994, p. 7) which provide a forum for addressing issues. These settings provide people the opportunity to interact with different others, gain self-awareness and learn new behaviors (Forsyth, 1990; Henry, 1992; Schneider Corey and Corey, 1997; Zastrow, 1997). For contact in the mixed group format to be successful, both balanced group membership and attention to process are important (Brown and Mistry, 1994).

Although the theory has been studied over these many years, the validity of the theory has not been sufficiently confirmed. Many of the Contact Hypothesis studies did not explore the effect of contact between groups in the workplace or in leisure settings. Many of the studies did not measure contact through direct observation or by directly asking participants about it (Winborne and Cohen, 1988). Therefore, any program interested in testing the contact hypothesis' relevance to eliminating racism and improving race relations must investigate the program's process through direct contact with participants.

FOCUS St. Louis and the Bridges Across Racial Polarization Program®

FOCUS St. Louis is an independent, nonprofit 501(c)(3) organization whose mission is to create a cooperative, thriving region by engaging citizens in active leadership roles to influence positive community change. It is committed to promoting a greater understanding among the 2.5 million people living in the 12-county, bi-state region. FOCUS' major roles are engaging citizens, influencing community policy, and developing leaders in the priority areas of good government, sustainable infrastructure, quality education, and racial equality and social justice. It operates five leadership development programs, engages citizens in community policy analysis, implementation, and problem solving, and operates the *Bridges Across Racial Polarization®* interracial dialogue program.

In the spring of 1993, two Leadership St. Louis program graduates met to discuss racial polarization in St. Louis and the perceived lack of interracial social contact among St. Louisans. They decided to pilot the concept of informal, interracial social gatherings, which they hoped would offer opportunities to develop new friendships. Beginning in September of 1993, 40 people initiated a series of interracial social gatherings over a nine-month period. Encouraged by their enthusiasm and the success of this experiment, *Bridges Across Racial Polarization®* (here forward referred to as *Bridges*) was created.

The goal of the *Bridges* program is to create better communication and understanding among all segments of the greater St. Louis community. The program's assumption is the community's quality of life is enhanced when people discover how much they have in common with others and how they can learn from perspectives different from their own. As a result of participating in a *Bridges* group, participants will meet and get to know people from other races whom they might not otherwise meet, break down barriers, experience and learn about different perspectives, and provide sounding boards for one another when divisive issues arise in the community. These relationships will create bridges of understanding and learning that will not only add richness to the lives of each other, but also to the entire St. Louis metropolitan region.

The *Bridges* program links individuals to a programmatic solution as way to tackle the pervasive and challenging social justice issue of racial polarization. The aspect of the *Bridges* program that best contributes to its success is its informal, low-key approach. With relationship building at its core, the *Bridges* program brings individuals together in each other's homes to share food and conversation with one another. It is a simple and basic way of interacting person to person.

Bridges is a voluntary program consisting of groups of eight to twelve people from a mix of racial backgrounds. The groups meet regularly on an informal, social basis, often in each other's homes. Participants get to know people from other races whom they might not otherwise meet, cross barriers, hear different ideas and perspectives, increase awareness and understanding, and provide a sounding board when divisive issues arise.

Ideally, each *Bridges* group consists of between 8 and 12 participants composed of people representing a racial/ethnic balance. This balance eliminates any sense of isolation among participants and leads to a greater interchange of ideas and discussion.

Each group has two co-hosts, (singles or couples), one person of color and one white person. The role of the co-hosts is to act as facilitators of the group's activities, rather than as the leaders of the group. The two co-hosts are responsible for scheduling and facilitating the gatherings and serving as the group's central contact. Before the group is initiated, co-hosts meet to discuss their role and to talk through the intent of the sessions and possible content. FOCUS provides the co-hosts with facilitation training and a program orientation session, which includes group dynamics, dialogue techniques, and information about the cycle of oppression, white privilege, and racism. The co-hosts do not have to host every session, nor are they responsible for setting the agenda or discussion topic for every session. However, they do have the responsibility to insure that the group meets and that there is a process in place for the group to function constructively.

When *Bridges* groups are formed, every effort is made to construct the groups with a balance of race and gender, as well as of singles and couples. A group roster is usually developed and distributed at the first gathering, so that group participants have a way to reach one another. This assists in the development of relationships and friendships outside of the group gatherings.

All interested program applicants are asked to submit a participation form. As soon as enough individuals to comprise a racially mixed group have been acquired, a group is formed. Often groups are comprised of complete strangers, and this can be both an asset and a liability for the program. Applicants are encouraged to take the initiative to seek out other interested participants and form their own groups. A challenge to note is the significantly greater interest in program participation by whites than by people of color. The program often has a waiting list for interested white participants, particularly white women. It has been harder to recruit and maintain African American participants in the program.

Potluck dinners are recommended with hosting responsibilities rotated throughout the group. This allows everyone to share some aspect of supporting the group for each gathering (either hosting the gathering or bringing some food and/or beverage for the meal). Potluck dinners also reinforce the social and personal aspect of the project so that it will not feel like a business meeting. Some groups also rotate the meeting content responsibilities so that the co-hosts do not have the entire responsibility for developing an agenda each time.

Each group decides how it wishes to function. This is a decision that the co-hosts ask the group to make at its first gathering. It is recommended that meetings be scheduled for two to three hours since the gatherings are usually over a meal. This allows for some social time as well as time for meaningful dialogue. It is recommended that the groups meet at least every eight weeks, if not more frequently. Groups do not have to meet at the same time nor have the same format each time they meet. Some groups assign an activity or a reading prior to the gathering, and then the co-hosts facilitate a dialogue centered on that topic. Other groups leave their discussion format fairly loose and talk about current events or personal experiences. Each group determines the content and format of their meetings depending upon the interests of participants.

Programs that effectively lessen racial inequities as part of an overall strategy to achieve a more just society are needed in the St. Louis region if the goal of active participation by all is to be reached. To date, the information collected on the impact of the *Bridges* program on its participants and on the community at large is primarily anecdotal. It is critical to determine how this program is actually impacting its participants and the St. Louis region with respect to race relations. This information will allow the program to be adapted and modified to ensure that it is best meeting the needs of its participants and most effectively decreasing racial polarization in the St. Louis region.

Hypotheses

The purpose of this research project was to discover what influence participating in a *Bridges* group had upon participants' attitudes, feelings and behaviors about interracial relationships. The evaluation team sought to address the following objectives and questions:

1. To discover participants' reasons for joining the program.

- What were the participants' initial expectations of the Bridges program?
- What were they hoping to get out of the experience?

2. To discover participants' actual experience with the program.
What is/was satisfying about the experience? What is/was frustrating?

- Why do participants continue to be involved in a group, or why did they leave the program?

3. To discover the impact of the program on participants.

- How does/did participation in the program influence participants' attitudes, feelings and behaviors about interracial relationships? How could the program be improved? How could the program have better met participants' expectations?

RESEARCH METHOD

Variables of Interest

There were several variables of interest in this study (see Table 1). The independent variable (IV) was participation in the *Bridges* program. The IV had three values: never assigned to a group; participated but no longer involved in a group (stopped out); continuous participation in a group.

The dependent variable (DV) was a sensitizing construct rather than a true variable. It is a construct that is decomposed into various elements, i.e., attitudes, feelings, and behaviors about interracial relationships as well as expectations of the *Bridges* program. The DV was measured by open-ended questions in the interview protocol designed for this project.

TABLE 1. Variables of Interest for the Study

	Variable Name	Operational Definition
Independent Variable	Type of participation in the *Bridges* program	Group 1: Never assigned to a group
		Group 2: Stopped out/participated in a *Bridges* group but no longer involved
		Group 3: Continuous participation in a *Bridges* group
Dependent Variable	Expectations for participating in *Bridges* program	Open-ended response
	Perceived gains from participating in *Bridges* program	Open-ended response
	Perceived change in attitudes about interracial relations	Open-ended response
	Perceived change in feelings about interracial relations	Open-ended response
	Perceived change in interracial relationships	Open-ended response
Intervening Variables	Type of *Bridges* group	Two values: Social group or Educational group
	Race of participant	Two values: African American European American
	Start date of group	Five values: 1993-1994; 1995-1996; 1997; 1998; 1999
	Leadership role in the group	Two values: Group leader or not group leader
	Satisfaction with *Bridges* program	Open-ended response
	Frustration with *Bridges* program	Open-ended response

There were several other variables of interest that were incorporated into the study. These variables were thought to be intervening variables that could modify the effect of participation in the *Bridges* program. These variables included type of *Bridges* group, race of participant, start date of group, and leadership role in the group. Each of these variables was scaled at the nominal level of measurement.

Sample and Sampling Plan

The study used a stratified sampling plan. The sampling frame for the study was constructed from the three types of *Bridges* program participants. This is the independent variable for the study that varies naturally.

A list of all participants in each group was compiled. This produced three lists of program participants: never assigned, stopped out, or continuous participation. The frames were further stratified by race. The numbers for each cell in the sampling plan are reported in Table 2.

From each of the six cells in the sampling frame, a random sample was selected. A sample size of 72 was used in order to achieve the maximum statistical power and for detecting program impact (Lawrence Erlbaum & Associates, 1988). The sample consisted of 24 respondents from each of the three program participants' groups (i.e., never assigned, stopped out, and continuous participation) and was further refined and selected from each of the six cells (i.e., Race X Program Participation) according to its proportion in the sampling frame.

Selected study participants were contacted about the project. The first contact was made by the Project Director through U.S. mail informing the potential participants about the study, and about a future telephone call to solicit their participation. A second contact was made through a telephone call from student research assistants hired by the project soliciting participation and scheduling interview appointments.

TABLE 2. Distribution of *Bridges* Program Participants for Developing Evaluation Sampling Plan

	Never Assigned	Stopped Out	Continuous Participation	Total
African Americans	5	54	36	95
European Americans	139	81	50	270
Total	144	135	86	365

Instrumentation

For this project, an interview instrument was developed and utilized. The instrument contained both forced-choice and open-ended questions and was content validated through two methods. First, it was face validated with a panel of experts constructed from the Steering Committee of the *Bridges* program and other outside experts on interracial relations. This validation was completed and resulted in the addition and modification of several questions. Second, the instrument was content validated by field-testing with a select group of *Bridges* participants. This step resulted in no additional changes to the interview instrument.

Because the instrument is an interview protocol, the student research assistants employed by the project were trained to insure their consistency and inter-rater reliability. Interviewers were trained for use of the instrument and sensitivity to the content on interracial relationships. Before data collection began, student interviewers demonstrated an 80% agreement on coding of interview data.

Data Collection Procedure

Data were collected through face-to-face interviews conducted by student research assistants hired by the project. Each interview lasted approximately one hour. Interviewers used the paper and pencil interview schedule developed for the project.

There were two student research assistants, one African American and one European American. Interviews were assigned randomly to the research assistants so as to minimize the interaction of race in the interviews. The students conducted twenty-five percent of the interviews jointly in order to test for inter-rater reliability; twenty-five percent of the interviews were conducted cross-racially; fifty percent of the interviews were conducted with same race interviewers. This approach allowed the project to control for the interactive effect of interviewer-interviewee race.

Data collection lasted approximately four months.

Data Analysis

Open-ended questions were content analyzed in order to develop research-grounded categories for possible recoding and aggregating the data for additional analyses. The forced-choice questions were used for analyzing the open-ended questions that were coded. Because the data are at the nominal level of measurement, chi-square analyses, point bi-serial correlations and Kendall's

Tau was conducted for these analyses. The decision rule for level of significance was set at .05 for a two-tailed test.

FINDINGS

Study's Respondents

There are several important findings about the study's respondents (see Table 3). First, the study's sample appears to be unbiased (*Bridges* participation-Year applied: r = .03; *Bridges* participation-Race: r = −.095; Year applied-Race: r = .002). Over time, the referral source for the *Bridges* program has expanded beyond the sponsor's group (X^2 = 17.261, df = 8, p < .028). Therefore, applicants to the *Bridges* program are coming from a wider range of referral sources. The sample of respondents drawn for this study was a fair representation of the population of *Bridges* program applicants and participants.

Second, the respondents appear to have similar density of racial networks (Density of Racial networks-Year applied: r = .132; Density of racial networks-*Bridges* Participation: r = .247; Density of Racial Networks-Race: r = −.088). Therefore, the sample of *Bridges* program applicants and participants are engaged in the same level of interracial interactions.

Third, continuous participants in the *Bridges* program had a different experience than both those who dropped out and those who were never assigned to

TABLE 3. Results of Correlation Analyses for Assessing Demographic and Programmatic Variables

	Year Applied	*Bridges* Participation	Race	Density of Racial Networks	Met Expectations
Bridges Participation	.03				
Race	.002	−.095			
Density of Racial Networks	.132	.247	−.088		
Met Expectations	−.083	−.758**	.044	−.094	
Change in Racial Networks	−.084	−.785**	.064	−.155	.877**

**correlation is significant at the p < .01 level

a group. Continuous participants reported having unmet expectations and contracted racial networks (*Bridges* participation-Met expectations: r = −.758, p < .01; *Bridges* expectations-Change in racial networks: r = −.785, p < .01). However, those whose expectations were met reported an expansion of their racial networks (Met expectations-Change in racial networks: r = .877, p < .01). There are several possible explanations for these results. Respondents may have come to the *Bridges* program with very high expectations that were not or could not be met. As a result of these unmet expectations, all study respondents reported becoming more purposeful in their interracial interactions. Those who continuously participated became more targeted and purposeful in their interracial interactions. Those who were never assigned to a *Bridges* group expanded their racial networks. Those whose expectations were met may have come to the *Bridges* program with constricted racial networks. Therefore, these individuals expanded their interracial networks by applying to or participating in the *Bridges* program.

Reasons for Applying and Joining Bridges

From open-ended interview questions, it was learned that all respondents had one overarching reason for applying to the *Bridges* program. People were interested in increasing their cultural understanding and sensitivity. Respondents expressed this theme in several different ways: ". . . a better understanding of people who are different, including their backgrounds and experiences . . . ," ". . . insight into really connecting through being educated and truly bridging the (racial) gap . . . ," and ". . . meeting other people and getting other viewpoints. . . ."

Study respondents held an array of views concerning their operational expectations for the program and the means through which the program would increase the participants' cultural sensitivity. One expectation centered upon composition of the groups and program participants. It was expected that groups would consist of a broad representation of ethnic clusters as well as a wide array of income and educational levels. There also was some expectation of participation in a structured program. Respondents expressed these views in several different ways: ". . . more diverse population, not as much as black and white, but more ethnic groups involved . . . ," ". . . more diversity with income and education levels . . . ," and ". . . structured guidelines for meetings. . . ."

Bridges participants (i.e., continuously involved and stopped out) seemed somewhat disappointed about group composition and program structure. They expressed a desire for interaction among the various *Bridges* groups. They also desired more program structure and guidance for group meetings. This may have been due in part to structural and scheduling problems that surfaced in several groups. *Bridges* participants expressed their disappointment through several suggestions: ". . . newsletter to share information across groups . . . ," ". . . maybe a one year initiative, shorter time span . . . ," ". . . program structure at three levels; participants choose according to their individual needs . . . ," and ". . . more focus with structure that builds trust early in the process of group formation. . . ."

In summary, study respondents held numerous expectations for their involvement in the *Bridges* program. They joined to increase their cultural sensitivity and span the racial divide. *Bridges* participants' expectations of involvement with a widely divergent group of individuals through a structured program were unmet. However, there appears to have been success in meeting their expectation for increasing their understanding of those who are culturally different from themselves.

Participants' Experience with Bridges

There were two factors that distinguished between participants' satisfaction and frustration with as well as contributed to continuous participation or stopping out of the *Bridges* program. These factors were the interpersonal connections in and the dynamics of the *Bridges* group.

The discriminator between satisfied and frustrated participants was interpersonal connections in the *Bridges* group. Those groups in which participants were satisfied were described as places in which membership was stable, continuously participating in the life of the group, friendly and interactive. Satisfied participants spoke of the ". . . relationships evolved over time . . ." and the ". . . closeness evolved among group members."

Those groups in which participants were frustrated were described as places in which people were unable to connect, unable (or unwilling) to find common meeting times, and unable (or unwilling) to discuss issues openly and in depth. Participants' dissatisfaction was frequently voiced as operational problems. However, there appears to have been a lack of commitment on the part of participants. Frustrated participants spoke of ". . . high rate of turnover . . . ," "People were dropping out . . . ," ". . . lost and added people over time . . . had to go through getting acquainted again . . . ," "nonsupport from (the program's sponsor)" and ". . . the group was too unstructured. . . ."

The discriminator between respondents who continuously participated in the *Bridges* program and those who stopped out was the processes of the group. Those groups in which participants were continuously involved with the program were described as places in which the group dynamic changed over time, having an atmosphere conducive to discussing difficult topics, open and comfortable. Continuous participants spoke of ". . . group dynamics have modified for the better . . . more group participation . . . ," ". . . openness of everyone, members are comfortable to speak openly to 'what's on your mind . . . ,' " and ". . . comfort zone . . . safe place to discuss cross racial issues."

Those groups from which participants stopped out of the *Bridges* program were described as places in which individuals were unable to connect or coalesce into a group, unfavorable to discussion of difficult issues, and unorganized. When exiting, subjects spoke of ". . . lack of time to delve into issues in more depth . . . ," ". . . not enough organization in group . . . ," ". . . the issues surfaced and attempts were made but real discussion fell through . . . ," ". . . lack of focus on real issues. . . ."

Table 4 reports analyses of the forced choice questions focusing upon impact of the *Bridges* program. As was previously reported, those whose expectations were met reported an expansion in their racial networks (Met expectations-Change in racial networks: r = .877, p < .01). Participants whose expectations were met also reported participating in *Bridges* groups with a greater variety of group activities and more frequent group meetings (Met expectations-Density of activities: r = .901, p < .01; Met expectations-Frequency of group meetings: r = .873, p < .01). Participants who reported an expansion in their racial networks also reported participating in *Bridges* groups with a greater variety of group activities and more frequent group meetings (Change in racial networks-Density of activities: r = .928, p < .01; Change in racial networks-Frequency of group meetings: r = .907, p < .01).

Because of the colinearity among several variables, an index was created for assessing group dynamics. This index variable was constructed by summing the responses of the following variables: frequency of group meetings, change in group dynamics, group cohesion, and group conflict. Positive group dynamics were associated with a greater variety of group activities, an expansion in racial networks and a participant having met her/his expectations (Group dynamics-Density of activities: r = .922, p < .01; Group dynamics-Change in racial networks: r = .974, p < .01; Group dynamics-Met expectations: r = .863, p < .01).

In summary, a positive group dynamic was the key to participants' successful experience in the *Bridges* program. Positive group dynamics were associated with participants' satisfaction and continuous, ongoing involvement in the program. Variety and frequency of meetings facilitated individuals connecting in the group. Stable membership facilitated interpersonal connections and trust that led to an atmosphere conducive to discussing difficult topics. This iterative, reinforcing circle of positive group dynamic led to participants' expectations being met, and subsequently to expansion of racial networks.

Impact of the Bridges *Program*

Study respondents were queried about the impact of their involvement in and suggestions for improving the program. The major influence of the *Bridges*

TABLE 4. Results of Correlation Analyses for Variables Assessing Program Impact

	Density of Racial Networks	Density of Activities	Frequency of Group Meetings	Change in Group Dynamic	Group Cohesion	Group Conflict	Change in Racial Networks	Met Expectations
Density of Activities	-.101							
Frequency of Group Meetings	-.103	.917**						
Change in Group Dynamic	-.133	.927**	.912**					
Group Cohesion	-.153	.927**	.921**	.995**				
Group Conflict	-.150	.93**	.911**	.995**	.995**			
Change in Racial Networks	-.155	.928**	.907**	.99**	.993**	.993**		
Met Expectations	-.094	.901**	.873**	.878**	.879**	.877**	.877**	
Group Dynamics	-.123	.922**	.883**	.986**	.98**	.985**	.974**	.863**

** correlation is significant at the p < .01 level

program was upon change in racial networks. As discussed earlier, those who continuously participated in the *Bridges* program constricted their racial networks, while those who were never assigned to a *Bridges* group expanded their racial networks (*Bridges* participation-Change in racial network: $r = -.785$, $p < .01$). It appears that everyone associated with the *Bridges* program became more purposeful in their racial networking. Those who continuously participated became more targeted and purposeful in their racial networking. Those who were never assigned to a *Bridges* group expanded their racial networks. Group process as the medium for creating changes in racial networks by developing interpersonal connections appears to have been successful. As one respondent stated, it was ". . . getting to know people and a new perspective" that produces the change.

Study respondents were asked for program improvement suggestions. Responses clustered into three suggestions. Participants desired more structure to the group experience, more support from the sponsoring organization and greater diversity in the participants. They desired more direction and leadership rather than the limited structure and constricted involvement provided by the sponsoring organization. Participants suggested dedicating a staff person to the *Bridges* program and providing ongoing leadership development for group co-hosts. Participants suggested greater diversity in the composition of the program participants. Diversity should extend beyond race to include socioeconomic status and age as well as a great inclusiveness of ethnic groups who participate in the program. Participants offered some of the following as suggestions for program improvement: ". . . could be more diverse in terms of race and socioeconomic backgrounds," ". . . structured guidelines for meetings," ". . . maybe a one year initiative, shorter time span."

DISCUSSION

This project investigated the impact of a racial dialogue program. It wanted to learn why participants joined, what their experiences were while in the program, and, ultimately, what difference participating made for these individuals. Participants and applicants alike came to the *Bridges* program with high expectations. As a result of their engagement with the program, participants and nonparticipants alike became more purposeful in their racial networking and interracial interactions. Participants became more focused in their racial networking; nonparticipants increased their involvement in racial networking. However, many participants expressed not having their expectations met through the program. Why?

Applicants and participants alike ostensibly stated their expectations at the end of their program involvement for increased cultural understanding and sensitivity. Many of the participants expressed their disappointment with the absence of a structured program. As several participants stated, they wanted to ". . . span the racial divide. . . ." Although stated as a goal of self-improvement, it appears that participants may actually have desired an action program. That is, participants may have come to the program looking for some type of initiative that would actively engage them in a behavioral process of changing racism and racial division in the community even though they spoke of cultural sensitization. But did the program have impact?

From both the statistical and the narrative data, it is clear that the *Bridges* program is successful. The key to its success is the group process. The discriminators for success are positive interpersonal connections and positive group dynamics. These indicators for success occur because of frequent interactions and varied group activities. In turn, these lead to participants' expectations being met, and, ultimately, racial networks expanding. In short, the contact hypothesis is substantiated by these findings! In order to reduce and eliminate racial polarization and racism, interracial interactions incorporating meaningful exchange must be increased throughout the community.

Finally, the program's goal of changing racial networks appears to be met. Participation changes racial networks through focusing and targeting the individual's racial networking. People who were never assigned to a *Bridges* group became purposeful in their racial networking by seeking out a broader array of interracial interactions. The program appears to stimulate the solution–action on the part of the citizenry to reduce racial polarization. Again, the data support the contact hypothesis.

These findings and conclusions must be read with some caution. First, the *Bridges* program is a small, targeted effort. It is uncertain if a large-scale effort could be as successful. However, presently the program has expanded and continues to expand its groups and the venues in which the groups are sponsored. These new groups should provide additional information about the generalizability of the program structure to an array of settings and sponsors.

Second, the participants in the *Bridges* program are a self-select group of individuals committed to reducing racial polarization and improving race relations in the community. It is unclear if the program would be as successful with a less motivated group. This is a venue for further, future research.

Third, this was a correlational study with post hoc measures. Future research should utilize quasi-experimental designs with multiple preenrollment measures and use of comparison groups. This would help test for the efficacy of the program. Future research should also investigate the group process of the program in order to document how the process creates the targeted changes. Documenting the process of contact will assist with improving our understanding of how it works, why it works and how to enhance it for improving our communities.

REFERENCES

Associated Press. (Wednesday, January 29, 1997) "Old Midwest, Northeast Cities Top List of Segregated Areas" *St. Louis Post-Dispatch.*

Brown, A. & Mistry, T. (1994) "Group work with 'mixed membership' groups: Issues of race and gender" *Social Work with Groups* 17(3), 5-21.

Forsyth, D. (1990) *Group Dynamics. Second Edition.* Pacific Grove, California: Brooks/Cole Publishing Company.

Henry, S. (1992) *Group Skills in Social Work. Second Edition.* Pacific Grove, California: Brooks/Cole Publishing Company.

Lawrence Erlbaum & Associates. (1988) S*tatistical Power Analysis Program.* Hillsdale, NJ.

Metropolitan Diversity Coalition and Confluence St. Louis. (1995) *Discovering Common Ground: Creating the Spirit of Community.* St. Louis: Public Policy Research Centers, University of Missouri-St. Louis.

Miller, J. & Donner, S. (2000) "More than just talk: The use of racial dialogues to combat racism" *Social Work with Groups* 23(1), 31-53.

Schneider Corey, M. and Corey, G. (1997) *Groups. Process and Practice. Fifth Edition.* Pacific Grove, California: Brooks/Cole Publishing Company.

Thomas, D. (1999) "Cultural diversity and work group effectiveness. An experimental study" *Journal of Cross-Cultural Psychology* 30(2), 242-263.

Winborne, W. & Cohen, R. (1998) *Intergroup Relations in the United States: Research Perspectives.* New York: The National Conference for Community and Justice.

Zastrow, C. (1997) *Social Work with Groups. Using the Class as a Group Leadership Laboratory.* Chicago: Nelson-Hall Publishers.

Social Justice and Welfare Reform:
A Shift in Policy

Sabrina W. Tyuse

SUMMARY. For six decades welfare entitlements were designated for the aid of poor children and since 1950, their caretaker. The current TANF program, however, represents a fundamental shift from child-focused aid programs to caretaker-focused work obligations. What are the economic and social consequences of a time-limited governmental reordering of responsibility for vulnerable children? More importantly, what impacts will caretaker-centered requirements and untested time limits have on the life chances of disadvantaged children? This article assesses from a social justice perspective previous income maintenance welfare initiatives, reviews their intended and actual outcomes, and explores the expected growing economic and social isolation of welfare recipients with current TANF policies. Following this assessment, future government initiatives as well social justice-type strategies to address the economic and social isolation of welfare recipients are recommended. *[Article copies available for a fee from The Haworth Document Delivery Service: 1-800-HAWORTH. E-mail address: <docdelivery@haworthpress.com> Website: <http://www.HaworthPress.com> © 2003 by The Haworth Press, Inc. All rights reserved.]*

Sabrina W. Tyuse, MSW, MA, PhD, is Assistant Professor at Saint Louis University, School of Social Service, 3550 Lindell Blvd., St. Louis, MO 63103 (E-mail: tyuses@slu.edu).

[Haworth co-indexing entry note]: "Social Justice and Welfare Reform: A Shift in Policy." Tyuse, Sabrina W. Co-published simultaneously in *Social Thought* (The Haworth Press, Inc.) Vol. 22, No. 2/3, 2003, pp. 81-95; and: *Practicing Social Justice* (ed: John J. Stretch et al.) The Haworth Press, Inc., 2003, pp. 81-95. Single or multiple copies of this article are available for a fee from The Haworth Document Delivery Service [1-800-HAWORTH, 9:00 a.m. - 5:00 p.m. (EST). E-mail address: docdelivery@haworthpress.com].

© 2003 by The Haworth Press, Inc. All rights reserved.
http://www.haworthpress.com/store/product.asp?sku=J131
10.1300/J131v22n02_07

KEYWORDS. Social justice, TANF, AFDC, welfare reform, social policy

INTRODUCTION

Public assistance is presently, and always has been, a much-debated issue because of its inherent:

1. how to provide assistance to those in need without,
2. encouraging if not promoting dependence for its intended recipients while ensuring the material welfare of poor children.

This dilemma is the crux of much social welfare policy debate. The Elizabethan Poor Laws of 1601, not unlike the Aid to Dependent Children (ADC) law of 1935 or the welfare reforms of the 1960s and 1990s, was designed to provide temporary assistance to those in need, by ensuring that aid would not erode the work ethic, denying assistance to able-boded, employable adults (Trattner, 1999). While much work has been done to measure the overall effectiveness of governmental aid programs (Blank, 1997; Danziger and Weinberg, 1994; Kenworthy, 1999), this paper adds a focus by assessing if these programs are socially just.

Van Soest (1995) defines social justice in terms of what a person owes society (legal), what people owe each other (commutative), and what society owes people (distributive). Other definitions of social justice are couched in egalitarian terms. Fiskin (1983), Flynn (1995) and Rawls (1971) define social justice in terms of each citizen having fair and equitable access to societal resources and opportunities. In Flynn and Rawls' conceptualization, as well as for the present researcher, socially just welfare reform policy embodies having access to necessary goods, services, and opportunities for poor and/or oppressed groups in society. Social justice then for the poor could lead to their improved social and economic status or equality of life chances (Fiskin, 1983; Wilson, 1987).

Studies on social justice and welfare reform have tended to focus on either the disparities of wealth resulting from our current economic system, or on the need for human service workers to enter the political debate on issues of welfare reform (Seipel, 2000; Stoesz, 2000). Stoesz (2000) discusses income disparities and the importance of asset building as a way to escape poverty. Research noted the absence of social work professionals (Stoesz, 2000) in social welfare policy debates and concludes that, to garner better services for those in need, social workers, human service professionals, and even religious leaders must enter political discussions, advocating for social change (Jacobson, 2001) in the design of social welfare policy (Lens and Gibelman, 2000; Seipel, 2000;

Stoesz, 2000). This analysis will review the current welfare reform initiative, TANF, as it relates to social justice strategies.

The American public was dissatisfied (Weaver, 2000) with the old Aid to Families with Dependent Children (AFDC) poverty program (Farkas, Johnson, Friedman, and Bers, 1996; Howard, 1992; Weaver, Shapiro, & Jacobs, 1995). This was because of the perception that it not only failed to lift welfare recipients out of poverty, but it also encouraged continued dependency (Murray, 1984) by not requiring recipients to work (Farkas, Johnson, Friedman, and Bers, 1996). The Clinton administration's response to dissatisfaction with the AFDC program was to sign the Personal Responsibility and Work Opportunity Act of 1996, which replaced AFDC with the Temporary Assistance for Needy Families Block Grant (TANF) program.

The TANF program created and defined new work requirements and time limits on the receipt of cash assistance, and the block grant provides states with a fixed amount of funds to assist needy families. The block grant differs significantly from the previous open-ended entitlement program, which provided assistance to eligible public assistance applicants. Moreover, this legislation gives recipients up to two years to obtain employment and up to five years of lifetime eligibility for federally funded cash assistance. TANF emphasizes a "work-first" strategy, in which programs are to move participants into employment status as quickly as possible through job search and short-term basic and remedial education training.

TANF eliminated a long-term welfare safety net, which for over 60 years under AFDC has provided the assurance of financial and material assistance to those in need. In fact, replacing the need-based AFDC programs with the time-limited TANF program represents a radical shift of government responsibility for poor children. Is elimination of a safety net socially just when underlying structural and economic conditions for continuing need exist?

To place the policy reversal of government responsibility for poor children in historical perspective, the original child support welfare program, Mother's Pension in the early twentieth century (1911-1935), was designed to provide financial support to poor mothers, usually poor widowed mothers, to allow them to remain at home to care for their children (Howard, 1992; Skocpol, 1992; Trattner, 1999). In 1935, ADC program benefits were federally supported for the aid of poor children. A caretaker grant was not added to the ADC program until the 1950s. The 1996 TANF policy represents a significant policy switch from child-focused entitlement aid programs to a time limited caretaker-focused work requirement.

What will be the economic and social consequences of the governmental abdication of continuing responsibility to poor children? More importantly, what impacts will caretaker-centered work requirements and strict time limits have on the life chances of disadvantaged children? This article assesses the social justice aspects of previous welfare initiatives, reviews their intended and actual outcomes, and explores what can be expected with current TANF policies. Specifically, it asks whether TANF policies, or societal mechanisms currently in place, will enable poor children to access basic maintenance resources and educational opportunities that can, over time, result in financial self-sufficiency?

Historical Background

From an historical perspective, it is important to note that both former and current welfare programs were *not* designed to end poverty, or even to address the underlying causes of poverty. The original policy intent of ADC was to "prevent destitution" or extreme poverty (Trattner, 1999). The Social Security Act of 1935 was a multifaceted set of social policies aimed to address massive structural and economic problems brought about by the Great Depression.

The Social Security Act of 1935 was designed to provide immediate but temporary financial relief to destitute Americans and to create jobs for the unemployed. The Act's three-pronged approach was targeted to provide:

1. aid to the elderly in the form of Old Age Assistance;
2. jobs for the unemployed in the form of work relief and unemployment insurance; and
3. assistance to widowed mothers and children through Aid to Dependent Children (ADC).

Initially, due to regional economic (Gordon, 1994; Piven and Cloward, 1997) and racial differences, most African Americans were not eligible for Social Security Act benefits. Powerful southern democrats argued, persuasively, that liberal social security benefits would undermine the work ethic of tenant farmers (Gordon, 1994; Piven and Cloward, 1997). The Social Security Act of 1935 excluded agricultural and domestic workers. African Americans comprised 50% to 60%, respectively, of these workers (U.S. Census Bureau, 1949). In 1950, Congress passed legislation (P.L. 81-734) by expanding the Social Security Act to include many excluded groups including agricultural and domestic workers.

Soon after the implementation of the Social Security Act, the United States entered into World War II. Because of defense industry labor needs during the war, women and minorities received unprecedented employment opportunities to fill skilled and semiskilled professions reserved for white males (Axinn and Stern, 2001; Day, 2000). Prior to the war, 40% of African American women and 25% of white women were in the labor force (Day, 2000), with an additional 44% of African American men being employed (Axinn and Stern, 2001). During the war however, 37% of all women found employment (Day, 2000). Nine of ten working age males, both white and African American were employed during World War II (Jaynes and Williams, 1989).

After the war, returning veterans displaced most employed women (Axinn and Stern, 2001; Axinn and Levin, 1982). Because of their wartime service and the need to support their families, returning veterans deserved to get either their old jobs back or new positions. Moreover, it was argued, women (and married women in particular) who were in those jobs should "step aside" and return home for traditional work to care for their families (Day, 2000).

African American males also experienced post-war employment reversals. Some African American males retained employment in the automobile industry (Georgakas and Surkin, 1998) and in the public sector (Day, 2000). Overall, however, African American unemployment rates increased steadily following the war. The African American unemployment rate rose by 53% to 5.9% in 1948 and to 9.0% in 1950 (U.S. Census Bureau, 1960).

Returning veterans were eligible for federal funds for education, home loans, business and farm loans, unemployment insurance, and employment services through provisions of the Servicemen's Readjustment Act of 1944 (Axinn and Stern, 2001; U.S. Congress, 1944), through the GI Bill. For white American veterans, access to education, a good job, and homeownership was underwritten by federal subsidies. For African American veterans, however, the future was not as fortunate. African American veterans, particularly southern African American veterans, did not take full advantage of GI benefits because of racial discrimination of GI benefit counselors (Onkst, 1998), who refused to grant them access to benefits to which all honorably discharged veterans were entitled (Onkst, 1998).

African American veterans employment experiences following WWII proved little changed from that preceding the war. Some showed declines. In southern states, technological advances in farming led to a 40% decrease in demand for laborers. As a result, between 1940 and 1970, four million African Americans, many to find support for their families, migrated from southern rural areas to large northern cities, including Detroit, Chicago and St. Louis (Lemann, 1992). Like European immigrants before them, African American migrants from southern states following WWII were mostly uneducated, illiterate, unskilled, and penniless. Unlike at the turn of the century, when settlement house workers, located in large cities like Chicago, Baltimore, and New York, addressed the adjustment needs of European immigrants, migrating African American families received little adjustment assistance (Trattner, 1999). While settlement house services could not be expected to alleviate the structural causes of poverty, services were designed to help socialize the immigrant families to their new environment (Segal and Brzuzy, 1998). With few exceptions African American migrants were largely ignored (Trattner, 1999) until the early 1960s (Trattner, 1999; Wilson, 1987).

African American families in northern cities generally lived in poverty. In fact, throughout the 1950s, more than 50% of African American families lived below the poverty line (Jaynes and Williams, 1989). In 1959, 18% of white families lived in poverty compared to 55% of African American families (Current Populations Report [CPS], 1991). By the early 1960s, the poverty rate for single female heads of households was more startling, with 40% of white households and 71% of African American households headed by women living in poverty (U.S. Census Bureau, 1997). This extreme level of financial deficiency eventually overwhelmed public resources. The public assistance rolls in many northern cities doubled between 1960 and 1970, from 6 million to 12 million recipients (Trattner, 1999).

American families, however, were largely unaware of the magnitude of African American poverty until a series of books (Galbraith, 1958; Harrington, 1962) and a *New Yorker* magazine documentary (MacDonald, 1963) delineated the conditions of the poor in America's affluent society. Fast on the heels of these reports came the "long hot summer" riots in Newark, Detroit, and Watts, joined by demonstrations in hundreds of African American communities (Trattner, 1999) across the country. Following the upheaval and civil protest, President Johnson convened a National Advisory Commission on Civil Disorders, the Kerner Commission, to determine the underlying causes for violent outbreaks and to recommend ways to prevent occurrences in the future (Trattner, 1999).

After seven months of research and investigation, the Kerner Commission presented a searing report to the President and to the nation. The Commission placed the causes of the riots and unrest squarely at white racism, poverty, segregation, and high unemployment of African Americans (U.S. Kerner Commission, 1968). The Kerner Commission called for social change efforts that would enable the poor, and African American poor in particular, to escape poverty (Trattner, 1999). The Commission called for full societal participation for African Americans, which must be granted through open access to societal resources, particularly education and employment opportunities, to housing, and welfare benefits.

At the same time that the Kerner Commission was researching and reporting its findings, the economies of large inner cities were undergoing dramatic change. The manufacturing industry, a major employer of African American males, left central cities to relocate in the suburbs, in the South, and in Third World countries (Wilson, 1996, 1987). Between 1967 and 1987, the city of Detroit lost 51% of its manufacturing companies, a total of 108,000 employment positions (Wilson, 1996). The number of African American males between the ages of 20 and 29 who were employed in the sector fell from three of every eight to one in five (Wilson, 1996).

In legislation (Economic Opportunity Act programs), ignoring the employment changes taking place in inner cities, Congress responded to African American unemployment and poverty over the next two decades by creating programs (Job Corps, Operation Head Start, Volunteers in Service to America, Upward Bound) that focused principally on individual deficits such as educational and work experience needs. AFDC was amended in the 1960s, providing expanded financial benefits, support services for families, financial benefits to two-parent family heads who had exhausted their unemployment benefits, and also a provision for rehabilitating public assistance recipients through training and employment programs. Legislation included the 1962 Manpower Development and Training Act (MDTA), the Work Incentive Program of 1967, the Comprehensive Employment and Training Act (CETA) of 1973, the JOB Training Partnership Act (JTPA) of 1982, and the Job Opportunities and Basic Skills Training (JOBS) program included in the Family Support Act of 1988. The JOBS program was replaced by The Personal Responsibility and Work Opportunity Reconciliation Act of 1996; also replaced was the Aid to Families with Dependent Children (AFDC) program with the Temporary Assistance to Needy Families (TANF).

While it is virtually impossible to uncouple the separate and combined effects of governmental programs and the civil rights gains of the 1950s, 1960s, and early 1970s to determine their economic impacts, the result was that from 13% to 26% of African American managed to escape poverty and enter the middle class (Thernstrom and Thernstrom, 1998; Jaynes and Williams, 1989). As noted earlier, although 55% of African American families lived in poverty in 1959, this number had declined to 32% by 1969 (Lemann, 1992), to 31% by 1972 (U.S. Census Bureau, 2000), to 26% by 1998, and to 23.1% in 1999 (Center on Budget Priorities, 2000). An impressive reduction in African American poverty had taken place, because African Americans were gaining access to expanded societal services and greater opportunities.

At least 25% of African Americans (Bane and Ellwood, 1986; Olson and Pavetti, 1996) were left behind and did not benefit from education, training programs, or civil rights opportunities. Trattner (1999) labeled this group the "underclass," and Wilson (1987) called them the "truly disadvantaged." These were the unemployed single males and welfare mothers cut off from mainstream society. They were concentrated in economically disadvantaged communities characterized by high rates of poverty and low rates of employment (Wilson, 1987). Depending on the individual state, Wilson's "truly disadvantaged" were 23% to 60% of the welfare caseload (Bane and Ellwood, 1986; Olson and Pavetti, 1996), a striking challenge to social and economic justice.

Today's Underclass: The Truly Disadvantaged

Those left behind and mired in poverty were most affected by a second shift to take place in the U.S. economy. Beginning in the 1980s and into the new millennium, the U.S. economy experienced a major shift from heavy manufacturing to a growing information and service economy. Job requirements of this shift affected inner cities disproportionately, resulting in poorer neighborhoods, troubled public schools, and fewer college-bound students (Wilson, 1996). The rising information and service economy required high levels of education and good communication skills. Left behind, particularly in poor, inner-city communities, were those on welfare who had lower levels of education coupled with little to no work experience (Holzer, 1996). States reported between 30% and 62% of welfare recipients possessed high school diplomas or General Education Development certificates (Harris, 1996, 1993).

Added to lower education attainment and lower level skills, the left behind lacked sufficient access to public modes of transportation (Kain, 1968; Stoll and Raphael, 2000; Wilson, 1987, 1996) and necessary information of job vacancies (Stoll and Raphael, 2000) to seek higher entry-level jobs in suburban areas (Kain, 1968; Stoll and Raphael, 2000; Wilson, 1987, 1996). Transportation and informational barriers, or spatial mismatch, as proposed by Kain (1968), refer to these combined effects of economic restructuring and residential segregation on access to employment for minorities living in central cities (Kain, 1968; Wilson, 1996, 1987). Minority females are the most severely affected this by spatial mismatch (Blank, 1997); economic restructuring has left minority women with the diminished employment opportunities also experienced by inner city men, and with a reduced supply of marriageable men (Wilson, 1987). Geographic location has limited employment prospects for poor, African American as well as Latina women (McLafferty and Preston, 1996).

Amidst unprecedented levels of employment in the 1990s initially continuing into the new century, poor single mothers find it difficult to escape poverty. As Table 1 aptly illustrates, while poverty levels fell sharply from 1973 through 1999, one quarter of white households and 41% of African American and Hispanic households headed by women continue to live in poverty (U.S. Census Bureau, 2000).

A myth prevailing is that poor single mothers refuse work (Edin and Lien, 1997). The opposite is true. Researchers report welfare recipients have little trouble finding employment (Harris, 1996, 1993; Spalter-Roth, Burr, Hartmann, and Shaw, 1995), and most work intermittently throughout their adult lives

TABLE 1. Families with Female Householder, No Husband Present–Below Poverty Level

	1973	1983	1989	1999
White, non-Hispanic	25.0	27.2	23.3	19.8
African American	56.5	57.0	49.4	41.0
Hispanic	57.4	55.1	50.6	40.7

Source: U.S. Census Bureau (2000). "Historical Poverty Tables – People."

(Edin and Lien, 1997; Olson and Pavetti, 1996). The chief problem for welfare recipients is *keeping* employment (Bane, 1997). Studies have found between 25% and 40% of welfare recipients lose their jobs within one year (Friedlander and Burtless, 1995; Hershey, 1997).

Reasons for job loss are related to: (1) personal and family problems, principally stable housing arrangements or substance abuse (Sisco and Pearson, 1994) and, importantly, (2) only low-wage employment is usually available for welfare recipients because of limited work experience and lower educational levels (Wilson, 1996, 1987). Jobs welfare recipients are capable of performing tend to be low-wage without benefits or are seasonal or part-time (Spalter-Roth et al., 1995), characterized by high turnover and layoffs (Edin and Lien, 1997). Most jobs, even full-time positions, for this population do not pay sufficient wages to raise them above the poverty line (Edin and Lien, 1997).

The TANF work-first policy requirement supports any job and, over time, results in needed work experience and in increased wage levels (Pavetti and Wemmerus, 1999). Labor market realities do not provide empirical support for the optimistic employment assumptions upon which work-first initiatives are based. The current work-first requirement is not designed to address systemic causes of poverty (Wilson, 1996, 1987) or structural barriers to living wage employment (Wilson, 1996, 1987) for leaving the welfare rolls. Not surprisingly, studies suggest that work-first participation results in short-term employment objectives (Bloom, 1997) while long-term employment continues to be an elusive goal for welfare recipients lacking marketable occupational training.

Is TANF a socially just policy response for those living in poverty-ridden neighborhoods characterized by poor educational opportunities and ever-decreasing employment prospects due to growing geographic isolation? Now is not the time to remove the basic welfare income support safety net when so much work still needs to be done to assist single-mother families, both in the short term with employment, and for the longer term with training, education, and access to opportunity.

Early TANF studies (Weaver, 2000; Blank and Haskins, 2001) report the program has shown some success in moving welfare recipients from welfare to work. For example, 60% (Sawhill, 2001) of former welfare recipients are now in the labor force. Whether this increase in work activity among welfare recipients is due to TANF program activities, a strong economy, recipient fear of "using up" their TANF eligibility, or some combination of all three is unclear. Will the "jobs" last? Will the jobs, over time, result in needed work experience and in increased wage levels (Pavetti and Wemmerus, 1999)? This is unclear. While recognizing that the TANF program has shown some success, the recommendations below are specifically targeted to address the growing economic and social isolation of welfare recipients but especially those who reside in larger inner city communities.

Discussion and Recommendations

Keeping in mind issues of need and dependency, as well as what constitutes socially just welfare reform policy, independent analyst (Seipel, 2000; Wilson, 1996, 1987) and government-sponsored officials (The Assembly Special Committee, 1992; Kerner Commission, 1968) have explored the underlying causes of poverty and have made similar recommendations:

1. increase employment opportunities for the poor;
2. increase educational opportunity and improve public education facilities;
3. reform the welfare system; and
4. increase the availability of low-income housing for the poor.

Wilson (1996,1987) called for similar increase to societal resources for those trapped in poverty.

To achieve fundamental social justice, by lifting the "truly disadvantaged" out of poverty, requires more than removing the welfare safety net by creating a welfare program that limits eligible children and their caretakers to a five-year lifetime income benefits. The current TANF policy fails to provide programs or policy incentives to improve access to basic goods, services, or opportunities for poor and oppressed groups in society. Moreover, many welfare recipients lack the necessary skills necessary to enter into or to successfully compete in the new technological service sector of the economy. The recommendations (Tyuse, 2000) below acknowledge the qualified success, to date, of the TANF program, but notes that it needs to go further by providing social justice-anchored strategies to improve the overall quality of job training to include public school education and private industry incentives needed to reduce long-term poverty. Because TANF represents a fundamental policy shift from child-focused aid programs to caretaker-focused work obligations, these recommendations are specifically targeted to address the growing economic and social isolation of all welfare recipients but especially those who reside in larger inner city communities. These measures represent social justice at work by improving access to basic goods, services, and opportunities for poor and/or oppressed groups, particularly poor families with children, in society.

Job Training Recommendations

1. Create federal job training programs designed to address the special needs of long-term welfare recipients (or those at risk, such as Wilson's "underclass") (Wilson, 1987), with basic skills that lead to GED completion.
2. Creation of federal job training programs designed to prepare qualified welfare recipients (i.e., those with at least a high school diploma) for jobs in the service sector. During the recent period of economic upswing, work-first training programs resulted in short-term employment with subsequent welfare reductions. Long-term employment and higher earnings increases continue to prove problematic for the untrained and the unskilled welfare recipients. Providing training for the new economy for this population is of utmost importance.
3. Enact job-training policies that link training completion to available employment opportunities, or a safety net until adequate employment is secured. Development of business partnerships should be encouraged through incentives. While such partnerships are difficult to develop and to maintain, local business input is essential for welfare recipients' labor market success. Moreover, job placement after program completion should be a necessary component of any training sequence.
4. Enact policies to improve the quality of present schools and new schools in central and inner city communities by providing necessary resources and qualified teachers to address the needs of students from disadvantaged backgrounds and neighborhoods (Wilson, 1996, 1987).
5. Develop more programs to create school-to-work transitions. Because the majority of students will not pursue post-secondary education, such programs are critical in public school systems in poor central and inner city communities. They should provide students with resume writing and interviewing skills, as well as training in appropriate attire and behavior needed in the work environment. In addition, students should be offered vocational courses and training in typing, auto repair, machine repair, computer and office machine skills, as well as linkages to nurse's aide training and other entry-level training in demand in the local labor market (Wilson, 1996).

Economic Development

Current economic policies and job training efforts have failed to address the employment realities of large, poor, inner city communities. Following are key recommendations (Tyuse, 2000) for federal and local government initiatives:

1. Develop programs in local environments that will stimulate job growth to address issues of high unemployment or non-employment of large segments of disadvantaged communities.
2. Improve central city residents' access to suburban job markets. For example, most communities do not have adequate public transportation linkages from the city to the suburban ring (Wilson, 1996).
3. Provide low interest loans for small business start-up endeavors by indigenous residents of disadvantaged communities.

Measures to alleviate employment isolation include the need for governments to encourage local development and new industry relocation to inner city communities. TANF represents a fundamental policy shift from child-focused aid programs to caretaker-focused work obligations. These recommendations address strategies designed to target long-term structural and economic deficiencies in communities in which welfare recipients tend to reside. These measures represent social justice at work by improving access to basic goods, services, and opportunities for poor and/or oppressed families and children in society.

REFERENCES

Axinn, J., & Levin, H. (1982). *Social welfare: A history of the American response to need.* (2nd. ed.). New York: Longman.

Axinn, J., & Stern, M.J. (2001). *Social welfare: A history of the American response to need.* (5th. ed.). New York: Longman.

Bane, M.J. (1997). Welfare as we might know it. *The American Prospect, 30,* 47-53.

Bane, M.J., & Ellwood, D.T. (1986). Slipping into and out of poverty. *Journal of Human Resources, 21*(1), 1-23.

Blank, R. (1997). *It takes a nation: A new agenda for fighting poverty.* Princeton, NJ: Princeton University Press.

Blank, R.M. & Haskins, R. (2001). The new world of welfare. Washington, DC: Brookings Institution Press.

Bloom, D. (1997). *After AFDC: Welfare-to-work choices and challenges for states.* New York: Manpower Demonstration Research Corporation.

Center on Budget and Policy Priorities. (2000). *Poverty rate hits lowest level since 1979 as unemployment reaches a 30-year low.* Center on Budget and Policy Priorities News Release. Washington, DC.

Current Populations Report. (1991). *Poverty in the United States.* U.S. Census Bureau.

Current Populations Report. (1999). *Poverty in the United States.* U.S. Census Bureau.

Danziger, S.H., & Weinberg, D.H. (1994). The historical record: Trends in family income, inequality, and poverty. In S. Danziger, G. D. Sandefur, & D.H. Weinberg, (Eds.), *Confronting poverty: Prescriptions for change* (pp. 18-50). Cambridge, MA: Harvard University Press.

David, M. (1999). *Principles of social justice.* Cambridge, MA: Harvard University Press.

Day, P.J. (2000). *A new history of social welfare* (3rd ed.). Boston: Allyn and Bacon.

Edelman P. (1997). The worst thing Bill Clinton has done. *The Atlantic Monthly, 279*(3), 43-46.

Edin, K., & Lien, L. (1997). *Making ends meet: How single mothers survive welfare and low-wage work.* New York: Russell Sage.

Farkas, S., Johnson, J., Friedman, W., & Bers, A. (1996). *The values we live by: What Americans want from welfare reform.* New York: Public Agenda.

Fiskin, J. (1983). *Justice, equal opportunity and the family.* New Haven, CT: Yale University Press.

Flynn, J.P. (1995). Social justice in social agencies. In *Encyclopedia of social work* (19th edition). Washington, DC: NASW Press, 2174-2179.

Friedlander, D., & Burtless, G. (1995). *Five years after: The long-term effects of welfare-to-work programs.* New York: Russell Sage Foundation.

Galbraith, J.K. (1958). *The affluent society.* Boston: Houghton, Mifflin Company.

Georgakas, D., & Surkin, M. (1998). *Detroit: I do mind dying: A study in urban revolution,* (Updated Edition). Cambridge, MA: South End Press.

Gordon, L. (1994). *Pitied but not entitled: Single mothers and the history of welfare, 1890-1935.* New York: Free Press.

Harrington, M. (1962). *The other America: Poverty in the United States.* New York: MacMillan.

Harris, K. M. (1993). Work and welfare among single mothers in poverty. *American Journal of Sociology, 99,* 317-352.

Harris, K. M. (1996). Life after welfare: Women, work, and repeat dependency. *American Sociological Review, 61,* 407-426.

Hershey, A.M., & Pavetti, L. A. (1997). Turning job finders into job keepers. *Future of Children, 7,* 74-86.

Holzer, H. (1996). *What employers want: Job prospects for less-educated workers.* New York: Russell Sage Foundation.

Howard, C. (1992). Sowing the seeds of "welfare": The transformation of mothers' pensions, 1900-1940. *Journal of Policy History, 4,* 188-227.

Jacobson, W.B. (2001). Beyond therapy: Bringing social work back to human services reform. *Social Work, 46*(1), 51-61.

Jaynes, G.D., & Williams, R.M. (1989). *A common destiny: Blacks and American society.* Washington, DC: National Academy Press.

Kain, J.F. (1968). Housing segregation, Negro employment, and metropolitan decentralization. *Quarterly Journal of Economics, 82,* 175-97.

Kenworthy, L. (1999). Do social-welfare policies reduce poverty? A cross-national assessment. *Social Forces, 77*(3), 1119-1120.

Kolko, G. (1962). *Wealth and power in America.* London: Thames and Hudson.

Lemann, N. (1992). *The promised land: The great Black migration and how it changed America.* New York: Vintage Books.

Lens, V., & Gibelman, M. (2000). Advocacy be not forsaken! Retrospective lessons from welfare reform. *Families in Society: The Journal of Contemporary Human Services, 81*(6), 611-620.

MacDonald, D. (1963, January 19). Our invisible poor. *New Yorker, 38,* 82-132.

McLafferty, S., & Preston, V. (1996). Spatial mismatch and employment in a decade of restructuring. *Professional Geographer, 48*(4), 417-467.

Morgan, J. (1962). *Income and wealth in the United States.* New York: McGraw-Hill.

Murray, C. (1984). *Losing ground: American social policy, 1950-1980.* New York: Basic Books.

Olson, K., & Pavetti, L. (1996). *Personal and family challenges to the successful transition from welfare to work.* Washington, DC: The Urban Institute.

Onkst, D. H. (1998). "First a Negro . . . incidentally a veteran": Black World War Two veterans and the G.I. Bill of Rights in the deep south, 1944-1948. *Journal of Social History, 31*(3), 517-538.

Pavetti, L., & Wemmerus, N. (1999). From a welfare check to a paycheck: Creating a new social contract. *Journal of Labor Research, 20*(99), 517-537.

Piven, F. F., & Cloward, R.A. (1997). *The breaking of the American social compact.* New York: The New Press.

Rawls, J. (1971). *A theory of justice.* Cambridge, MA: Harvard University Press.

Sawhill, I. (2001). From welfare to work: Making welfare a way station, not a way of life. *Brookings Review, 19*(3), 4-7.

Segal, E.A., & Brzuzy, S. (1998). *Social welfare policy, programs, and practice.* Itasca, IL: F.E. Peacock Publishers, Inc.

Seipel, M.O. (2000). Tax reform for low-wage workers. *Social Work, 45,* 65-72.

Sisco, C.B., & Pearson. C.L. (1994). Prevalence of alcoholism and drug abuse among female AFDC recipients. *Health & Social Work, 19*(1), 75-77.

Skocpol, T. (1992). *Protecting soldiers and mothers: The political origins of social policy in the United States.* Cambridge, MA: Harvard University Press.

Social Security Act of 1935, Pub. L. No. 74-271, 49 Stat. 620.

Spalter-Roth, R., Burr, B., Hartmann, H., & Shaw, L. (1995). *Welfare that works: The working lives of AFDC recipients.* Washington, DC: Institute for Women's Policy Research.

Stoesz, D. (2000). Renaissance. *Families in Society: The Journal of Contemporary Human Services, 81*(6), 621-628.

Stoll, M.A., & Raphael, S. (2000). Racial differences in spatial job search patterns: Exploring the causes and consequences. *Economic Geography, 76*(3), 201-223.

Thernstrom, A., & Thernstrom, S. (1998). Black progress: How far we've come—and how far we have to go. (Black America: Progress & Prospects). *Brookings Review, 16*(2), 12-16.

Trattner, W. I. (1999). *From poor law to welfare state: A history of social welfare in America.* (6th ed.). New York: Free Press.

Tyuse, S.W. (2000). *Previous training and the employment of welfare recipients: An analysis of California's Greater Avenues for Independence (GAIN) Program.* Unpublished Doctoral Dissertation, University of Michigan, Departments of Sociology and Social Work, Ann Arbor, MI.

U.S. Census Bureau. Census of Population. (1960). Population Mobility: States and State Economic Areas. Washington: U.S. Government Printing Office.

U.S. Census Bureau. (1997). Current Population Survey. Historical Poverty Tables–People.

U.S. Census Bureau. (2000). Current Population Survey. Historical Poverty Tables–People. *http://www.census.gov/income/histpov/hstpov02.txt*

U.S. Census Bureau. (1949). Historical Statistics of the United States, Government Printing Office.

U.S. Census Bureau. (1975). Historical Statistics of the United States, Government Printing Office.

U.S. Congress, Public Law 346, 78th Cong., 2nd sess., June 22, 1944.

U.S. Department of Labor, Bureau of Labor Statistics. (2001). Web: *stats.bls.gov*

U.S. Kerner Commission. (1968). *Report.* New York: National Advisory Commission on Civil Disorders.

Van Soest, D. (1995). Peace and social justice. In R. L. Edwards. (Ed.-in-Chief), *Encyclopedia of social work* (19th ed.), 3, pp. 1810-1817. Washington, DC: NASW Press.

Weaver, R.K. (2000). *Ending welfare as we know it.* Brookings Institution Press: Washington, DC.

Weaver, R. K., Shapiro, R.Y., & Jacobs, L.R. (1995). *Public Opinion Quarterly, Welfare. (The Polls-Trends), 59*(4), 606-628.

Wilson, W.J. (1987). *The truly disadvantaged: The inner city, the underclass, and public policy.* Chicago: University of Chicago Press.

Wilson, W.J. (1996). *When work disappears: The world of the new urban poor.* New York: Knopf: Distributed by Random House, Inc.

"Human-Sized" Economic Development: Innovations in Missouri

Margaret S. Sherraden
Betsy Slosar
Antonina Chastain
Joseph Squillace

SUMMARY. Traditional approaches to community development have bypassed many poor communities. This paper reports on findings from a statewide survey of 171 organizations in Missouri about innovative approaches to community economic development (CED). These "human-sized" CED approaches include homeownership, microenterprise, saving, and neighborhood development. Although enthusiastic, respondents identify challenges to service delivery, including funding, reaching low-income families, staff recruitment and training, economic educa-

---

Margaret S. Sherraden, PhD, is Associate Professor, University of Missouri-St. Louis.

Betsy Slosar, MSW, is Economic Development Director, International Institute of Metropolitan St. Louis.

Antonina Chastain, BSW, is Eastern Coordinator, Missouri Association for Social Welfare.

Joseph Squillace, MSW, is Health Policy Analyst, Citizens for Missouri's Children.

Address correspondence to: Margaret S. Sherraden, Department of Social Work, University of Missouri-St. Louis, 8001 Natural Bridge Road, St. Louis, MO 63121 (E-mail: sherraden@umsl.edu).

An earlier version of this paper was presented at the 47th Annual Program Meeting, Council on Social Work Education, Dallas, Texas, March 8-11, 2001.

[Haworth co-indexing entry note]: " 'Human-Sized' Economic Development: Innovations in Missouri." Sherraden, Margaret S. et al. Co-published simultaneously in *Social Thought* (The Haworth Press, Inc.) Vol. 22, No. 2/3, 2003, pp. 97-117; and: *Practicing Social Justice* (ed: John J. Stretch et al.) The Haworth Press, Inc., 2003, pp. 97-117. Single or multiple copies of this article are available for a fee from The Haworth Document Delivery Service [1-800-HAWORTH, 9:00 a.m. - 5:00 p.m. (EST). E-mail address: docdelivery@ haworthpress.com].

© 2003 by The Haworth Press, Inc. All rights reserved.
http://www.haworthpress.com/store/product.asp?sku=J131
10.1300/J131v22n02_08

tion, building partnerships, serving rural areas, and ensuring that the poor have a voice in their own development. Accordingly, recommendations for enhancing CED include increases in support to assist communities and households generate greater wealth, community participation, partnerships among public and private for-profit and nonprofit entities, access to information and education on CED, public awareness, and attention to rural issues. *[Article copies available for a fee from The Haworth Document Delivery Service: 1-800-HAWORTH. E-mail address: <docdelivery@haworthpress.com> Website: <http://www.HaworthPress.com> © 2003 by The Haworth Press, Inc. All rights reserved.]*

KEYWORDS. Community economic development, community participation, asset building

INTRODUCTION

After a decade of economic prosperity and declining unemployment rates, many communities in urban and rural areas of Missouri continue to confront severe economic and social problems. Traditional approaches to community development have bypassed poor communities, raising awareness that new and more effective approaches to economic and social development in poor neighborhoods are needed.

This paper explores innovations in "human-sized" community economic development (CED).[1] CED is a strategy that integrates economic and social development to increase tangible assets and build capacity, to increase life chances and empower low-income and low-wealth people and their communities (Sherraden & Ninacs, 1998). Examples of CED strategies include homeownership, microenterprise, business incubators, savings and investment mechanisms, financial services, economic education, commercial and industrial development, consumer and producer cooperatives, land trusts, community infrastructure improvements, job creation and training, technical assistance, and supportive social services.

Three key features characterize this approach (Sherraden & Ninacs, 1998; Rubin & Sherraden, forthcoming). First, where social development and economic development traditionally have been viewed as distinct and separate processes, CED integrates the social and the economic (Midgley, 1995). All too often, separate focus results in economic development efforts directed to select sectors of a community, leaving others with the same or diminished resources. As economic development efforts increase employment, homeownership, and savings accumulation, they also provide resources that fuel and sustain social development. In the process, community involvement and social capital is created that provides the social relations upon which further development is possible (Woolcock, 1998). Local capacity for development is expanded through the creation of institutional structures that facilitate and sustain economic renewal (Beverly & Sherraden, 1997).

Second, CED aims to increase assets and other tangible resources in low-income and low-wealth households and communities and to create institutional structures that facilitate and encourage locally directed wealth building. Asset building provides long-term resources to produce economic stability, to continue economic and social improvement, to increase hope for the future, and to enhance intergenerational welfare (Sherraden, 1991, p. 148; Page-Adams & Sherraden, 1997).

Third, CED differs from traditional economic development models that promote top-down development. Attracting outside businesses into a community through financial incentives may increase economic activity, but does not necessarily involve or benefit local communities. The CED approach emphasizes a bottom-up empowerment approach that involves a broad array of community stakeholders. Community members are key partners who work in partnership with public, nonprofit and private entities. Thus, this approach is a "human-sized" economic development approach that differs in fundamental ways from traditional economic development approaches.

This paper reports on innovations underway in Missouri in community economic development. Specifically, we report on efforts to build assets through homeownership, small business (or microenterprise), savings, and other community development activities (Boshara, 2001; Shapiro & Wolff, 2001).

BACKGROUND

In 1994, a group of practitioners came together to form the Community Economic Development Committee under the auspices of the Missouri Association for Social Welfare (MASW).[2] Initially the committee focused on welfare-to-work proposals, but soon began to address severe lack of economic opportunity in disadvantaged communities. Since then, over 200 individuals and organizations from across the state have joined the CED committee to promote new approaches to economic development in urban and rural communities. The Committee sponsors regional and state forums and conferences on CED; drafts and advocates for new legislation; helps develop linkages among public, nonprofit, and for-profit agencies; and disseminates information on "human-sized development" to legislators, state agency staff, and the public (Sherraden et al., forthcoming).

In 1999, committee members launched a baseline survey to assess types and levels of CED activity and key challenges confronted by organizers. The results of the survey contribute to our understanding of CED implementation and help guide advocacy and education efforts of CED practitioners.

CED Committee members, staff, and students, with assistance from researchers at the University of Missouri-St. Louis and St. Louis University, developed, implemented, and analyzed the survey.[3] Funded by research grants from the Center for Social Justice at St. Louis University and from the University of Missouri at St. Louis, the study surveyed organizations in the public, nonprofit, and for-profit sectors that were likely to be engaged in CED activities. Locating these organizations was complicated by the fact that CED projects were being implemented in public, nonprofit, and for-profit organizations that span the social and economic development "divide." Researchers generated a database that included community action agencies, historic preservation groups, community development corporations, housing organizations, microenterprise programs, human services, business development organizations, economic development groups, banks, and university extension services. Approximately 880 organizations across the state of Missouri were identified as *potentially* being engaged in CED activities with low-income populations.

The survey instrument was a self-administered mail questionnaire.[4] The first section of the survey concerned the respondent organization, including range of services offered, clientele, funding, staffing, and participation in community development programs. The second section concerned the specific CED activities undertaken by the organization, including homeownership, microenterprise, savings and financial services, and neighborhood development. Each section contained close-ended and open-ended questions related to service provision, target population, challenges, and support needed.

In May of 1999 the initial mailing of 880 surveys was sent to the executive director or person with knowledge of the organization's programs. Three months later a second mailing was sent to 270 nonrespondent organizations, chosen because they were among the types of organization most likely to be engaged in CED (based on information from the first wave of survey returns). Of all returned questionnaires (n = 199), 171 were involved in some CED activity. Response rates varied widely by type of organization. For example, only three percent of financial institutions responded, while 39 percent of community development organizations responded. The overall response rate was 23 percent. The low response rate is due to a lack of CED activity–as we defined it–in most of the organizations originally surveyed.

Survey data were analyzed using Statistical Package for the Social Sciences (SPSS), and open-ended comments (147 total pages) were analyzed using a qualitative analysis program, ATLAS-ti, according to an initial coding scheme derived from background research on CED and supplemented with codes that emerged in analysis.

ORGANIZATIONS INVOLVED IN CED

The types of organizations are wide-ranging. Respondents often selected more than one category to describe their organization, but community development and economic development organizations were mentioned most often (Figure 1).

Geographical catchment areas include counties (26%), municipalities or small towns (29%), and regions (30%). Seven percent serve the whole state and eight percent serve neighborhoods (Table 1). The majority of organizations that responded are nonprofit (62%), followed by public or governmental (35%), and for-profit organizations (3%).[5] Funding sources include public

FIGURE 1. Type of Organization (n = 171)

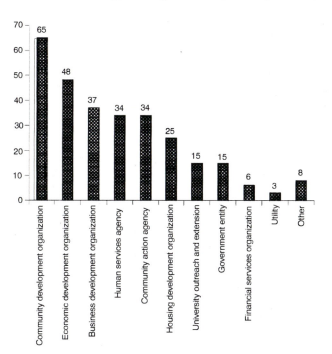

sector funds (58%), private sector grants (22%), fees or earned income (12%), and other sources (8%) (Table 1).

Organizations reported that 71 percent of their participants are White, 20 percent are African American, three percent are Hispanic, one percent is Asian American, one percent is Native American, and four percent are unspecified (Table 1). Several respondents were unsure of the exact ethnic and racial background of participants, but reported serving a variety of minority, refugee and immigrant populations, including Russians, Bosnians, Somalis, Iranians, Vietnamese, and Koreans, including one organization that serves "many African and Middle Eastern cultures; our clients speak 14 different languages."

TABLE 1. Organizations Engaged in CED, 1999

	Percents
Catchment Area (n = 169)	
State	7
Counties	26
Small towns	29
Regions	30
Neighborhood	8
Tax Status (n = 169)	
Nonprofit	62
Public	35
For-profit	3
Funding Sources (n = 153)	
Government funding	58
Private grants	22
Fee for service	12
Other sources	8
Percent of Budget in CED (n = 168)	
1 to 25	54
26 to 50	10
51 to 75	6
76 to 100	30
Race/Ethnicity of Clients (n = 157)	
White	71
African American	20
Hispanic	3
Asian	1
Native American	1
Other	4

Most of the organizations are small, although the size varies widely. The number of employees ranges from one part-time person in one organization to 6,000 full-time employees in another (median is six full-time employees). Slightly over half (51%) of the agencies also have part-time employees (median is two part-time employees). Over one-third of the organizations (36%) use volunteers (median is 12 volunteers).

More than half of the organizations (54%) devote less than one-fourth of their budget to CED. Many in this group were just beginning to get involved in CED. At the other extreme, about a third (30%) of the agencies devote more than three-fourths of their budget to CED. Thirty-two agencies are members of the Missouri Community Development Corporation Association, a CDC trade association created by the state to spur local CED initiatives.

Many of the organizations receive state and federal funding for community economic development. State funding sources include the Neighborhood Assistance Program (NAP), state tax credits for donors to approved community service, crime prevention, education, job training, or physical revitalization; the Community Bank/CDC Tax Credit Program; Missouri Community Development Corporation grants for housing, human service projects, economic development, job creation, welfare to work, and infrastructure improvements; and the Youth Opportunities Program, tax credits for youth crime prevention (Missouri Department of Economic Development, 2001). Municipalities or governmental entities reported receiving Rural Economic Assistance Program support to hire professional economic developers. Many respondents were located in Missouri or Federal Enterprise Zones, which provide access to other development tax credit programs. Forty organizations received funds through the Missouri Community Development Block Grant program, offering grants to improve local facilities, address health and safety concerns, and develop a greater capacity for growth benefiting low- to moderate-income persons. Agencies reported other federal funding, not addressed in the survey because of its focus on state support.

COMMUNITY ECONOMIC DEVELOPMENT IN MISSOURI

Results of this survey provide insight into the range of CED activities underway, as well as some of the challenges to CED in Missouri. Of 171 organizations reporting CED activities with low-income populations, 139 offered in-depth information on their CED programs. These respondents filled out in-depth sections on housing (60), microenterprise (38), savings or financial development (15), neighborhood development (63), or other kinds of CED activity (38). Summarized below are the types of services they deliver, challenges they confront, and respondents' suggestions for improvements.

The largest number of respondents (60) provide home ownership services for low-income participants in Missouri. Among these services are counseling for home ownership, home construction and rehabilitation, assistance with home repair, credit counseling, closing cost assistance, home loans, and other support, including weatherization, distribution of information on housing programs, and research on rural and farm worker housing. While the focus of the survey was on homeownership, many organizations also reported that they are engaged in rental unit construction and rehab and in rental management.

Organizations also deliver a broad array of microenterprise services. Defined as sole proprietorships, partnerships, or family businesses with five or fewer employees, microenterprises generally lack access to commercial lending and require less than $25,000 in capitalization (Langer et al., 1999, xii). A total of 38 responding organizations provide microenterprise services, primarily involving economic education, technical assistance and business planning. To a lesser degree, they facilitate bank loans or offer micro loans themselves. Other support services include formation of peer support networks, business incubators, market development, and mentoring.

A small number of organizations (15) provide savings and financial services to low-income participants, such as economic and financial education, Individual Development Accounts (IDAs),[6] and credit counseling. One program organizes savings clubs, and another operates a community bank. With the exception of consumer credit counseling agencies, which were not included in the survey, savings programs for the poor is a relatively new field. With passage of state legislation in 1999 that supports IDAs, and ongoing funding of the federal Assets for Independence Act (AFIA), it is likely that numbers of savings and financial education programs will expand.[7]

A large number of organizations (63) reported being involved in some kind of neighborhood development that fit the survey's CED definition. Their primary activities are community organizing, business district activity, planning and marketing development, and Enterprise Zone projects. Twenty-three of these organizations develop and distribute business capital (not microenterprise related). A few operate land trusts, undertake infrastructure projects, and engage in various neighborhood development projects.

Across these types of CED, survey respondents reported very similar challenges, which often reflect inadequate physical, economic, and social infrastructure. Survey respondents described discouragement in the face of huge development tasks. They work with families with large debt, many of whom find it difficult to imagine how they will ever become savers or homeowners. Agencies working in communities hard hit by disinvestment in a fiscally competitive environment find it challenging to plan for progressive community development. Nonetheless, the surveys also suggest optimism about emerging models and the potential for real advancement among participants and communities if certain challenges are met.

Table 2 identifies the common challenges encountered by organizations engaged in homeownership, microenterprise, and savings and financial programs.

Time and again, respondents mentioned difficulties in obtaining sufficient resources for:

1. funds for low-income household development (e.g., homeownership and microenterprise);
2. funds for program development (e.g., staff salaries and program overhead); and
3. funds for community development projects (e.g., transportation and infrastructure).

Some respondents emphasized the need for more funding for organizational development, but there was more emphasis on the need for program funding. Adequate funding for loan programs, subsidies, incentives, and outright grants would increase assets in households and communities. While many focused on support for programs, some emphasized the importance of direct funding to participants. As one respondent phrased it, "Money, money, money to people–not agencies!"

Slightly more than half of the respondents (55%) working in home ownership programs mentioned the need for funding, especially for home repair and general maintenance. As one respondent wrote:

> It is a challenge finding programs to help them keep their home. If they experience financial hardship they're at risk of losing everything. Keeping up with repairs and maintenance for older homes is an issue.

TABLE 2. Common Challenges to CED Practice, 1999 (Percents)

	Home Ownership N = 60	Micro-enterprise N = 38	Savings and Financial Services N = 15
Funding	55	58	47
Participant recruitment and retention	45	42	60
Staff recruitment, training and retention	38	32	33
Economic education	40	26	47
Agency collaboration	–	–	47

Others cited a lack of capital for home loans. Also mentioned were resources for credit counseling and credit repair (48%) and homeownership training (40%). According to one respondent, "Low income buyers have a higher percentage of poor credit history and little to no savings."

Respondents from microenterprise programs identified funding for operations (58%) and loan capital (55%) as the greatest challenges. They expressed frustration that funders do not see microenterprise development as a priority and that banks are reluctant to take risks with low-income entrepreneurs. Among their recommendations is development of a micro-loan pool available and accessible in all counties throughout the state. One respondent pointed out that "many of the people who need business capital are just above the levels for (traditional microenterprise) programs and below the levels needed for standard loans." Others emphasized that many programs require equity, which many potential participants lack.

For programs offering savings and financial services, funding is less problematic than participant recruitment; nevertheless, seven singled out difficulties in obtaining matching funds for IDA programs. This may be less of a problem after Missouri's IDA program begins to provide tax credits to donors who contribute to matching funds.[8] This optimism is guarded, however. As one respondent pointed out, IDA programs may have the same difficulty recruiting donors as other tax credit programs:

> We are very interested in setting up an Individual Development Account program for low-income families. However, we already have tax credits from the neighborhood assistance program [NAP] and can't raise funds for that.

Finally, many respondents pointed out that low levels of funding for program operations hamper service delivery. Organizations report the need for supplemental grants to operate in a way that truly helps their participants.

Reaching Low-Income Families

Another important challenge facing CED programs is effective outreach and methods for working with people with low incomes and low wealth. Respondents report that as participants churn through the bureaucratic mill of agencies, paperwork, and rejections, some have become discouraged and distrustful. This distrust creates serious obstacles to recruiting potential participants. Others are reluctant to seek help because they are embarrassed about debt and financial troubles, many believing that seeking help may be risky.

Others believe they will not qualify and doubt that their credit record can ever be cleared up. One survey respondent put it this way:

> It is difficult to help individuals address their past credit and debt issues, while also trusting our agency's programs to really help them.

Respondents from home ownership programs report that potential participants are often reluctant to utilize the full range of housing services, especially those that help them clean their credit records. They often do not fully utilize the credit counseling provided. In other cases, participants may have had bad experiences and do not trust official or formal assistance programs. As one respondent wrote, "clients often do not trust government programs." Contributing to this reluctance, people do not want to reveal low incomes: "When we have workshops, attendance is low. Some do not attend for fear of embarrassment." This is common in both rural and urban areas. According to another respondent, "As the neighborhood continues to gentrify, low-income families become increasingly reluctant to self identify."

In some cases, potential participants' fears about debt may be accurate. For example, debt can make it difficult to qualify for homeownership programs:

> Participants tend to have too much debt to qualify for programs. Agencies often screen 70 applicants to find ten qualifiers. . . . People qualifying for mortgages on "fixer-uppers" have no funds for needed repairs. [When] participants are over-committed on resource allocation, housing tends to lose out when money is stretched.

Adding to lack of trust and high debt, potential participants often do not understand the CED approach. While they may be familiar with job programs (e.g., Job Corps) and income maintenance programs (e.g., TANF and Food Stamps), typically they are unfamiliar with the CED methods and they lack easy access to the few alternatives that might exist (Midgley & Livermore, 1998).

Finally, CED programs generally involve a longer term commitment than other programs. For example, there are usually several steps a family must undertake before they can purchase a home or start a microenterprise. These may include credit repair, financial education, mentoring, or counseling. These cannot be done all at once, nor can they usually be accomplished by one organization. They may involve several family members. The process can lead to participants becoming discouraged. These difficulties also produce a certain frustration among staff who are trying to help. For example, in microenterprise programs, retention of participants is labor intensive and involves working on serious credit problems before business planning can be seriously undertaken. One respondent explained:

> Most low-income families don't come to us. If they do, the general desire for success and the skills (technical, analytical, production) needs a lot of teaching to [help them] compete in the marketplace. It takes time and much one-on-one. Often they are unwilling to complete the necessary written work and expect this work to be completed for them. . . .

Recruiting participants is difficult in savings and financial education programs, according to respondents, because of participants' lack of access to formal banking and savings institutions. Many potential savers have more experience with so-called "fringe banking," such as check cashing and payday loan outfits, or informal saving (Caskey, 1994). According to some respondents, it takes outreach and education to help people with limited financial resources understand and trust these new opportunities for saving. People need to be acquainted with the idea of saving. In order to engage them, it takes "identifying and accessing other resources and helping participants to consider those resources without being overly 'directive' or creating 'dependence.' " Apprehension about the motives of savings programs exacerbates recruitment difficulties. As one respondent wrote, "Potential participants were leery of the program, thinking that it was too good to be true."

Eight respondents pointed out that once in the savings and financial education programs, participants tend to save at low rates. It is difficult for participants to meet various financial obligations and emergencies without hindering their ability to save. They report that families frequently have little extra to put into savings, although staff try to assist families manage their finances to enable some day-to-day savings. However, it was unclear from the surveys whether all of these organizations provide matches for participant savings as is customary in an IDA program.[9]

In sum, difficulties in participant recruitment reflect several inhibiting factors, including lack of awareness, low incomes, large debt and bad credit, lack of trust, and embarrassment.

Staff Recruitment and Training

The challenges of participant recruitment and the layers of challenges faced by poor families and communities can easily overwhelm staff, especially those without cross-training in social *and* economic development. Respondents reported considerable difficulty recruiting and retaining employees with the appropriate mix of skills. In microenterprise, for example, staff need experience and training with small business development, but also need "people skills," including cross-cultural skills. It is challenging to find the right balance that fits participants' needs. Level of experience is often more important than educational background. They report that lack of training and burnout sometimes leads to poor staff attitudes. As a result, some staff focus on participant deficiencies, believing the principal obstacle is the participants themselves–their lack of initiative, dependency, and apathy. As one respondent observed, "(We) need to change the attitude of the families. They don't want to improve their credit rating, won't attend counseling sessions. The hardest to deal with are the young families–older ones are trying harder and are making progress toward economic sustainability."

Other respondents recognized these problems, but focused on reasons behind them: the challenge of living poor in America and the history of exclusion from institutions that enable household and community asset accumulation, especially for people of color (Sherraden, 1991; Oliver & Shapiro, 1995; Conley, 1999). Survey respondents pointed to inflexible rules and inadequate funding, lamenting their inability to really help.

Finally, several suggested that staff themselves are frustrated by a lack of voice and influence in policy implementation. They reported that officials in public agencies, the banking sector, and funding organizations do not permit program staff to make key implementation decisions. They believe that solutions are imposed from the top instead of consulting those with a direct stake in the community and those most affected–people living in poverty. Of particular concern is the availability of flexible funding streams that might allow programs to provide support at the appropriate time and in the appropriate manner. Several respondents argue that they are more familiar with the local context and consumer/participant constraints than are funders, therefore, they should have the latitude to decide how to implement programs.

Lack of funding makes it more difficult to attract, train, and retain qualified employees who can deal with these frustrations. One respondent said it is difficult to compete with states that provide better salaries in this field. He described losing a business counselor to a neighboring state within days of receiving the survey in the mail. The counselor had created over 70 jobs in the past four years. Providing opportunities for professional development is difficult without adequate funding, as one person noted: "There is not enough money to keep the entire staff fully and thoroughly trained."

Economic Education and Training

One of the biggest challenges to providing economic education and training to participants is the fact that the educational materials themselves are generally inadequate—usually not written in language that is plainly understood by participants who have low literacy levels. One respondent cited the need for more appropriate books, worksheets, pamphlets and videos on financial education topics. The need is great, according to survey respondents, for comprehensive staff training opportunities, technical consultation, and a clearinghouse for resources.

In microenterprise programs, staff find it difficult to offer economic education for microentrepreneurs (Table 2), but even more find it difficult to provide in-depth technical assistance (36%). Specifically, participants need assistance in managing loans, accounting, budgeting, legal issues, tax concerns, management, marketing, and use of computers and computer programs. Sometimes these can be covered in classes and support groups, but often individuals require one-on-one attention. Staff are not able to provide all the training needed, and organizations report a great need for mentors and volunteers.

One respondent suggested creating a pool of mentors who would donate their time on either a short-term or long-term basis to work with people starting businesses similar to their own. Peer support works well, provided it is sustained and supported by staff, according to respondents. However, approximately a fourth of the microenterprise assistance providers pointed to the difficulty of organizing and staffing groups. The challenge is on both the staff side—finding staff with good group work skills—and on the participant side because lack of transportation and child care make regular participation difficult.

Microenterprise agencies serving immigrants and refugees encounter slightly different issues related to economic education. While these groups often possess education and expertise in their businesses, their credentials and experience are often not recognized and they frequently do not understand regulations and procedures for establishing and operating businesses in the United States. Language and culture present additional barriers. Therefore, some respondents report that there should be greater flexibility in the credentialing process for new Americans attempting to ply a trade, such as cosmetology or plumbing, in which they had attained expertise and status in their home countries.

Collaboration and Partnerships

Several respondents reported a lack of coordination, collaboration and partnerships among service providers, state and local agencies and the business sector. Excessive paperwork and complicated procedures in multiple organizations bogs down service delivery, keeping participants who do qualify for programs on long waiting lists. "Bureaucratic red tape and governmental [regulations]," in the words of one respondent, get in the way of even the most determined participants and devoted staff. To some extent this results from long-established patterns where social and economic development were addressed through separate bureaucracies. In the old model, social service agencies provided "social assistance" and advocated for disadvantaged families and communities, while economic development agencies helped develop physical infrastructure, retain businesses, and attract and create new business and investment. Seldom would an economic development agency work with a social service agency because their "clients" and technologies were different. CED practitioners responding to the survey suggest that the CED model makes it necessary for organizations to work collaboratively across this "divide." According to respondents, there is considerably more room for policy innovation that encourages cross-sector collaboration in CED.

Respondents from savings and economic education programs appeared to be particularly concerned about the difficulties of building collaborative relationships with other organizations. This may affect savings programs in particular because they are relatively new–agencies are still working to develop the tools and procedures for effective service delivery. One person observed, "Some local agencies are more cooperative in promoting these programs and referring clients than others." However, several respondents recognized the importance of coordination, collaboration and sharing information among emerging programs.

Serving Rural Areas

Respondents reported challenges serving participants in rural areas. Those working in rural areas perceive an urban bias, believing that cities garner the lion's share of resources and attention from state and federal programs. A common perception is that federal and state funding are channeled through Jefferson City to urban areas and county seats and do not pass through to benefit rural areas. As one respondent noted, "Most federal dollars are channeled through the state, which in turn, doesn't fund rural areas." A lack of rural infrastructure, such as housing, transportation, and communications, impedes the capacity of programs to provide adequate services to rural participants.

According to rural respondents, urban bias magnifies the challenges discussed earlier. CED programs are scarce. Support services, such as credit counseling and repair, are often unavailable. Travel and transportation barriers increase service delivery obstacles. In many rural areas, it is simply unrealistic to require low-income microentrepreneurs to attend weekly training and support groups that may take an hour or more of travel. Agencies should develop alternative training and mentoring methods and provide the resources to support these initiatives. For example, one respondent noted that being the only program in a large rural area makes it difficult to require the same level of participation in training as urban agencies might require: "We are spread over a ten county area and do not feel we can ask someone only borrowing $50 to lose a day's pay to come to monthly educational meetings."

Lack of resources in rural areas contributes to underdevelopment, which respondents argue leads to further deterioration, as local talent–both staff and local residents–leaves for greater opportunities in urban and suburban areas. Acute shortages of skilled workers in rural areas follow. Respondents suggested that if a greater proportion of funds were spent in rural areas, then, in the words of one respondent, "jobs (within commuting distance), good roads, and small business would be spread around the state. High school graduates would not have to leave home to get a job, and college graduates would come back home to work after finishing school."

Several respondents commented on the need for more information on funding sources, "best practices" in CED, training for staff, and technical assistance. This was an especially common issue for rural respondents who frequently feel "out of the loop."

Voice

Some respondents feel that lack of "voice" exacerbates difficulties in community development. Tight restrictions by state government and other funders prohibits organizations from being able to offer the kinds of support that respondents believe will really assist people. Local community leaders and residents are not consulted or included in decision making:

> Who best would know what our needs are than the people living within the community? Outsiders come in and don't hear our voice. They want to tell us our needs and disregard our [ideas about] community betterment.

This reluctance to involve local communities in decisions may contribute to apathy noted by several respondents. They believe that their difficulties in trying to motivate community members to work together for the betterment of their neighborhoods is partly a result of not being listened to by those with local authority or in positions of power.

For these reasons effective community participation is difficult to encourage and sustain. Creating an atmosphere of inclusiveness is difficult. It is particularly challenging to get people to work together at different levels–from the political arena to volunteers. Yet community development requires collaboration by a variety of stakeholders, such as community organizations, council members, county officials, mayors and others from both public and private sectors. A solution offered by one respondent would be for community members to be trained in team building, and for teams of volunteers to work together to accomplish tasks beneficial to the community as a whole. However, it is difficult to plan and implement long-term strategies when day-to-day exigencies claim most of people's time and energy. Nonetheless, the majority of respondents noted that greater communication across local organizations (horizontal) and between local and regional/state organizations (vertical) would improve chances for effective development.

Neighborhood Development

Many respondents pointed out that neighborhood development is a necessary foundation for successful asset building. They mentioned the need for more jobs and job training, as one respondent who said that microenterprise may fulfill a dream for a few individuals, but it is not practical for most people. At the same time, opportunities for advancement in employment are crucial, as this respondent pointed out:

> Most low-income families are easy to serve. The problem is not within the family, but the system. After we place people in entry-level jobs they become discouraged because of lack of advancement due to poor technical skills. The system prevents gaining technical skills if they do not have a G.E.D., regardless of their ability. We are setting them up for failure.

Respondents wrote that lack of jobs leads to an inadequate tax base for local physical infrastructure and basic services. Many communities lack adequate roads, bridges, sewers, surface and wastewater control, fire departments, libraries, schools, child care, and medical facilities. As one respondent pointed out, "In the rural counties we serve, we have difficulties assisting our families in overcoming barriers such as transportation and childcare."

Access to information for CED is also a concern. Two respondents wrote that despite improved access to census data, it is difficult to obtain adequate data about neighborhoods. Others said they needed help in assessing community needs. Others want access to ideas and "best practices" models and methods.

BUILDING "HUMAN-SIZED" COMMUNITY ECONOMIC DEVELOPMENT

In sum, despite their relatively recent introduction, CED strategies for increasing household and community assets in low-income communities are being implemented by a substantial number of organizations in Missouri. While committed to these innovations, respondents in organizations providing CED services articulated several serious challenges. CED requires a change in philosophy and methods for participants, staff, and funders. Further, its processes are still relatively new and require considerable changes to program models and implementation. Survey respondents were cautiously optimistic about the emerging model of CED, and the model of economic development is slowly changing and new ideas are gaining currency. As one respondent observed, "Greater differences of opinion exist today versus ten years ago concerning what constitutes 'desirable' development."

Based on the survey responses, several concrete recommendations for building "human-sized" CED are offered here. First, financial support and technical assistance should be increased for "human-sized" CED. On one hand, additional funding can support development of household assets that will enable families to be equal partners in their own and their community's economic development. On the other hand, more funding can build organizational capacity to deliver CED services. This can be accomplished in a number of ways. Economic development agencies can help local service providers compete successfully for tax credits for CED. In addition, more direct funding streams for development of low-income households and communities is required along with statewide access to low-interest revolving loan funds. Seed funding could attract more federal, state, and private foundation grants. Creation of community foundations may be able to foster more "human-sized" CED, especially in rural areas. Finally, CED programs need more support for operations. The labor-intensive nature of working with low-income families in distressed communities requires fiscally healthy agencies that can provide adequate salaries and training for staff in both the "soft" skills of helping people and the "hard" skills of financial management. These investments could produce long-term benefits by assisting families and communities to generate wealth from within.

Second, communities should participate as full partners in CED policy-making, program design, and program implementation. Effective voice from below will help make programs more relevant to local circumstances.

Third, collaboration and partnerships among public and private for-profit and nonprofit entities engaged in CED work with low-income communities should be encouraged, perhaps rewarded. Collaboration would increase organizations' ability to meet both the social and economic needs of households and communities. Providing incentives could minimize competition, increase rewards for collaboration, and streamline case management among organizations serving the same participants. Continued collaboration and networking through statewide associations will increase political clout, pool expertise and resources, and provide continuing opportunities for joint training and projects.

Fourth, communities want increased access to information and education on "human-sized" CED. A statewide clearinghouse for education and training materials about CED could provide more up-to-date information on CED initiatives and "best practices" throughout the United States and the world. Such a clearinghouse could also generate more effective information and training materials on financial services, saving, homeownership, and business development for low-income and low-wealth populations. Moreover, to generate support among policy-makers, legislators and state department staff should be informed regularly about CED strategies and results.

Fifth, it is also important to raise public awareness about CED. This will help to recruit volunteers with skills and expertise in asset building strategies, including homeownership, microenterprise, savings and household finance, and neighborhood development.

Finally, assistance to rural areas should be increased to provide additional support for homeownership, microenterprise, and savings that will assist with housing shortages, employment and business shortages, and disinvestment. Special efforts are needed to develop innovations, disseminate "best practices," and reach low-income, low-wealth rural populations–aided by the use of new technologies such as the Internet, teleconferencing, and distance learning.

This article describes the range of organizations that have adopted CED strategies in their work with poor households and communities. Although survey respondents suggest that there are difficult challenges to effective implementation, they also emphasize that development of tangible assets and capacity building in poor households and communities offer a viable and important alternative to traditional economic development.

NOTES

1. This term was coined by Peter De Simone, Executive Director of MASW.
2. The Missouri Association for Social Welfare, founded in 1901, is a broad-based, statewide citizens' membership organization whose purposes are research, coalition building, public education, and advocacy through the state (www.masw.org).
3. Contact the authors for a copy of the survey instrument.
4. Reviewed for ethical compliance by the Human Subjects Committees at the University of Missouri-St. Louis and St. Louis University, the questionnaire underwent a two-stage pretest by seven organizations that responded with feedback about the design and content. It was disseminated under the auspices of the Missouri Association for Social Welfare, with the CED project director and faculty from the two universities as co-signers.

5. Sampling decisions account for the small number of for-profit organizations that responded: the survey was sent only to for-profit organizations that are on the CED mailing list and some others that committee members believed were involved in CED. The for-profits that responded are utilities and management consultants involved in community development activities.

6. Individual Development Accounts (IDAs) are matched savings accounts for low- and, moderate-income individuals and families for long-term investment strategies, such as home ownership, business capitalization, and post-secondary training and education (Sherraden, 1991).

7. More information on IDAs, which are called FDAs in Missouri's legislation, is available from the Community Development Program of Department of Economic Development. AFIA is administered by The U.S. Department of Health and Human Services.

8. Missouri's program provides $4 million per year in 50% tax credits, which can leverage a maximum of $8 million in funding for IDAs per year. Further information is available on the Missouri Department of Economic Development Webpage: *www.ecodev.state.mo.us/cd/sda/default.hotmail*

9. Other research suggests that savings occurs when there is a match, even among the very poor (Schreiner et al., 2001).

ACKNOWLEDGMENTS

The authors are grateful for financial support for this study from the Ewing Marion Kauffman Foundation, the Emmett J. and Mary Martha Doerr Center for Social Justice, Education and Research at Saint Louis University, and the University of Missouri-St. Louis Research Fund.

Many people were instrumental in designing, implementing, analyzing, and writing this report. Special thanks go first to the CED Committee and its many members who have been meeting since 1994 to discuss methods to promote social and economic development to Missouri's low-income communities. Dr. Susan Tebb, Dean of the School of Social Service at St. Louis University, provided assistance with the design of the survey and with Human Subjects review at St. Louis University. The authors also want to thank Dianna Moore, Director of Community Development, Department of Economic Development, for her valuable suggestions and the agencies that pretested the survey instrument and offered suggestions for improvement, including Justine Petersen Housing and Reinvestment Corporation, St. Louis Association of Community Organizations (SLACO), Economic Opportunity Corporation (ECO) of Greater St. Joseph, The Family Asset Building Program (FAB) of Heart of America Family Services, Economic Development Department of the City of Thayer, Northside Community Center, and the Community Reinvestment Department at Mercantile Bank. Peter De Simone, Executive Director of MASW, provided invaluable guidance and ideas throughout the project, as well as Lelia Lancaster, MASW Administrative Assistant, who assisted in compiling and writing the report.

REFERENCES

Beverly, Sandra G. & Michael Sherraden. 1997. Investment in human development as a social development strategy. *Social Development Issues 19* (1), 1-18.

Boshara, Ray. 2001 (December). Building Assets: A Report on the Asset-Development and IDA Field. Washington, DC: Corporation for Enterprise Development.

Caskey, John P. 1994. *Fringe Banking: Check-Cashing Outlets, Pawnshops, and the Poor*. New York: Russell Sage Foundation.

Conley, Dalton. 1999. *Being Black, Living in the Red: Race, Wealth, and Social Policy in America*. Berkeley, CA: University of California Press.

Langer, Jennifer A., Jacqueline A. Orwick, & Amy J. Kays. *1999 Directory of U.S. Microenterprise Programs*. Microenterprise Fund for Innovation, Effectiveness, Learning and Dissemination (FIELD), The Aspen Institute, in collaboration with the Association for Enterprise Opportunity. Washington, DC: Aspen Institute.

Midgley, James. 1995. *Social Development: The Developmental Perspective in Social Welfare*. London: Sage.

Midgley, James & Michelle Livermore. 1997. The developmental perspective in social work: Educational implications for a new century. *Journal on Social Work Education 33* (3), 573-586.

Missouri Department of Economic Development. 2001. *Community Development Group: Program Resource Guide*. Jefferson City, MO: Department of Economic Development (*http://www.ecodev.state.mo.us/cd/booklet/Resource2.pdf*).

Oliver, Melvin L. & Thomas M. Shapiro. 1995. *Black Wealth/White Wealth*. New York: Routledge.

Page-Adams, D. & M. Sherraden. 1997. Asset building as a community revitalization strategy. *Social Work 42*, 423-434.

Rubin, Herb & Margaret S. Sherraden. Forthcoming. Community economic and social development. In Weil, M.O. (ed.), *Handbook of Community Practice*. Thousand Oaks, CA: Sage.

Schreiner, Mark, Michael Sherraden, Margaret Clancy, Lissa Johnson, Jami Curley, Michal Grinstein-Weiss, Min Zhan, & Sondra Beverly. 2001 (February). Savings and Asset Accumulation in Individual Development Accounts. St. Louis, MO: Center for Social Development.

Shapiro, Thomas M. & Edward N. Wolff (eds.). 2001. *Assets for the Poor: The Benefits of Spreading Asset Ownership*. New York: Russell Sage Foundation.

Sherraden, Margaret S., Betsy Slosar, & Michael Sherraden. 2002. Innovation in social policy: Researcher, practitioner, advocate, and student collaboration. *Social Work 47* (3), 209-224.

Sherraden, Margaret S. & William C. Ninacs (eds.). 1998. *Community Economic Development and Social Work*. Binghamton, NY: Haworth Press.

Sherraden, Michael. 1991. *Assets and the Poor: A New American Welfare Policy*. Armonk, NY: ME Sharpe.

Woolcock, M. 1998. Social capital and economic development: Toward a theoretical synthesis and policy framework. *Theory and Society 27* (2), 151-208.

The Homeless in Missouri in the '90s:
A Continuing Challenge to Social Justice

John J. Stretch
Larry W. Kreuger

SUMMARY. Homelessness in the United States continues to grow despite unprecedented prosperity. Even with a wide array of services, shelters are not stemming the tide. The answer is a massive recommitment by both federal and state governments to increase the steadily shrinking supply of low-income housing. The policy remedy is for every family to have an entitlement to safe, sanitary, and affordable housing. Homelessness is a national disgrace. It is both preventable and remediable. *[Article copies available for a fee from The Haworth Document Delivery Service: 1-800-HAWORTH. E-mail address: <docdelivery@haworthpress.com> Website: <http://www.HaworthPress.com> © 2003 by The Haworth Press, Inc. All rights reserved.]*

KEYWORDS. Homelessness, homeless services, homeless policy, homeless research, housing subsidy, social justice

John J. Stretch, PhD, is Professor of Social Work, School of Social Service, Saint Louis University, 3550 Lindell Boulevard, St. Louis, MO 63103 (E-mail: stretchj@slu.edu).

Larry W. Kreuger, PhD, is Associate Professor of Social Work, School of Social Work, University Missouri-Columbia (E-mail: kreugerl@missouri.edu).

[Haworth co-indexing entry note]: "The Homeless in Missouri in the '90s: A Continuing Challenge to Social Justice." Stretch, John J., and Larry W. Kreuger. Co-published simultaneously in *Social Thought* (The Haworth Press, Inc.) Vol. 22, No. 2/3, 2003, pp. 119-134; and: *Practicing Social Justice* (ed: John J. Stretch et al.) The Haworth Press, Inc., 2003, pp. 119-134. Single or multiple copies of this article are available for a fee from The Haworth Document Delivery Service [1-800-HAWORTH, 9:00 a.m. - 5:00 p.m. (EST). E-mail address: docdelivery@haworthpress.com].

© 2003 by The Haworth Press, Inc. All rights reserved.
http://www.haworthpress.com/store/product.asp?sku=J131
10.1300/J131v22n02_09

CONTEXT

In the decade of the prosperous 1990s, the American economy outpaced the world in growth, productivity, and general well-being. Inflation remained at record lows, and unemployment was, for most Americans, practically nonexistent. But amid all this prosperity, one segment of our society has continued to be left behind: the homeless. A survey of 26 cities, including St. Louis, by The United States Conference of Mayors (1999) reveals that fact all too clearly.

Why are people homeless? The lack of affordable housing continues to lead the list, but other causes are substance abuse, low-paying jobs, domestic violence, mental illness, poverty, changes and cuts in public assistance, the lack of access to affordable health care, and the lack of needed services.

At its root, however, homelessness is a housing problem. The United States Conference of Mayors (1999) report highlights both the absolute scarcity and the unaffordability of safe and sanitary housing for low-income individuals and families. Requests for assisted housing by low-income families and individuals increased in 70 percent of the cities during 1998. City officials estimate that low-income households spend close to half of their income just on housing.

As for the booming times, city officials reported mixed views with respect to the effect of a continuing strong economy on problems of both hunger and homelessness. Some say there is little or no impact. Some say in the long run the strong economy will lead to improved conditions. Still others say that the strong economy has made things worse, especially with respect to increased housing costs that lead to less and less affordable housing.

What can be done? In the short run, shelter beds, food pantries, and existing housing supply for low-income families must be kept on track. Our research, collaborated by some and challenged by others (Bingham, 1987; Hope, 1986; Jencks, 1994; Ropers, 1988; Wright, 1989), shows that housing stability is the prime anchor in serving the homeless effectively.

Continued funding for the essentials is our only safety net in the long run. In the interim, we need a comprehensive initiative to end homelessness through a massive federal, state, and local partnership to reestablish the severely depleted supply of affordable housing, to stabilize homeless families, and to prevent future homelessness.

At the state level, we must increase the dedicated homeless funding for the Missouri Housing Trust Fund. We must simultaneously create living-wage jobs and the necessary career ladders with job training to bring the homeless into the universal benefits of the new economy. We must also provide targeted services for mental health, drug abuse, and domestic violence fully commensurate to the demonstrated need.

Our progressive voluntary sector must forge partnerships with political leaders to develop local, state, and national initiatives to eradicate a 20-year American scandal: homelessness amid plenty in the richest country in the world.

BACKGROUND OF THE RESEARCH

Since the mid 1980s, there have been resource investments in families who have suffered from uprootedness and the attendant crisis of homelessness (Hutson and Clapharn, 1999). For example, in St. Louis, Missouri, economically troubled homeless families have differentially benefited from concerted case management efforts by a network of both public and private agencies to deal with the multiple problems of homeless families. Until quite recently, there were little systematic data which charted the immediate and long-range impacts of case-managed community networked resources (Danesco and Holden, 1998). Human service providers and their funders, therefore, had scant efficient ways to assess the immediate and long-range impacts of programs aimed at helping the homeless who resided in shelters or to monitor the functioning of the formerly homeless in the community after their initial homeless crises had been resolved (Stojanovic et al., 1999).

After briefly reviewing homeless shelter based services in St. Louis, one of the largest and oldest systems of shelter care in the state, we discuss our empirical findings on the impact of shelter-based services compared to housing-based subsidies. Presented next are our reasons for downsizing shelter-based services and instead focusing scant resources on prevention. In the appendix are some representative best practices of homeless service initiatives. Finally, we discuss a prevention-based policy option, which we recommend be instituted at the federal and state levels.

In this paper we examine human need for a home and what typically is at risk when people lose a place of residence (Figure 1). Next we summarize a historical rationale for shelter-based services for homeless families in the United States. The concept "family" is inclusive of two-parent, single-parent, or single-person household. Ten factors are identified representing views on the functions and benefits of shelter services. Later developed are our argument for downsizing shelter-based services and the empirical support for increased permanent housing subsidies focusing on prevention of future homelessness.

RATIONALES FOR SHELTER-BASED SERVICES IN THE UNITED STATES

A review of recent literature and the experience of the authors, based on over twenty-five years of study of homeless families, posit the following general reasons for shelter-based services:

1. Shelter-based nightly quarters are preferable to sleeping in harsh conditions under bridges or in cardboard houses (Bidinnotto, 1991);
2. Shelters provide emergency living quarters on a temporary substitute basis for low-income, often minority families who cannot afford other living arrangements and who suffer from random and unpredictable natural events such as fires and disasters or from largely unpredictable political or economic events such as foreclosures, evictions, and condemnations (Karger and Stoez, 1990);
3. Shelters provide short-term solutions to immediate survival needs for food, clothing, and bedding for people who have lost their place of residence (Kreuger, 1987);
4. Shelters offer protection for potential victims of crimes of street violence such as rape or drive-by shooting and other serious environmental trauma (Institute of Medicine, 1988);
5. Shelters offer security as stopping off havens for low-income persons who are passing through and for the indigent who would otherwise be sleeping on park benches (Wright, 1989);
6. Shelters provide safe destinations for abused women and abused or neglected adolescents who are contemplating seeking help (Institute of Medicine, 1988);
7. Shelters often offer a mechanism for getting safer housing through placements, subsidies, and vouchers (Stretch and Kreuger, 1992);
8. Shelters offer a minimal line of defense against the harsh economic and political reality of politicians whose economic policies cause gentrification and the subsequent loss of low-income housing and the various economic rewards of greed (Karger and Stoez, 1990);
9. Shelters provide support for law enforcement officers who are able to drop off intoxicated persons or drug abusers who need a place to sleep it off rather than using hospital or jail space (Blau, 1992); and,
10. Shelters offer a last line of defense for persons of color who might be systematically discriminated against in the search for apartment rentals, those discriminated against for mortgage and home repair loans, and those redlined by banks (Blau, 1992).

NEEDS OF THE HOMELESS

The basic needs of homeless persons seeking to reestablish a family through permanent housing in a stable community are often complex and, by necessity, require a range of targeted services, confirmed by a survey of homeless men and women in New York.

FIGURE 1. The Functions of a Home, Risks, and Consequences of Losing a Permanent Residence

Functions of Home	Risks Due to Loss	Consequences
Physical shelter	Hydration/sustenance	Exposure, heat stroke
Place for belongings	Security	Need to carry possessions, health risks
Recovery	Comfort, healing	Fatigue, poor judgment
Haven/protection	Privacy	Crimes against person/property
Primary relationships	Affection, stability	Stress, separation anxiety
Autonomy	Control over environment	Anxiety, angst, depression
Privacy	Control of personal space	Dehumanization, discrimination
Growth/development	Family interaction	Delayed development, separation anxiety
Recreation	Physical well-being	Fatigue, sleep disorders
Dignity	Self-esteem	Difficulty making decisions, poor judgment

(Huttman, 1993; Jahiel, 1992)

Homeless Men and Women Report Their Needs for Help

As efforts to help the homeless move beyond the provision of basic temporary shelter, it is important to understand a homeless person's perspective on need for assistance. Responses from a representative sample of 1,260 men and women interviewed in New York shelters reveal multiple needs not readily met by a single service agency. Those reporting a specific need for help on each of 20 items are shown in Figure 2 (Herman et al., 1994).

How Many Homeless Are There, Both Nationally and in Missouri?

The problem of counting hard-to-reach homeless individuals and families is complex (Carr, 1991; Jencks, 1994). The multiple and range of needs of the homeless, including vulnerability, psychiatric disabilities, poverty, uprootedness, alcohol and other substance abuse, transience, and other social and behavioral factors, make accurate censuses quite difficult (Burt and Cohen, 1989). There are numerous empirical and epidemiological problems associated with daily censuses or other periodic attempts to enumerate hard-to-reach homeless populations. Weigard (1985), Momeni (1990), and Blau (1992) have examined these methodological problems in detail.

In Missouri and probably typically in other jurisdictions, one standard strategy for enumerating shelter residents, other homeless persons, or services intended for the homeless involves the compilation of an up-to-date listings of all available primary and secondary shelters and services provided. Next, shelter operators and service personnel must be contacted and surveyed in an at-

FIGURE 2. Needs of the Homeless

Finding a place to live	87.1	Problems with drugs	18.7
Having a steady income	71.0	Learning to get along better with other people	18.5
Finding a job	63.3	Nerves and emotional problems	17.9
Improving my job skills	57.0	Learning how to protect myself	17.6
Learning how to get what I have coming from agencies	45.4	Learning how to read and fill out forms	17.3
Getting on public assistance	42.1	Legal problems	15.0
Health problems	41.7	Drinking problems	13.0
Learning how to manage money	40.2	Getting around town	12.4
Getting along with my family	22.8	Getting veteran's benefits	9.6
Getting on SSI/SSD	20.8	Problems with the police	5.1

tempt to count all actual homeless individuals and families. Once point-in-time count data are aggregated, additional efforts are typically made to extrapolate from a single point-in-time period to a longer one, typically a year. Several estimation procedures have been derived for these purposes, with their validity and reliability critiqued by others (for example, Coughlin, 1988; DeSimone, Gould, and Stretch, 1993; Jahiel, 1992).

Procedures of more recent Missouri statewide shelter censuses by the Missouri Association for Social Welfare in 1993, 1994, 1996, and 1998 used the following formula to derive an estimated total annual homeless count.

1. First, from a survey of shelter operators and other involved professionals, a total number of shelter beds is derived (Total Shelter Beds or TSB). Shelter beds are often cited as one basic proxy of the number of homeless persons served.
2. Second, a Mean Reported Shelter Occupancy (MRSO) is calculated based on a survey of shelter operators. In Missouri in 1993 the MRSO was .8927. This figure means an average of 89% of the shelter beds were used.
3. Third, a factor is derived which expresses an approximate number of non-sheltered homeless persons in an area proportionate to those occupying shelter beds (Rate Non-Sheltered, or the RNS). The United States Department of Housing and Urban Development (HUD) used an RNS factor of 2.3. The Department of Social Services in New York State reported in 1984 an RNS of 2.49; in contrast, the Health and Welfare Council of Central Maryland reported an RNS of 2.9. An average RNS would be 2.5.
4. Finally, a multiplier is derived, accounting for the probable number of homeless in an area during one year, yielding an Annual Homeless Rate

(AHR). This multiplier accounts for the finding that some people are homeless all year long; others are only episodically homeless. An estimate of the annual rate compared to the periodic data was derived by Jahiel (1992) in an extensive review of the literature. He utilized 2.65 as the most appropriate annual multiplier.

The final total annual homeless count is an estimate based on the several criteria outlined above. The count matches closely figures cited in the literature for an approximate percentage of the population likely homeless during one year per 1,000 in the general population (Jahiel, 1992; Jencks, 1994).

Initially in Missouri for 1993, the formula estimated 28,280 individuals were homeless. Estimates from HUD of 1,000,000 point-in-time homeless nationally (2,650,000 annually) would produce an estimate for Missouri of 53,950 homeless annually. Finally, Jahiel (1992) estimates that about 1.75% of the population are homeless at any point. This would yield a national count of 4,463,932 homeless at any point (255,081,838 * 1.75% = 4,463,932) and approximately 11,829,420 homeless annually in the United States. The Jahiel derived estimate yields a rate for Missouri of 90,871 point-in-time homeless and 240,808 annually homeless.

Over one's lifetime, an alarmingly large numbers of Americans experience some form of homelessness. Through a telephone study, researchers Link et al. (1993) established a lifetime prevalence of literal and hidden homelessness of 14%, or 26 million persons, with a five-year prevalence of 4.6%, resulting in an estimated count of 8.5 million. Findings showed no larger incidence for men or women, African Americans or Caucasians, or urban or rural people. Extrapolating to Missouri translates into 520,000 over a lifetime and 170,000 over a five-year period. (DeSimone, Gould, and Stretch, 1993). From 1993 through 1998, homelessness in Missouri increased (DeSimone, Gould, and Stretch, 1999) (see Table 1). No matter which estimator is adopted, homelessness in the United States is a serious social problem of major public concern.

Long-Term Outcome Assessment at the St. Louis Family Haven Shelter

The Homeless Continuum Model (Hutchison et al., 1986) was the foundation for the development of a computer-assisted management information model based on social work best practices to assist families break the cycle of homelessness. A series of case management social work treatment strategies were developed over time based on a 5-stage model:

1. Preventive Stage;
2. Crisis Intervention Stage;

3. Stabilization Stage;
4. Resettlement/Transitional Housing Stage; and,
5. Community Reintegration Stage.

The United States Department of Health and Human Services in 1984 formally recognized the Homeless Continuum Model (HCM) as an effective expansion of shelter-based services which went well beyond simply providing food and periodic shelter. The model currently remains the basic approach of the homeless service coordinators in St. Louis. The rationale behind the model's progressive service stages was based on facilitating persons with family responsibilities through and out of the immediate crisis of homelessness to achieve family self-sufficiency. The general strategy in the City of St. Louis is a public-private commitment to solve the complex needs of homeless families. The HCM became fully operational through a ten-year commitment by the Midland Division of The Salvation Army to establish a computer-assisted system to chart and evaluate policy support to assist homeless families achieve self-sufficiency.

Since the opening of the 54-bed Salvation Army Family Haven, a long-term residential program was aimed at preventing, ameliorating, and correcting the effects of homelessness on families through an intensive case management approach. For a five-year period, we developed and implemented a computer-assisted evaluation model which tracked services to and outcomes for 875 homeless families. The research effort, supported by a HUD grant, was a partnership with The Salvation Army and the community (Stretch and Kreuger, 1992). Evaluation of the HCM is one of the very few longitudinal, empirical assessments of shelter, services, and housing supports. We cite in detail its continuing best practices and policy relevance components, as well as current policy inadequacies.

Our policy-practice evaluation employed a cross-walked analysis of field interview data, computerized shelter records, and data from several Missouri state and local computer databases describing the current status, amount of sta-

TABLE 1. Estimated Count of Missouri's Homeless

Year	1993	1994	1996	1998	1998
Homeless persons per day	28,280	22,000	21,355	32,500	Sheltered: 11,500 Unsheltered: 7,000 Doubled-up: 14,000
Homeless persons per year	53,950	58,600	56,765	62,650	Sheltered: 25,650 Unsheltered: 8,000 Doubled-up: 29,000

bility, and social functioning of former shelter families (Stretch and Kreuger, 1990). The design did not entail experimental manipulation, although retrospective comparisons on a limited number of key variables were carried out on a panel of families. Likewise, the study did not allow for strictly causal inferences, due partly to the nonexperimental composition of the comparison groups and to the inability to utilize probability sampling selection procedures. While there were longitudinal data elements asked of individual families which provided indications of cohort changes over time, the basic research cohort design was point-in-time.

Population and Sample

Out of 875 total families served, 450 families (51%) who had resided at the shelter were selected eligible of the target population located and interviewed. The final population of 450 cases were families receiving housing placements considered by The Salvation Army staff as permanent (Section 8, other public housing, rented or purchased housing, and other permanent housing arrangements). The 450 of the 875 families served are considered the best-served families. Searches through Missouri state databases, city and county housing offices, and telephone directories produced a pool of 256 of 450 (57%) families in the metropolitan area available for interviewing. Of the 256 families, 201 (78.5%) were interviewed at their places of current residence.

Selecting among best-served formerly homeless families resulted in systematic selection biases in the final data set of 201 cases. The final 201 interviewed families were by design selected by nonprobability sampling procedures (their availability). Generalizations to the entire 450 best-served formerly homeless families and any inferences beyond these families to the 875 total families served are guarded.

FINDINGS

Data from 201 field interviews indicated an average time since leaving the shelter of 1,294 days (median 1,331 days), or about 3.5 years. Almost two-thirds, 64% (129), of the former shelter families interviewed currently resided in Section 8 housing. Seventeen percent (35) resided in private rental or purchased units; 2% (4) were in homeless shelters in the city; and the remaining 16% (33) resided in other public assistance settings. Over one-third, 37% (74), reported living in permanent residences upon termination of shelter residence. Another approximate one-third, 37% (74), reported living in just one residence since staying at the shelter.

The mean average of different residences lived in at time of interview for all cases was 2.28. Reasons for selecting current residences included 34% (68) who cited no other option; 17% (35) who cited quality of the housing unit; and 12% (24) who indicated required family size of the housing unit. Monthly rent paid by the families ranged from none to $525. About 30% (61) of respondents in public, shared, or other nonrental units paid no rent. The remaining 70% (140) respondents paid an average rent of $119. Questions about unmet housing needs indicated approximately 57% (114) of respondents expressed continuing housing needs. These respondents included 23% (27 of 114) who indicated a need for furniture or appliances, and 22% (26 of 114) who cited a need for larger housing. Other needs included financial help with utilities, maintenance/repairs, lower rent, and difficulties with the neighborhood. Asked about problems encountered in applying for housing assistance, almost a third, 30% (61), indicated applying for assistance was an issue. However, no single problem dominated a list of difficulties, which included expiration of Section 8 certificate, ineligibility for Section 8, and high local rents. A summary of key findings follows.

1. Where were formerly homeless families, who once received intensive shelter-based services, living up to 5 years later?

Of the 201 formerly homeless families, approximately 64% (129) resided in federally subsidized (Section 8) housing; 17% (35) were in private rental or purchased units; 2% (4) were in homeless shelters in the city; and the remaining 16% (33) were in other public assistance settings.

2. How many recipients of intensive shelter-based services experienced additional homeless episodes since leaving the shelter?

About one in six (16%; 33) experienced additional homeless episodes.

3. Did the families who rerooted and maintained stable residences receive more shelter-based services than those who become homeless again?

No, there was no statistically significant relationship between amount of shelter-based service and additional homeless episodes ($t = .859$, $df = 187$, $p = .39$).

4. Did amount of time elapsed since receiving shelter-based services have an impact on whether families recycled into homelessness?

Yes, families who become homeless again had previously received services an average of 3.5 years earlier, compared to those who were not homeless, who averaged 1.5 years since services (t = 4.23, df = 199, p = .004).

5. Did any one factor distinguish those who became homeless again from those who did not?

Yes, those who received federal housing subsidy (Section 8 certificate) housing placement at termination were likely to reroot into the community and avoid becoming homeless again, compared to families who did not receive a Section 8 certificate.

The factors discussed in 1-5 above were correlated as indicated.

Probabilities were calculated utilizing the Bonferroni adjustment, taking into account the total number of correlations computed to minimize Type I error.

6. What other factors were empirically related to successful rerooting by formerly homeless families?

Examined were family supports including amount of education, employment status, participation in job training, and amount of income including Aid to Families with Dependent children and food stamps. All were found unrelated to the likelihood of additional homeless episodes. Formerly homeless families who were residentially stable, however, were not likely to become homeless again, when compared to those who experienced multiple residential occupancies (Chi-Square 11.45, df = 1, p < .001).

7. If residential instability was highly correlated with homelessness, did housing subsidies have an impact on residential stability?

Yes, those receiving a federal housing subsidy were much likely to have moved than those not receiving the subsidy (Chi-Square 10.94, df = 1, p < .001). In addition, those who received a subsidy moved less often than those who did not (t = 4.98, df = 199, p < .001).

Our research assessing the impact of shelter-based services on homeless families principally found that many formerly homeless families had successfully rerooted. Those who became homeless again evidenced general residential instability, which in turn was statistically significant related to lack of a housing subsidy (Table 2).

Contrary to our expectations, we found that amount of shelter-based services was unrelated to rerooting. Type of permanent housing placement (specifically Section 8) was crucial in preventing additional homelessness. Finally, we found that the shelter-based services work in the short run (very few fami-

TABLE 2. Factors Tested Against Key Outcomes of Successful Rerooting

Rerooting	Moves	Chronic	Services	Subsidy	Since
Moves	.453*				
Chronic	.054		−.093		
Services	−.072	−.161	.045		
Subsidy	−.363*	.333*	−.074	.212	−.499
Since	.202	.344*	.061	−.434	.283*
Share	.335*	.374*	−.079	−.152	.211

* = significant at .05 level (a)

lies immediately recycled into homelessness), but the impact of services without a permanent housing subsidy was not likely to last.

In our judgment, the outcome evaluation pointed to a need for permanent housing supports, both to reroot securely those once homeless and, more importantly, to prevent additional homeless episodes. Our data do not empirically support the use of intensive shelter services as a sole strategy to prevent additional homeless episodes. Our conclusions have been subsequently corroborated in a homeless prevention study by the Inspector General of the United States (Kussenrow, 1991).

A CASE FOR DOWNSIZING SHELTER-BASED SERVICE

Since the time of what would now be termed "organized social services" under the Elizabethan Poor Law, shelters and shelter-type services have existed. The English Poor Laws of the 16th century were more honestly straightforward than the modern United States poor laws of the 21st century. The poor house and the almshouse were meant to get the homeless out of sight. They were also designed to provide the least amount of humane support for the greatest number of poor homeless people.

Today in the United States, the richest industrial nation, we witness a continuing policy debate on how many and what kind of worthy and unworthy homeless inhabit our cities and countryside (Blau, 1992). We have observed conservative policy makers terminologically diminishing or doing away with large segments of the unhoused and ill housed (Weigard, 1985). By twisting definitional parameters, policy makers have managed to exclude hundreds of thousands of homeless individuals, families, and children from our consciousness as homeless or poorly housed and in need of prevention programs (Kreuger and Stretch, 1995). Thus out of sight politically, the homeless, especially children, are too often out of mind programmatically (Schmitz and Wagner, 1996). This public policy denial must not continue (Wright, Rubin, and Devine, 1998).

Added to the political definitional confusion is the lack of clarity for homeless policy objectives. The federal government, in the current policy climate of devolution of social welfare responsibility, views homelessness as primarily a state issue. The states in turn see homelessness as a local issue. To ease the social conscience of the body politic, a new chimerical beast has been invented–privatization. Public-private partnership is too often just a facile neologism for dumping public sector responsibility on churches, United Ways, and other private sector charities. Beginning in the 1980s and continuing apace through the 1990s, the federal government began to cut back drastically on housing expenditures for the poor, but the private sector did not take up the slack. The election rhetoric of Republican President George W. Bush echoes this same policy theme for the new millennium.

A few shelters have developed complex specializations in serving the range of homeless populations. Notably, fewer shelters have evolved elaborate medical, dental, psychiatric, and long-term social services to meet basic needs. Age and gender segregate most shelters. There are social-psychological and ethical implications of gender- and age-based allocation of public space, only now beginning to be researched (Gutheil, 1992; Spain, 1992).

Sometimes a shelter will provide a full range of social and rehabilitation services, which include community placement, follow-up, subsidized housing, and other care. At first blush, the shelter movement, at least for some, appears to be doing the job. There is little long-term empirical research, however, supporting the effectiveness of even the best shelters. No official government entity systematically collects and reports impact and outcome data on a national, regional, or statewide basis. The most damning aspect of shelter provision is that homeless persons who seek them out have absolutely no entitlements to their services and no redress if they are turned away. With no clarity of social purpose and no common criteria for assessing social impact, the hodgepodge, mainly private charity, shelter system today may actually serve to hide lack of impact under a public-private partnership umbrella. Growth in public efforts to provide low-income housing solutions both to prevent and to eradicate homelessness have been hindered by uncertain, inadequate, and dwindling federal and state appropriations to match demand during the 1990s. Yet to be fully determined is the impact of welfare reform (Kreuger, 2000). There is no policy relief in sight (Stretch, 2000).

Our fundamental position is that shelters and shelter-based services are in the main performing a maintenance function, obscuring the basic need for permanent housing and associated social services. Shelter-based services, even the most successful, deflect the argument that the federal government must commit vastly more housing resources and social service professionalism to eradicate forcibly the absolute shame of homelessness and its grinding down of the human spirit.

We have an epidemic of homelessness in the United States. It is an outrage to social justice. Homelessness is both politically and socially acceptable, partially because we in the private social service sector are unwittingly hiding the homeless from public view in shelters.

Shelters give unwarranted social comfort to the body politic while continuing to perpetuate a myth. The myth is that by graduating from a shelter, most of the homeless, through good old American bootstrapping, can return and reroot in their native communities. To the contrary, our data, yet to be contradicted, indicate this is true only for those fortunate few who received adequate housing and social service supports (Stretch and Kreuger, 1992).

REFERENCES

Bidinnotto, R.R. (1991). Myths about the homeless. *Reader's Digest,* June, 99-103.

Bingham, R., Green, R., and Sammis, B. (1987). *The homeless in contemporary society.* Beverly Hills, CA: Sage.

Blau, J. (1992). *The visible poor: Homelessness in the United States.* New York: Oxford University Press.

Burt, M. and Cohen, B. (1989). *America's homeless: Numbers, characteristics, and programs that serve them.* Washington, DC: The Urban Institute.

Carr, J. (Ed.) (1991). Counting the homeless: The methodologies, policies, and social significance behind the numbers. [Special issue]. *Housing Policy Debate,* 2(3).

Coughlin, E. (1988). Studying homelessness: The difficulty of tracking a transient population. *The Chronicle of Higher Education,* October 19, 1998, 24-25.

Danesco, E. and Holden, W. (1998). Are there different types of homeless families: A typology of homeless families based on cluster analysis. *Family Relations,* 47(3): 159-165.

DeSimone, P., Gould, T., and Stretch, J. (1993). *Homelessness in Missouri: Eye of the storm?* Jefferson City, MO: Missouri Association for Social Welfare.

DeSimone, P., Gould, T., and Stretch. J. (1999). *Homelessness in Missouri: Report to the Missouri housing development commission.* Jefferson City, MO: Missouri Association for Social Welfare.

Gutheil, I.A. (1992). Considering the physical environment: An essential component of good practice. *Social Work,* 37(5): 391-396.

Herman, D., Struening, E., and Barrow, S. (1994). Self-reported needs for help among homeless men and women. *Evaluation and Program Planning,* 17(3): 249-256.

Hope, M. and Young, J. (1986). *The faces of homelessness.* Lexington, MA: D.C. Heath.

Hutchison W., Searight, P., and Stretch, J. (1986). Multidimensional networking: A response to the needs of homeless families. *Social Work,* 31(6): 427-430.

Hutchison, W., Stretch, J., Smith, P., and Kreuger, L.W. (1992). Social networking with homeless families. In Jahiel, R. (Ed.), *Homelessness: A prevention-oriented approach.* Baltimore: The Johns Hopkins University Press.

Hutson, S. and Clapharn, D. (1999). *Homelessness: Public policies and private troubles.* New York: Cassell.

Huttman, E. (1993). The homeless and 'doubled-up households.' In Hallett, G. (Ed.), *The new housing shortage: Housing affordability in Europe and the USA.* New York: Routledge.

Institute of Medicine (1988). *Homelessness, health and human needs.* Washington, DC: National Academy Press.

Jahiel, R. (1992). *Homelessness: A prevention-oriented approach.* Baltimore, MD: The Johns Hopkins University Press.

Jencks, C. (1994). *The homeless.* Cambridge, MA: Harvard University Press.

Karger, H.J. and Stoez, J. (1990). *Welfare policy in America.* New York: Greenwood Press.

Kreuger, L.W. (1987). Tracking health services for the homeless: Issues in information management. Paper presented at the Annual Program Meeting (APM) of the National Institute for Information Technology: Health Related Services. Myrtle Beach, FL.

Kreuger, L.W. (2000). *A survey of providers of shelter services for homeless persons concerning the impact of welfare reform.* Columbia, MO: School of Social Work, University of Missouri-Columbia.

Kreuger, L.W. and Stretch, J. (1995). *Housing and homelessness.* In Midgely (Ed.), *Controversial issues in social welfare policy.* New York: Allyn and Bacon Publishers.

Kussenrow, R. (1991). *Homeless prevention programs.* Washington, DC: Department of Health and Human Services, Office of Inspector General.

Link, B. et al. (1993). *Lifetime and five-year prevalence of homelessness in the United States* New York: Columbia University and New York Psychiatric Institute.

Momeni, J. (1990). *Homelessness in the United States: Vol. 2,* New York: Greenwood Press.

Ropers, R. (1988). *The invisible homeless.* New York: Human Services Press.

Schmitz, C. and Wagner, J. (1996). The interconnection of childhood poverty and homelessness: Negative impact/points of access. (Revised, 2000). APM of the Council on Social Work Education, Washington, DC.

Spain, D. (1992). *Gendered spaces.* Chapel Hill: University of North Carolina Press.

Stojanovic, D., Shinn, B., Labay, M., and Williams, N. (1999). Tracing the path out of homelessness: The housing patterns of families after exiting shelter. *Journal of Community Psychiatry,* 27(2): 199-208.

Stretch, J. (1985). Children of the homeless. APM of the 3rd National Social Work Conference, New Orleans, LA.

Stretch, J. (2000). The have-nots have been left behind in boom times, *St. Louis Post Dispatch,* March 23 Editorial. C-19.

Stretch, J. and Kreuger, L.W. (1990). As the twig is bent: An empirical study of homeless children. *Health Progress,* June. 63-65; 77.

Stretch, J. and Kreuger, L.W. (1992). Five-year cohort study of homeless families: A joint policy research venture. *Sociology and Social Welfare.* 19(4): 73-88.

The United States Conference of Mayors (1999). *Hunger and Homelessness Report.* Washington, DC.

Weigard, R. B. (1985). Counting the homeless. *American Demographics* (December) 34-37.

Wright, J., Rubin, B., and Devine, J. (1998). *Beside the golden door: Policy, politics, and the homeless.* New York: Aldine de Gruyter.

Wright. S.D. (1989) *Address unknown: The homeless in America.* New York: Aldine de Gruyter.

APPENDIX. Examples of Best Practices of Homeless Service Initiatives

1. Seattle, WA (1999). *Coordinated Strategy to Prevent Homelessness.* The United States Conference of Mayors: Washington, DC.

2. Bangor, ME (1999). *Community Development Block Grant Success Stories.* The United States Conference of Mayors: Washington, DC.

3. St. Louis, MO (1999). *Coordinated Strategy to Prevent Homelessness.* The United States Conference of Mayors: Washington, DC.

4. 1999 Best Practices Nominations (1999). *Nomination Detail Reports.* The United States Conference of Mayors: Washington, DC.

Immigrant and Refugee Communities: Resiliency, Trauma, Policy, and Practice

Cathryne L. Schmitz
Michelle Vazquez Jacobus
Catherine Stakeman
Grace A. Valenzuela
Jane Sprankel

SUMMARY. Children and families from immigrant and refugee communities entering new lives in the United States are at risk of traumatic adjustment. Federal policies impact them directly and indirectly, privileging some while challenging others. It is incumbent upon social workers, as professionals committed to social and economic justice, to comprehensively understand the range of obstacles facing immigrants and refugees and empower them in their struggle to make a healthy adjustment. This article weaves together multiple policy and practice strands with

---

Cathryne L. Schmitz, PhD, is Associate Professor, School of Social Work, University of Southern Maine, Portland, ME 04104 (E-mail: cschmitz@usm.maine.edu).

Michelle Vazquez Jacobus, MSW, JD, is Assistant Professor, Department of Social Work, University of Southern Maine, Portland, ME 04104.

Catherine Stakeman, MSW, PhD, is Assistant Professor, Department of Social Work, University of Southern Maine, Portland, ME 04104.

Grace A. Valenzuela is Assistant to Superintendent for Multicultural Affairs, Portland Public Schools, 331 Veranda Street, Portland, ME 04103.

Jane Sprankel, LCSW, is Director of Admissions, School of Social Service, Saint Louis University, Saint Louis, MO 63103.

[Haworth co-indexing entry note]: "Immigrant and Refugee Communities: Resiliency, Trauma, Policy, and Practice." Schmitz, Cathryne L. et al. Co-published simultaneously in *Social Thought* (The Haworth Press, Inc.) Vol. 22, No. 2/3, 2003, pp. 135-158; and: *Practicing Social Justice* (ed: John J. Stretch et al.) The Haworth Press, Inc., 2003, pp. 135-158. Single or multiple copies of this article are available for a fee from The Haworth Document Delivery Service [1-800-HAWORTH, 9:00 a.m. - 5:00 p.m. (EST). E-mail address: docdelivery@haworthpress.com].

© 2003 by The Haworth Press, Inc. All rights reserved.
http://www.haworthpress.com/store/product.asp?sku=J131
10.1300/J131v22n02_10

discussion of the needs, strengths, and traumas experienced by immigrant and refugee individuals and families. The responses of a small metropolitan community to the needs of diverse immigrant and refugee populations are presented as an exemplar. *[Article copies available for a fee from The Haworth Document Delivery Service: 1-800-HAWORTH. E-mail address: <docdelivery@haworthpress.com> Website: <http://www.HaworthPress.com> © 2003 by The Haworth Press, Inc. All rights reserved.]*

KEYWORDS. Refugees, immigrants, trauma, resiliency, social policy

INTRODUCTION

Worldwide, ethnic and geographic conflicts are displacing the largest number of refugees in history. By the mid-1990s, there were 40 million refugees, including 20 million outside their homeland (Hokenstad & Midgley, 1997). This displacement "is perhaps the most serious crisis facing human kind today" (p. 110). Global changes in the social, economic, and political landscape have combined with the 1965 Immigration and Nationality Act (INA), resulting in a shift in the immigrant and refugee populations entering the United States (U.S.) (Kamya, 1997). The INA intensified the focus on kinship ties as a basis for immigration, increasing the number of women, children, and older adults in this population.

The transition from homeland to a new country is a stressful experience for immigrants and refugees. For many immigrants and refugees, the loss of friends, family, community, and country is followed by arrival in a new land, finding a home, encountering a new language, adjusting to a new and different environment, and locating employment. For some, the process of migration is made more traumatic when it involves violent experiences or the abrupt departure from their homeland (Drachman, 1995).

The experiences and concerns of immigrants and refugees often overlap. Immigrants, individuals and families granted legal permanent residence by a host country, face the stress of acculturation, loss, and change (Kamya, 1997). Refugees, those fleeing their homeland under circumstances of persecution or oppression, face even greater stressors. Fearing persecution, refugees cross national boundaries searching for safety (Kamya, 1997). They may leave their homeland in order to survive (Hench, 2001a) and suffer from the effects of trauma, persecution, and violence (Ajdukovic & Ajdukovic, 1993).

Immigrant and refugee individuals and families are a diverse group with unique sociocultural backgrounds and needs (Norton-Staal, 1994). They are, as a rule, an asset rather than the burden they are frequently perceived to be

(Benson, 1990). Refugees are "capable of helping themselves . . . [and] often re-create their communities while in exile. . . . They also support each other economically" (Hokenstad & Midgley, 1997, p. 110). Yet, there are concerns and issues which accompany immigrants to the U.S. These are additive and multilayered, with interactions across the individual, family, community levels, and movement between the implications and responses of policy and practice. While many immigrants and refugees adapt to their new life without additional assistance, others need services (Drachman, 1995), supports, and resources from the community. During phases of migration, families and individuals may face the effects of violence as well as the loss of networks, income, physical and emotional security, and support services (Djeddah, 1995; Hokenstad & Midgley, 1997). Cultural traditions oftentimes clash with new circumstances (Hench, 2001b) and stress becomes a common experience.

Immigrants and refugees are increasingly heterogeneous. Their needs, as they flee violence and economic oppression, interact with the profession of social work, with social workers playing a vital role in the provision of services that "enhance the welfare of refugees throughout the world" (Hokenstad & Midgley, 1997, p. 111). The commitment of the profession to strengthening diverse populations and the emergence of social justice as an organizing value of social work practice (*Code of Ethics*, National Association of Social Workers, 1996, revised 1999; *Curriculum Policy Statement* of the Council of Social Work Education [CSWE], 1992; New Educational Policy and Accreditation Standards, 2002) places social work at the center of the response to the global shifts in populations (Hokenstad & Midgley, 1997). The focus on the intersection of, and interaction between, the individual and the social, the complexities of culture and ethnicity, and the promotion of social and economic justice (Hokenstad & Midgley) can orient the response.

The social justice perspective, strengths model, and multicultural practice methods precipitate the empowerment of people to actively participate in change efforts. Moving into practice with immigrants and refugees from these perspectives provides a focus for assessing the applicability of theories, practice methods, and service delivery arrangements from a social justice context (Swenson, 1998), and provides a framework for integrating policy practice. Just services are built from strengths, are culturally informed, and operate from an empowering base. An array of practice methods, congruent with social justice perspectives, is available to social workers responding to the needs of newly arrived immigrants and refugees. These interventions can be applied while working with individuals, families, groups, and communities.

"The strengths perspective demands a different way of looking at individuals, families and communities. All must be seen in the light of their capacities, talents, competencies, possibilities, visions, values, and hopes, however dashed and distorted these may have become through circumstance, oppression, and trauma" (Saleebey, 1996, p. 298). For social justice to prevail, social workers must acknowledge and honor the unique characteristics and circumstances of immigrant and refugee populations who seek assistance in adjusting to their new environment.

Within cross-cultural practice, the social worker accepts culture as paramount to helping the relationship. Culture can be understood as the method by which we receive, rationalize, and give meaning to our own unique experiences in the world (Saleebey, 1994). The National Association of Social Workers (2001) has recently proposed standards for cultural competence in social work practice that include an expectation for developing knowledge and skills that reflect an understanding of the role of culture *and lived experiences* in the helping process. NASW expectations of cross-cultural practice also include empowering diverse populations to access needed goods and services as well as advocating for language appropriate information and referrals, without which newly arrived immigrants and refugees are less informed about rights, responsibilities, and resources.

BACKGROUND

United States (U.S.) immigration laws set the stage for the justice experienced by, and meted out to, immigrants. Thus, an understanding of immigration law is crucial for social workers working with the immigrant community. Harsh immigration policies can complicate adjustment (Drachman, 1995), and social work, as a profession, plays a role in advocating for economically and socially just policies (Hokenstad & Midgley, 1997).

World migration patterns, heavily influenced by "the conscious design of U.S. immigration and naturalization laws" (Lopez, 1996, p. 37), are reflected in the racial and ethnic composition of the nation. "Federal law restricted immigration to this country on the basis of race for nearly one hundred years, roughly from the Chinese exclusion laws of the 1880s until the end of the national origin quotas in 1965" (p. 37). Nativist sentiment ebbed and flowed with war and economic transitions culminating in the 1882 Chinese Exclusion Act, which expanded to eventually encompass all people from Asia. There were parallel efforts that attempted to exclude people from Africa. The early 1920s witnessed efforts to establish quotas for immigrants from specified regions and with the depression came "mass deportations of people of Mexican descent . . . more than half of them U.S. citizens" (p. 37). Although racial restrictions were *dismantled* in 1965, "arguably racial discrimination in immigration law continues" (p. 37).

The INA of 1952 was a response to post-war nationalism and a reaction to the influx of immigrants. It codified many existing provisions into one federal act, regulating and monitoring immigration as well as the behavior of immigrants once in residence. The act imposed numerical limits on immigrants from various countries; organized a government body and procedure whereby immigrants could be itemized, contained, and controlled; and instituted procedures both for recognizing immigrants as legitimate or *naturalized* citizens of the United States and for deporting those who were not so considered. Since 1952, the INA has been modified and supplemented on several occasions, at times curtailing and at other times expanding, the rights and benefits of immigrants and refugees (Padilla, 1997).

The Immigration Reform and Control Act of 1986 (IRCA) further modified INA restrictions and regulations such that some 2 million long-term undocumented workers were legalized, most of who were from Mexico, Central America, and the Caribbean (Padilla, 1997). Also in 1986, as a part of the Omnibus Budget and Reconciliation Act of 1986, *legal* immigrants were entitled to receive Medicaid benefits, as long as they otherwise met criteria for eligibility. With the passage of the Immigration Act of 1990 (P.L. 101-649), temporary protective status was granted on a case-by-case basis to people from countries suffering from armed conflict or natural disasters. Immigration from the northern regions of Latin America was expanded (Rolph, 1992).

In 1996 Congress passed a tripartite of bills, which included the Personal Responsibility and Work Opportunity Reconciliation Act (PRWORA) (P.L. 104-208), the Illegal Immigration Reform and Immigrant Responsibility Act (IIRIRA) (P.L. 104-193), and the Anti-Terrorism and Effective Death Penalty Act (AEDP) (P.L. 104-32). These three acts work cumulatively to restrict the benefits, freedom, and opportunity of immigrants in the U.S.–particularly those immigrants whose legal status is in question. The PRWORA has been especially devastating for immigrants as one aspect of the bill forbids immigrants who arrived in this country after August 22, 1996, from receiving federal means-tested benefits, such as Medicaid, Temporary Assistance for Needy Families, and food stamps during the first 5 years of their stay in the country unless they became U.S. citizens. *This prohibition includes those who enter and reside in the country legally.* There are exemptions to this rule but they are few and are not qualified for easily (Richardson & Fox, 1998, as cited in Reidy, 2000).

The IIRIRA, through its increasingly stringent regulations on the admission of immigrants, and through its expansion of INS powers to detain and deport immigrants, has also exacted a toll on immigrants. Among its provisions, the IIRIRA imposed new limitations on the acceptance of refugee and asylum seekers by expanding the power of INS officials to summarily deny a proper

hearing. Under the IIRIRA, *legal* immigrants, who leave the country and return (even for a brief vacation or family visit), are subject to investigation and
possible imprisonment without due process if they have any kind of a criminal
record–including minor infractions (Progressive, 1997).

Overall, the 1996 reforms have been particularly damaging for immigrants
with limited economic means. While immigration laws have always restricted
immigrants at risk of becoming a *public charge*, prior to 1996 a person could
counter this classification by showing evidence of their nondependence on the
U.S. benefits system (Stickney, 1998). The 1996 changes, the provisions of the
PRWORA, and the IIRIRA act together to significantly alter the admissibility
of evidence in such a way as to make the public charge classification unavoid-
able for all but the most financially secure and well-established immigrants
(Fox & Zimmerman as cited in Stickney, 1998).

Refugees: Politics and Numbers

The Refugee Act of 1980 (P.L. 96-212) gave legal status to asylees and refugees. It established the Refugees Resettlement Program, which provided
funds for income support, health services, job training, and social services for
refugees. In this act, a *refugee* was designated as a person who was granted
permission while *outside* the U.S. to enter the U.S. legally because of harm or
feared harm in her/his country of origin due to her/his race, religion, nationality, political opinion, or membership in a particular social group. An *asylee*, by
contrast, was granted legal status from *within* the U.S. because s/he had suffered from or feared harm upon return to her/his country of origin due to
her/his race, religion, nationality, political opinion, or membership in a particular social group. The Refugee Act declared that the number of refugees/asylees
would be determined annually by presidential determination and that agents
from the Immigration and Naturalization Service (INS) would be responsible
for making the determination. The implementation of this law has been selec-
tive and petitions for refugee status have generally been regarded much less
skeptically than those for asylum status (B. Stickney, personal communication, January 2001). Although not officially or objectively outlined as such, the
standards for being accepted as a refugee are much less stringent than those for
being accepted as an asylee once in the U.S.

Generally, Eastern European immigrants have been granted refugee status
liberally with as many as 65,000 individuals admitted yearly. By contrast, the
limit on admission of refugees from the African continent has historically been
set low, with a maximum of 2,000 throughout the 1960s, 1970s, and 1980s–time
periods in which many regions in Africa, such as Chad, Liberia, Angola, and
Sierra Leone, were undergoing severe turmoil and civil war. In 1992, during

the crisis in Somalia, the number remained low (3,000), increasing only in the late 1990s to 5,000 and then to 7,000. Although the number for the African continent increased in the year 2000 to 12,000 and in 2001 to 20,000, there are still some 3 million African refugees living in Africa under dire and threatening circumstances. The contrast between the treatment of refugee petitions from Nicaragua and El Salvador has also been striking. While approximately 75-80% of refugee/asylum applicants from Nicaragua in the 1980s were accepted, only 2-3% from El Salvador were accepted during those times (B. Stickney, personal communication, November 2000).

ISSUES OF CHILDREN AND FAMILIES

Worldwide, immigrants and refugees are too often exposed to extremely stressful and traumatic experiences, not only when they are forced from their homes, but throughout their displacement. Almquist and Brandell-Forsberg (1995) suggest that the more difficult the refugee/immigrant experience, the more complex the adaptation process. Immigrant and refugee populations can be described as suffering from traumas and stresses, persecution and danger, losses and isolation, uprooting and violent change. Lives are further stressed as the result of a lack of adequate housing, poor or unfamiliar diet, separation and loss of family members, changes in financial status, loss of social status, and loss of jobs or the inability to transfer skills (Ajdukovic & Ajdukovic, 1993).

The more divergent the cultures of the homeland and the adopting country, the greater the potential for difficulty with adjustment (Drachman, 1995). Lack of control over their lives and feelings of helplessness, as well as problems with health status, can compromise the psychological status of immigrant and refugee individuals and families. Domestic violence including child abuse, marital discord, substance abuse, economic hardship, school problems, and parent-child conflict have all been reported as consequences of the stress of relocation (Ajdukovic & Ajdukovic, 1993; Drachman, 1995; Jacob, 1994). The complexity and interaction of effects, combined with a lack of culturally appropriate resources, further compromises adjustment (Ajdukovic & Ajdukovic 1993; Weiss & Parish, 1989). In addition, cultural differences and unfamiliarity with the customs of the U.S. limit access to social, legal, and medical services (Wong, 1987).

More than three-quarters (80%) of refugees are women and children (Djeddah, 1995). The problems they experience are those of other poor women and children in developing countries: inadequate food and drinking water, malnutrition, anemia, respiratory diseases, unregulated fertility, high birth rates, and high rates of maternal and child mortality. The well-being of mothers directly impacts the health of children. Since gender-based inequality is intensified within an environment of extreme violence, attention to women's empowerment and the safety and security of children is vital (Djeddah, 1995).

Roles and Relationships

The literature has identified several arenas in which role change or loss occurs, including economic, gender, family power, and life cycle (Foner, 1997; Pettys & Balgopal, 1998). Immigrants as well as refugees are influenced by the policy and values of the dominant culture in the arenas of marriage, family, and kinship, as disseminated by the mass media, the schools, and other institutions. Issues around dating and marriage, as well as family responsibilities, are challenged when children are exposed to cultural values and norms of the U.S. (Pettys & Balgopal, 1998). The educational system further precipitates gender conflict by exposing girls to co-education and new roles (Norton-Staal, 1994).

The shifting of economic and power arrangements along with changes in the traditional marriage patterns contribute to the changes in gender roles (Norton-Staal, 1994). While immigrant women may experience an elevation in status by gaining more economic freedom, the earning power of males may decline, further reducing male authority and drastically changing the dynamics within the family. Women find they have more power and are eager to adopt values that enhance their positions just as young people generally support new norms that provide greater freedom (Pettys & Balgopal, 1998).

Intergenerational relationship patterns are impacted as well. The maintenance of cultural heritage and traditional values can conflict with struggles to assimilate (Norton-Staal, 1994). Relationships can be disrupted as children learn a new language and adapt to new values. Children may accrue power within the family while elders may experience a decline in status when they no longer have control over valued resources (Pettys & Balgopal, 1998). The loss of roles and familiar economies may cause a crisis of identity (Norton-Staal, 1994). In her book *The Spirit Catches You and You Fall Down*, Anne Fadiman vividly describes how these changes are seen among a particular group of immigrants, the Hmong. Fadiman describes how a former Hmong judge, who is now an assembly line worker in a box factory, frames the dilemma, "When you have no country, no land, no house, no power, everyone is the same" (Fadiman, 1997, p. 206); and how a former battalion commander describes the consequence, "We have become children in this country" (Fadiman, 1997, p. 206). A role-play paints the picture:

> ... [the presenter] cast them [six members from the audience] as a grandfather, a father, a mother, an eighteen-year-old son, a sixteen-year-old

daughter, and a twelve-year-old daughter. "Okay," she told them, "line up according to your status in your old country." Ranking themselves by traditional notions of age and gender, they queued up in the order . . . with the grandfather standing proudly at the head of the line. "Now come to America," said Dr. Lee. "Grandfather has no job." Father can only chop vegetables. Mother didn't work in the old country, but here she gets a job in a garment factory. Oldest daughter works there too. Son drops out of high school because he can't learn English. Youngest daughter learns the best English in the family and ends up at U.C. Berkeley. "Now you line up again." As the family reshuffled . . . its power structure turned completely upside down with the youngest girl now occupying the head of the line and the grandfather standing forlornly at the tail. (Fadiman, 1997, pp. 205-206)

The normative developmental changes in immigrant and refugee family relationships are coupled with the additional challenges of acculturation and adaptation to a new society (Tseng & Fuligni, 2000). A subtle mix of messages exists regarding the degree to which one is to assimilate. Although some diversity is expected in terms of maintaining cultural norms and practices, there is also an expectation that one is to assimilate into the mainstream. English language acquisition for children may create strain within the family, but lack of English speaking skills can cause difficulties and create barriers to accessing information and resources (Wong, 1987). Within immigrant families from East Asia, the Philippines, and Latin America, for example, children rapidly learn and adopt the English language, whereas their parents may maintain use of their native languages. This puts the children in an unfamiliar position of control as the primary means of interaction with mainstream society (Tseng & Fuligni, 2000). These double messages create confusion for immigrant and refugee parents and their children (Pettys & Balgopal, 1998). In cultures that emphasize collectivism and family, adaptation of some family members to Western values of privacy and individualism can drive wedges into the family, creating not only familial conflicts, but also interpersonal conflicts.

Children and Adolescents

For child and adolescent immigrants and refugees the dilemmas can produce competing processes–the developmental processes of growth pitted against the dramatic experiences of escape and displacement (Ajdukovic & Ajdukovic, 1993; Garbarino, Dubrow, Kostelny, & Pardo, 1992). Immigrant and refugee children and adolescents experience the losses of important others, financial capacity, parental support/protection, and home. The impact of these losses is layered and additive. Stress is increased with disruptions in education, family separation, and the impact of living with distressed adults (Ajdukovic & Ajdukovic, 1993; Almquist & Brandell-Forsberg, 1995). Children may be at high risk of mental health issues because they are more vulnerable and dependent on adults for their care while their coping skills are developing (Ajdukovic & Ajdukovic, 1993). Refugee children exposed to persecution show symptoms of post-traumatic stress disorder (PTSD), anxiety, depression, sleep disturbances, dependency, and difficulties with concentration (Almquist & Brandell-Forsberg; Garbarino et al., 1992). Lower socioeconomic status, longer period of displacement, homes in a conflict zone, and larger families may contribute further to heightened difficulty with adjustment (Ajdukovic & Ajdukovic, 1993).

Counteracting the above mentioned stressors, a positive personality disposition, and a supportive family and community all contribute protective factors. These factors help children develop resiliency in surviving trauma (Ajdukovic & Ajdukovic, 1993). Children immigrating with families exhibit a resilience that is more illusive for children facing horrors and disruption without familial support (Garbarino et al., 1992). At times, family members can provide witness for the traumatic experiences of children (Almquist & Brandell-Forsberg, 1995). Some children in war-torn areas, however, may have been exposed to traumatic incidents that are not known to their parents (Almquist & Brandell-Forsberg). Even very young children have the ability to talk about traumatic experiences and memories, but children may not do so until asked and even then usually will not do so in front of their parents (Almquist & Brandell-Forsberg).

FAMILY AND COMMUNITY RESPONSES

While shifting family patterns may cause stress, family relationships, values, and history provide support and strength in transitioning to the new country. Families come to their adopted country in search of peace, security, and success (Hench, 2001b); and family goals and hopes for the future provide a basis for planning. Community-based assistance that works with the family, and within cultural traditions, facilitates the adaptation of refugees to the new environment (Norton-Staal, 1994). A family or family-like environment is a source of care, protecting individuals from the negative impact of stress (Djeddah, 1995). A study of a community of Southeast Asian immigrants in Garden City, Kansas, reflects the value of extended family support. Living in crowded conditions, adult family members all worked while older children and the elderly provided childcare. The pooling of resources led to a gradual improvement in conditions for all members of the family (Benson, 1990).

Experiences post-migration, including the effects of social policies, family life, relationships, isolation, and the success or failure of plans and goals, affect adjustment (Jacob, 1994) as immigrants and refugees cope with new cultural systems cognitively, attitudinally, and behaviorally (Kamya, 1997). The interaction of coping mechanisms and the migration process are multilevel involving internal resources, availability of support, and stressors experienced (Kamya, 1997). Intervention designed to remediate the disruption can facilitate the reorganization of the common experiences of trauma and loss.

Examination of the relationship between stress and coping within immigrant populations reveals a connection between stress, self-esteem, spiritual well-being, and coping (Kamya, 1997). Assimilation of non-European immigrants may be more complex and require direct intervention (Wollons, 1993). Refugees of countries in Latin America, Africa, and Asia experience additional stress due to discrimination based on physical features (Jacob, 1994). Wollons' study (1993, p. 197) of Mexican American assimilation indicates the importance of infusing hope and "teach[ing] children to believe in the power of their own heritage." Mindful of the implications for practice with African immigrant/refugee populations, professionals need to exhibit a sensitivity to, and express an interest in, the spiritual well-being of African immigrants and refugees (Kamya, 1997).

Social Services

The demand for public and private social services among refugees has been increasing (Jacob, 1994). Socially just services are needed to assist immigrant and refugee communities in coping with not only past traumas and conflicts, but also stresses associated with adjusting to their new environments. For service delivery to be accessible and appropriate, it must include full disclosure of rights, responsibilities, and resources. For service to be accessible and appropriate, information must also be provided in the languages of the immigrant and refugee populations. Without access to language appropriate information, either through the use of a trained interpreter or written material in one's own language, immigrants and refugees remain dependent on others with limited ability to fully participate in their own adjustment.

The justice model provides guidance for a broad range of activities such as case management; advocacy; individual, organizational, and community support, empowerment, and development; mediation; supervision and agency directorship; and development of change agents (Swenson, 1998). The range of supportive services similarly encompassed in a social justice approach includes education, counseling, disease prevention, and reproductive health care (Djeddah, 1995). There are several important issues to consider in guiding services for immigrant consumers. Why did s/he leave her/his country of origin? Was s/he forced out? Did s/he flee? Did s/he arrive in the U.S. legally? If not, what are the safe ways to provide her/him assistance and support? If so, how can we protect her/his legal status and maximize her/his opportunities? What kinds of adjustments has s/he had to go through? What is the extent of cultural, linguistic, locational, social, religious, economic and personal adjustment s/he has endured? How has her/his role in society and in her/his family changed? What is the nature of the continued adjustments s/he is likely to face? What supports and connections can we provide her/him to soothe the trauma of relocation? What work can be done to enable a continuation of her/his native practices and customs, as well as association with people from similar backgrounds?

Therapeutic interventions must be adapted to fit within the framework of the cultural norms of immigrants and refugees. Ethnically or multiculturally sensitive practice recognizes the significance of race and cultural as integral to understanding a person in his/her environment, race and ethnicity are recognized as central to a person's daily interactions within her/his environment and to her/his sense of self. Multicultural practice provides both social workers and vulnerable populations with an appreciation for their particular cultural experience and identity (Swenson, 1998).

Therapeutic interventions need adaptation to fit within the framework of the immigrant and refugee cultural norms. Responding to a range of different consumers in culturally appropriate ways is complex. It involves learning new ways of thinking about global constructs; it requires patience with self and others; it requires watching and listening for how people experience themselves in the context of their own life experiences; and it requires rethinking some of the well-known assumptions about the social work profession (Green, 1999). Culturally competent, ethnically sensitive services are grounded in knowledge of historical context and current policies and events. Therefore, interventions within a cultural context must include understanding the experiences, perceptions, and needs specific to a given immigrant or refugee community.

Culturally competent practitioners move beyond the ethnocentric view, disconnecting from Western models of services and presentation where necessary. The labeling of services must be framed in language familiar to the traditional community. To accomplish this, social workers must have more intimate knowledge of the various immigrant and refugee populations, and access to culturally appropriate community resources that can meet the needs of the populations being served. The ability to help others find and make use of resources is a critical skill for social workers working with marginalized and oppressed populations (Green, 1999).

Culturally appropriate programs are designed to fit the needs of the particular immigrant and refugee group. Crisis intervention models, for example, have been adapted in culturally appropriate ways to help refugee populations cope (Weiss & Partish, 1989). Sensitive and responsive programs for immigrant and refugee populations should include services which not only help children cope with stress, but also empower mothers. Children need assistance to facilitate continuing their education, reestablishing peer relationships, and developing new peer relationships (Ajdukovic & Ajdukovic, 1993; Almquist & Brandell-Forsberg, 1995). Further, programs to improve communication skills help families better negotiate the circumstances of their changed lives. Healing can then occur as people are pulled together to relearn trust and heal within the context of community and family.

Social workers are particularly well-prepared and well-versed in the skills necessary for working with immigrant and refugee communities (Hokenstad & Midgley, 1997). They can provide counseling services; engage in policy and advocacy activities that impact the lives of immigrants and refugees; support community-building activities; and facilitate the development of refugee organizations (Hokenstad & Midgley, 1997). Social work professionals, as mental health counselors, case managers, and problem solvers, respond to the PTSD, depression, grief, trauma, and other mental health concerns of immigrants and refugees (Hokenstad & Midgley, 1997; Van Soest, 1997). They can also mediate the transitions. A model used by a school in Miami provides an example. Social work interns mediated a transition for Haitian families to the norms of the school system in the U.S. The mediation was bidirectional, educating school personnel as well as family members about each group's relative values, expectations, and goals. By so doing, the relationship between the Haitian parents and school personnel was greatly improved as they learned to better communicate with and appreciate each other's struggles and successes (Bronstein & Kelly, 1998).

Where services can be provided in the first language of immigrants and refugees, it greatly increases accessibility (Jacob, 1994). Therefore, social workers who speak the language and understand/belong to the culture of a particular immigrant community are an invaluable resource. They have been found to decrease feelings of vulnerability among a group of immigrant clients (Weiss & Partish, 1989) while providing education and facilitating communication. According to Bronstein and Kelly (1998), the presence of social work interns who were from the same culture and spoke the language of the immigrant population served, were, at least in part, responsible for the success of their program. The impact of ethnic similarity may change in relation to acculturation status (Mokuau, 1987). Ethnic similarities have been found to be more significant for newly arrived immigrant/refugee families than for those families who are well-established.

COMMUNITY EXEMPLAR

Context

Nestled in New England at the crossroads of the urban and the rural, Portland is unlike any other city or town within the state of Maine. With a population of 65,000, it is the state's largest city, with some districts exhibiting characteristics of inner-city urban life. Portland's peninsula is the city's most densely populated area. It has a high rate of poverty, homelessness, substance abuse, and crime. Many of the city's social service agencies, including City Hall itself, are located on the peninsula.

While the state of Maine is the *whitest* in the nation according to the most recently released 2000 Census Report, Portland is remarkably diverse. Since the turn of the century, Portland has been a magnet for immigrants from Greece, Ireland, Italy, Poland, and other countries in Europe. In addition, like many other cities and towns in the state, Portland has a significant population of residents of Franco-American heritage. Furthermore, the city has a small number of African Americans who have been natives of Maine for three generations or more. However, it is in the last 20 years that this diversity has changed exponentially.

Portland has become a resettlement site for primary and secondary refugees from many parts of the world. Portland's Office of Refugee and Immigration Services resettles 250 primary refugees (adults and children) annually. The steady increase in the number of secondary migrants (refugees moving to Portland within a year of their arrival in the U.S.) and relocated people (immigrants or former refugees in the country for over a year) further expands the population. Anecdotal evidence and a recent article in the *Portland Press Herald* (Hench, 2001a) cite three primary reasons why Portland has become a magnet for immigrants and refugees: safety, good schools, and accessibility of services. The small size of the city, accompanied by more manageable social problems, less aggressive racism, and better schools facilitate the transition (Hench, 2001a, 2001b).

Over 90% of the refugees resettled to Maine live in Portland. From the late 1970s to late 1980s, refugees from Afghanistan, Cuba, Southeast Asia (Cambodia, Laos, and Vietnam), and Eastern Europe (Czechoslovakia, Poland, and Russia) settled in Portland. With the 1990s, the city witnessed the arrival of refugees from Africa (Congo, Eritrea, Ethiopia, Rwanda, Somalia, and Sudan), and from the former Yugoslavia.

Refugees resettling from other U.S. cities are often part of the ethnic communities that are already established in the Portland area. This provides essential support for maintaining the culture, language, and religion of these immigrants' homeland (Hench, 2001a). Family and friends provide further support as individual families try to adjust (Hench, 2001b). A human rights activist who came to Portland as a refugee more than a decade ago states, "Refugees are always trying to create a community to replace the ones that were lost to war, ethnic cleansing, religious and political persecution, and famine" (Hench, 2001a, p. 4a). Within 6 months, most refugees in the area have an apartment and are working (Hench, 2001b). Still, time is needed to rebuild bridges to family and community for those who have suffered the violence of war and forced relocation. This healing requires the rebuilding of trust and the discovery of potential.

The response of the city of Portland to this influx of immigrant/refugee individuals and families has been multidirectional, providing a range of short- and long-term interventions. The network of services and resources has emerged piecemeal in response to perceived need. The range of services, however, is comprehensive, responding to the needs of recent arrivals, as well as children and families now settling into the community. The private nonprofit agency, Catholic Charities, focuses on the needs of new refugees while the schools, city, and nonprofit organizations work to provide the resources and supports that facilitate adjustment and recovery. Available programs range from trauma recovery; to language and job training/placement; to advocacy and empowerment.

Refugee Resettlement Services

Refugee resettlement services are provided in Maine by Catholic Charities, the largest private social service agency in the state. Since its inception, approximately 5,000 refugees have been resettled. Currently, 70% of Portland's refugees are Muslim and face the challenges of living in a region largely unfamiliar with their culture and religion. Further, as refugees, most have come to the U.S. under circumstances of tremendous adversity, have been witness to horrific violence, and have suffered great loss. As a result, symptoms of PTSD are commonly seen among Portland's refugee community.

Catholic Charities begins its sponsoring services when the agency sends representatives to the airport to meet new arrivals. Housing is then arranged as quickly as possible and a resettlement plan, which includes initial contact with governmental services and employment agencies, is prepared. The program serves individuals and families for one year, extending beyond the federally required six months. Within 90 to 120 days, most refugees (90%) become self-sufficient.

Furnished housing (federal regulations only require beds) and clothing are provided for the family. Benefits available to qualifying refugees include Medicaid for the first eight months, food stamps, and low-income housing. Services provided by Catholic Charities include cultural orientation, readying children for school, and identifying medical services; case managers are assigned to each household to help with issues of readjustment; and a psychiatric nurse familiar with the cultural issues is on staff to meet the needs of individuals experiencing PTSD.

Portland Public Schools and Community Support Responses

Portland Public Schools, in its mission, vision, and belief statements, stresses the significance of community in providing a holistic education for all its students. This philosophy has supported the development of a broad range of programs and services that support families and children while building inclusive community services. The multidimensionality is reflected in the range of services available–language development, academic support, esteem building, family empowerment, health assessment, adult education, and grief recovery. With the help of these services, parent-community partnerships have strengthened, and professional development has been provided for personnel from the schools and collaborating community service agencies. In the process, inter-organizational collaboratives have formed to creatively respond to the rapidly growing needs of the community.

The Portland public school system has witnessed and responded to double-digit increases in the enrollment of students who speak a language other than English. In fact, from August 2000 to January 2001, 316 students from diverse linguistic backgrounds entered the district, a 50% increase over the same time period in the previous year. Over the past five years the language minority student enrollment has increased by 146%, an average annual increase of 29%. As of January 2001, Portland Public Schools' Home Language Survey indicated that over fifty languages other than English are spoken in the district. In a district serving 8,000 students, this represents 12% of the enrollment.

In response to the great influx of students and families from diverse ethnic and cultural backgrounds, the Portland public school system coordinates and collaborates with existing programs, community-based organizations, and institutions of higher education. A partnership has formed between the district and Portland Housing Authority's Educational Centers. The Centers provide homework support for children and youth from the third grade through high school. Support is available daily until 7:00 p.m.

Portland's public schools also house a Multilingual Intake Center, which registers new students who have been identified as "language minority" through a Home Language Survey. The Center initiates students with a "one-stop" registration where all required forms are completed, a school nurse conducts initial health screening, and English language fluency assessments are administered. The Center is located on the peninsula, a home to many newcomers. Convenient, centralized registration occurs in an atmosphere of welcome and comfort. The data gathered informs enrollment projections, budget preparation, and educational planning.

The Center provides services to assist students in the development of their English language skills and the attainment of academic success. Activities enhance classroom instruction, curriculum, and assessment. Literacy instruction is provided through

1. literature-based reading programs and integration of visual and performing arts at the elementary level;
2. a project-based instructional program at the middle school level; and
3. career planning at the high school level.

Books and materials are available on loan to staff, parents, and community members in multiple languages. The Multicultural Multilingual Center also provides assistance in obtaining legal guardianship for children who arrive in the U.S. unaccompanied by adults.

Another valuable service the schools enable in the Portland area is The Portland Partnership. The Partnership is a nonprofit organization involving local businesses and parents, through which partnerships between the school and the community are established; and volunteers who can act as mentors, classroom aides, tutors, library aides, technology specialists, and guest speakers are solicited and trained. The Portland Mentoring Alliance is another business-community organization that supports students at the Portland high schools. Its mission is to identify students who will benefit from the consistent mentorship of a caring and responsible adult.

Last year, Portland Public Schools also received federal funding for its 21st Century Community Learning Centers. The project is a consortium of five of the district's schools where 70%-85% of students receive free or reduced lunch. The focus of the project is to extend learning for underachieving students, including many English language learners, by providing after-school, summer school, and vacation week programs.

At Portland High School, a program entitled Upward Bound identifies students from low-income families, or those who would be the first generation to go to college, and supports them in their academic work to ensure graduation from high school and acceptance at a four-year institution of higher education. Many of the students served by Upward Bound come from diverse linguistic and cultural backgrounds.

In all of its work with diverse populations, the development and maintenance of self-esteem and pride in ethnic identity is a constant objective. To support this objective, Portland High School has created the International Club. The Club provides a forum for connecting students with common experiences. Participants share cultural traditions and support one another in navigating their new school, the school culture, and the culture of the larger society. In the spring, the International Club puts on a cultural show where students from various countries showcase their music, dances, costumes, and other traditions. School staff, parents, and community members are invited to witness the event. It is a venue whereby students' cultural identities receive solid validation.

A Parent Advisory Council (PAC) ensures the participation of bilingual or non-English speaking parents in the schools and in the education of their children. There are six different PACs representing major groups in the district: Khmer (Cambodian), Russian, Serbo-Croatian, Spanish, Vietnamese, and an African PAC serving Somalis, Sudanese, and other families from the continent of Africa. Parent/Community Specialists who are members of the major linguistic and cultural groups run the PACs. Adjusting and negotiating the culture of their adopted country, and developing fluency in a new language, can be stressful for immigrant families. Understanding this, the PAC's monthly workshops and/or classes focus on a range of issues designed to assist parents as they transition to life in the adopted country. Examples of workshops and classes include developing employment-seeking strategies, passing the U.S. citizenship test, finding and/or buying a house or an apartment, and learning how to protect one's self from consumer fraud.

The Portland Public Schools system provides other services for adults as well. Adult education classes are offered for those whose first language is other than English. With the assistance of this program, many newcomers have found employment opportunities as translators and support personnel. The University of Southern Maine also provides services through a pilot partnership, The Extended Teacher Education Program. Through this program refugees gain the certification needed to qualify for teaching positions.

Another collection of services afforded adult members of the Portland Public Schools' community is the professional development activities provided through district-wide workshops, school-based training, newsletters and bulletins, and graduate credit course offerings. Two after-school workshops are offered monthly. One focuses on language and academic issues related to English language learners, and the other on culture. Curriculum has been developed to foster increased cross-cultural understanding. Specific workshops include Refugee and Immigrant Women in Transition; Child Rearing Practices in Cambodia, Vietnam, Somalia, and El Salvador; Africa Is Not a Country; In Between Worlds: Voices of Asian-American Youth; What Is a Refugee?; and Understanding Confucian Values.

The Center for Grieving Children

At Riverton Elementary School, a program assisting former refugee children cope with grief and loss is offered in collaboration with another Portland agency, the Center for Grieving Children (CGC). Three years ago, after a tragic death, a social worker from the public schools and CGC sought funds to provide services to the diverse immigrant and refugee cultural groups in the city. The program was created for children who have experienced multiple losses as a result of witnessing war crimes against family members. Group support, art therapy, and therapeutic play activities are offered. CGC provides intervention, which incorporates a strength-based resiliency response grounded in a client-centered philosophy.

To better understand the needs of refugee children and families, a panel composed of representatives from the refugee communities meets with CGC's facilitators annually. Participants from the various cultural groups educate CGC staff, consultants, and board members. Training is provided regarding the culture's attitude about and experience with death, and the rituals and practices related to death and mourning. CGC board members and staff learn culturally based methods for supporting children and families in maintaining traditions. Through this training, group facilitators communicate with and assist children and families expand their repertoire of responses and reactions.

Other Community Resources and Collaboratives

The Immigrant and Legal Advocacy Project (ILAP). ILAP is Maine's only nonprofit legal services agency assisting low-income noncitizens and their U.S. citizen family members with immigration law and related legal issues. Through its Immigration Clinic, ILAP offers attorney consultations, immigration application assistance, and brief intervention to resolve minor immigration complications. For persons who have complex immigration cases, ILAP offers full legal representation. Individuals before the Immigration and Naturalization Service (the INS), the State Department (the U.S. Consulate abroad), and persons in removal proceedings at the Immigration Court of Boston, the Board of Immigration Appeals, and in the Federal Courts are represented. ILAP assists criminal defense attorneys representing noncitizens in criminal matters, in order to help prevent noncitizens with U.S. citizen family members from becoming deportable because of criminal charges. Education and outreach services, workshops for immigrant community groups, and training on immigration law and related matters for service providers who work with noncitizens are also provided.

New Mainers Mentoring Project. The New Mainers Mentoring Project, sponsored by Portland's Department of Health and Human Services' Social Services Division, is in the process of implementation. Recognizing that new immigrants to the U.S. often arrive with education and skills, but without the knowledge needed to continue their careers in the U.S., this project was organized by a community collaborative of the Community Improvement Through Employment Project and business, social service, and education leaders. It was designed to meet the needs of highly skilled, professional immigrants. These individuals are partnered with mentors familiar with U.S. trades, regulations, and procedures. By working with mentors who share their native cultural understanding, but also understand the economic and social systems in the U.S., new immigrants are better able to realize their potential. The goal is to help new immigrants find jobs that more closely match their skill level. The program is developing curriculum on mentoring, cross-cultural relations, and career development.

Health Services. There is a range of health services available including an international clinic at Maine Medical Center that provides medical assistance to refugee families. The clinic provides initial and continuing medical assistance for adults. There is also a pediatric clinic. In addition, the Department of Mental Health and Mental Retardation has an office in the Portland area with a representative who understands and provides services within a cultural context.

Refugee Organizations. There are various refugee groups and churches providing services and assistance formally and informally. Many of the cultural groups are integrated into the PACs. Small, community-based organizations serving disenfranchised populations in the city have developed responses respectful of the needs of immigrant and refugee populations. In addition, there are ethnic specific groups. For example, the African Community Organization works within the community to help recent arrivals with their adjustment to new community boundaries within the adoptive country. The Sudanese and Serb communities are examples of communities that have recently succeeded in establishing their own church, space, and leader.

IMPLICATIONS AND CONCLUSION

The services and resources of Portland, Maine, illustrate one community's actions and reactions to the rapidly expanding needs. Although not specifically designed as such, the city of Portland has been able to provide a cohesive response to the needs of the diverse immigrant and refugee populations resettling into the area. A comprehensive range of services is offered to meet the legal, educational, health, and social service needs of the individuals and families. Gaps in the formal service system are met by the informal developments of the cultural community to which the individuals and families belong. Because it is a small city, a high degree of collaboration and cooperation exists. The collectivity of the families and communities facilitates communication and cohesion. Organizations work together and community members share knowledge of resources. As the city grows, however, a formal mechanism will likely be needed to maintain the cohesiveness and comprehensiveness of the service system.

The experiences of Portland, Maine, are echoed in other communities. Services develop in a piecemeal fashion in response to immediate perceived needs. Quickly, however, practitioners recognize that agencies cannot deliver services in a vacuum. Networks of health, social, and legal service providers come together with issues of advocacy, policy development, availability, and access as the cornerstone of their agenda. The development of a network of services provides a mechanism for facilitating the entry and settling of immigrants and refugees.

These lessons teach us that networks and collaboration provide a "lifeline" in practice with immigrants and refugees. Comprehensive service development and provision moves practitioners beyond the use of direct practice skills to the development and inclusion of policy and advocacy skills. The just practitioner, who works with immigrant and refugee populations, is quickly reminded of the connection between direct practice and policy.

On a daily basis, practitioners working with immigrants and refugees face policies that prevent access to needed services. Participation in networks and collaborations affords the just worker the opportunity to influence the development of policies that directly affect client access to services. Together, agencies have a broader range of resources to influence policy as well as practice. In addition, practitioners have a forum for sharing the wealth of knowledge garnered through practice. This assists with the further development of informed and culturally sensitive practice.

Refugee and immigrant families not only need the sponsorship that eases transition, but also the services of programs which assist children and families with trauma recovery, legal advocacy, education/employment, and health care. From this initial framework, designed to meet the immediate needs, communities have formed collaboratives, which can provide a source for concerted, comprehensive expansion and development. Further, multidisciplinary approaches are critical to the provision of effective services for immigrant and refugee communities. Such services recognize that the legal, social, physical, and mental health needs, as well as the economic and cultural issues of immigrant communities, must all be considered in the design and implementation of any responsive program. In *ideal* programs, members of the refugee and immigrant communities are pivotal in the development and delivery of services. Finally, exemplary programs must take care to constantly assess community functioning and evaluate the impact of the services and resources–not by monitoring statistics, but by truly incorporating the ideas of the immigrant communities served and by regularly assessing this community's interaction with and perception of the program.

Just practice with immigrant and refugee populations requires an understanding of the complex interactions between personal and global history, including the past and continued trauma experienced by the individuals and families. Empowering practice is grounded at the intersection of the culture, values, and norms of the country of origin and the receiving country. Thus, services and supports must be tailored to meet the unique needs of the growing populations of immigrant and refugee children and adults, some of whom have experienced unimaginable horrors. A holistic community response is comprehensive, providing personal and political advocacy in combination with community building, empowerment, and recovery/healing services.

As this article was going to press, the horrific incidents of September 11, 2001, occurred. What the nation's responses, at the governmental, community, and personal levels, will mean for the future of immigrants and refugees, particularly those of Middle Eastern descent, cannot be fathomed at this time. One thing, however, can be definitively declared–the deprivations of social justice or restrictions on civil liberties that have been experienced by immigrants will, most likely, be furthered by this crisis. It is, therefore, even more vital for social workers to respond to the *call to arms* with our own call for justice–to represent and advocate for the millions of immigrants and refugees in this country who, though having absolutely no relationship to the events of September 11, will, nonetheless, likely be harshly punished by the country's responses to them.

REFERENCES

Ajdukovic M. & Ajdukovic, D. (1993). Psychological well being of refugee children. *Child Abuse and Neglect, 17*, 843-854.

Almquist, K. & Brandell-Forsberg, M. (1995). Iranian refugee children in Sweden: Effects of organized violence and forced migration of preschool children. *American Orthopsychiatric Psychiatric Association, 65*, 225-236.

Benson, J. (1990). Households, migration and community context. *Urban Anthropology, 19* (1-2) 9-29.

Bronstein, L. R. & Kelley, T. B. (1998). A multidimensional approach to evaluating school-linked services: A school of social work and county public school partnership. *Social Work in Education, 20* (3), 152-165.

Council of Social Work Education. (1992). *Current Standards and Curriculum Policy Statements.* Available from: *http://www.cswe.org*

Djeddah, C. (1995). Refugee families. *World Health, 48* (6), 10-12.

Drachman, D. (1995). Immigration statutes and their influence of service provision, access and use. *Social Work, 40,* 188-197.

Fadiman, A. (1997). *The spirit catches you and you fall down: A Hmong child, her American doctors, and the collision of two cultures.* New York: Farrar, Straus and Giroux.

Foner, N. (1997). The immigrant family: Cultural legacies and cultural changes. *International Migration Review, 31,* 964-978.

Garbarino, J., Dubrow, N., Kostelny, K., & Pardo, C. (1992). *Children in danger: Coping with the consequences of community violence.* San Francisco, CA: Jossey-Bass Publishers.

Green W.G. (1999). *Cultural awareness in human services.* Boston, Allyn and Bacon.

Hench, D. (2001a, January 21). Better life beckons in Maine: Refugees who resettle here say Portland is known for good schools and racial tolerance. *Maine Sunday Telegram,* pp. 1a, 4a.

Hench, D. (2001b, January 21). Refugee families lured by safety, jobs in Portland. *Maine Sunday Telegram,* p. 4a.

Hokenstad, M. C. & Midgley, J. (1997). *Issues in international social work: Global challenges for a new century.* DC: NASW Press.

Jacob, A. (1994). Social integration of Salvadorian refugees. *Social Work, 39,* 307-312.

Kamya, H. (1997). African immigrants in the United States: The challenge for research practice. *Social Work, 42,* 154-165.

Lopez, I. F. H. (1996). *White by law: The legal construction of race.* New York: New York University Press.

Mokuau, N. (1987). Social workers' perceptions of counseling effectiveness for Asian American clients. *Social Work, 32,* 331-335.

National Association of Social Workers. (2001). *Standards for cultural competence in social work practice.* DC: NASW Press.

National Association of Social Workers. (1996, revised 1999). *Code of Ethics.* Available from: *http://www.socialworkers.org/pubs/code/code.asp*

Norton-Staal, S. (1994). African refugee families. *Issues, 95* (1). Available from: *http://www. unhcr.ch/issues/children/rm09512.htm*

Padilla, Y. C. (1997). Immigrant policy: Issues for social work practice. *Social Work,* 42, 595-607.

Pettys, G. & Balgopal, P. (1998). Multigenerational conflicts and new immigrants: An Indo American experience. *Families in Society, 79,* 410-414.

Progressive. (1997). *No justice for immigrants, 61* (11), 8-10.

Reidy, M. F. (2000). Health services for immigrant children. *Journal of Health Care for the Poor and Underserved, 11* (3), 276-284.

Rolph, E. (1992). Immigration policies: Legacy from the 1980s and issues for the 1990s. Santa Monica, CA: Rand Corporation.

Saleebey, D. (1994). Culture, theory, meaning, narration. *Social Work, 39,* 351-360.

Saleebey, D. (1996). The strengths perspective in social work practice: Extensions and cautions. *Social Work 41,* 296-396.

Stickney, B. (January, 2001). Personal communication.

Stickney, B. (1998). Whither family unity? A post IIRIRA update. *Immigration Briefings, 98* (112), 1-28.

Swenson, C.R. (1998). Clinical social work's contribution to social justice perspective. *Social Work, 43,* 527-538.

Tseng V. & Fuligni, J. (2000). Parent out of lesson language use and relationships among immigrant families with East Asian, Filipino, and Latin American backgrounds. *Journal of Marriage and Family, 62,* 465-476.

Van Soest, D. (1997). *The global crisis of violence: Common problems, universal causes, shared solutions.* Washington, DC: NASW Press.

Weiss B. (1989). Culturally appropriate crisis counseling: Adapting an American method for use with Indo Chinese refugees. *Social Work, 34,* 252-254.

Wollons, R. (Ed.). (1993). *Children at risk in America: History, concepts, and public policy.* New York: State University of New York Press.

Wong, D. (1987, November/December). Preventing child sexual assault among Southeast Asian refugee families. *Children Today, 16* (6), 18-22.

Doing Justice:
Women Ex-Offenders as Group Facilitators, Advocates, and Community Educators

Faye Y. Abram

Jann L. Hoge

SUMMARY. Many social work practitioners see social support groups as a mainstay of direct/clinical practice yet make little or no connection between their work with these groups and social justice practice. This article examines a community-based support group process for women ex-offenders and family members that integrates social justice activities. It focuses on the women ex-offenders as group facilitators, advocates, and community educators. The research also highlights their specific so-

---

Faye Y. Abram, PhD, MSW, ACSW, is Associate Professor at Saint Louis University, School of Social Service, 3550 Lindell Blvd., St. Louis, MO 63103 (E-mail: abramfy@slu.edu).

Jann L. Hoge, PhD, MSW, ACSW, is Assistant Professor at Marygrove College, Department of Social Work, 8425 West McNichols Road, Detroit, MI 48221 (E-mail: jhoge@marygrove.edu).

The authors would like to thank Mary McCafferty, Courtney McDermott, Sr. Regina Siegfried, ASC, and Sr. Jackie Toben, SSND, for their assistance in preparing this article.

This article reports on a research project funded by Saint Louis University School of Social Service Emmett J. & Mary Doerr Center for Social Justice Education and Research.

[Haworth co-indexing entry note]: "Doing Justice: Women Ex-Offenders as Group Facilitators, Advocates, and Community Educators." Abram, Faye Y., and Jann L. Hoge. Co-published simultaneously in *Social Thought* (The Haworth Press, Inc.) Vol. 22, No. 2/3, 2003, pp. 159-176; and: *Practicing Social Justice* (ed: John J. Stretch et al.) The Haworth Press, Inc., 2003, pp. 159-176. Single or multiple copies of this article are available for a fee from The Haworth Document Delivery Service [1-800-HAWORTH, 9:00 a.m. - 5:00 p.m. (EST). E-mail address: docdelivery@haworthpress.com].

© 2003 by The Haworth Press, Inc. All rights reserved.
http://www.haworthpress.com/store/product.asp?sku=J131
10.1300/J131v22n02_11

cial change activities and suggests complementary activities for social justice practitioners working with them. *[Article copies available for a fee from The Haworth Document Delivery Service: 1-800-HAWORTH. E-mail address: <docdelivery@haworthpress.com> Website: <http://www.HaworthPress.com>* © 2003 by The Haworth Press, Inc. All rights reserved.]

KEYWORDS. Female ex-offenders, social justice, support groups, advocacy, community education

INTRODUCTION

Many social work practitioners see social support groups as a mainstay of direct/clinical practice yet make little or no connection between their work with these groups and social justice practice. Swenson (1998) identifies activities to promote social justice within direct practice and suggests that social workers facilitate the organization of mutual aid groups to take collective action. Similarly, Pearlman and Edwards (1982) provide a case example of a group process that advances social justice by enabling clients to develop their own resources, take their own actions, and advocate for themselves. This article reports on an evaluation of a community-based program for women ex-offenders and family members that integrates advocacy and community education in a support group process. It focuses on the women ex-offenders as group facilitators, advocates, and community educators. This research highlights the social change activities of the women themselves and suggests complementary actions for social justice practitioners working with them.

From a social justice perspective, female ex-offenders deserve focused attention because they, like currently incarcerated women, tend to be a very disadvantaged and vulnerable population. According to the Bureau of Justice Statistics' report on women offenders (1999), approximately two-thirds of women confined in local jails (64%), state prisons (67%) and federal prisons (70%) are women of color; approximately two-thirds have young children (70% of women in jails, 65% in state prisons, 59% in federal prisons); nearly half have never been married (48% of women in jails, 47% in state prisons, 34% in federal prisons); and one-third are either widowed, separated or divorced (37% of those in jails, 36% in state prisons, 37% in federal prisons) (p. 7).

Further evidence of the vulnerability of women offenders is that prior to entering prison, many were poor and using alcohol and/or other drugs. Of those in state prisons, "about 37% of women had incomes of less than $600 per month [significantly less than poverty level income] prior to arrest . . . [and] nearly 30% of female inmates reported receiving welfare assistance. . . ." Further disadvantaging them, "about half of the women offenders confined in state prisons had been using alcohol, drugs or both at the time of the offense . . . [and] nearly 1 in 3 women serving time in state prisons said they committed the offense which brought them to prison to obtain money to support their need for drugs" (Bureau of Justice Statistics, 1999, pp. 8-9).

Female offenders' involvement in drugs is reflected in the type of offenses for which they are incarcerated. The Bureau of Justice Statistics (1999) reports that 30% of women offenders in local jails, 34% of those in state prisons, and 72% of those in federal prisons are incarcerated for drug offenses, while 58% of women offenders in jails, 38% of those in state prisons, and 20% of those in federal prisons are serving time for a property or public order offense. In contrast, only 12% of women offenders in jails, 28% of those in state prisons, and 7% of those in federal prisons are confined for violent offenses (p. 6). In short, "most women in prison are not violent criminals. They are substance abusers whose criminal behavior is integrally linked to their addiction. The majority of them are charged with drug offenses or drug-related property offenses" (Women's Prison Association & Home, Inc., 1995).

Formerly incarcerated female offenders resemble the population of women currently serving a jail or prison sentence. Women ex-offenders have been described as one of the poorest and most underserved population in our society (Dressel & Barnhill, 1994; Eaton, 1995; Greene, Haney, & Hurtado, 2000). "The pressures on women exiting the correctional system are overwhelming. These women are often homeless, penniless, and struggling to remain drug free. They receive little pre- or post-release planning or support to help them reunite with their families" (Women's Prison Association & Home, Inc., 1995, p. 8). Similarly, Wilson and Anderson (1997) report that "female ex-offenders experience more reentry and financial problems than do their male counterparts. Additional problems include reestablishing relationships with their children and other family members, performing the dual roles of breadwinner and parent, and coping with the more negative societal attitudes toward female offenders than toward male offenders" (p. 346).

In addition, some existing programs and policies have restrictive eligibility requirements or provisions that exacerbate the difficulties faced by women ex-offenders and their families. For example, the Personal Responsibility and Work Opportunity Reconciliation Act of 1996 (Public Law 104-193) stipulates (unless the state passes a law opting out of the provision) that those with drug felony convictions are permanently and for their lifetime ineligible for federal cash welfare (i.e., TANF: Temporary Assistance for Needy Families) and food stamps. This policy, as Rubinstein (1996) noted, not only continues to punish those who may be successfully employed, law-abiding, in drug treatment and/or abstaining from drugs, but it also hurts children and causes entire families to suffer.

If deprivation of economic, political, social, and psychological resources provides compelling reasons to intervene for social justice (Rawls, 1971), then female ex-offenders and their families clearly deserve focused attention. Nevertheless, from a review of the clinical and research literature on female ex-offenders and their families, Singer and associates (1995) conclude that programs and "services rendered to them have been woefully deficient" (p. 103). Relatively few aftercare programs address the unique substance abuse problems of women ex-offenders; oftentimes they simply replicate programs developed for men (Austin, Bloom, & Donahue, 1992; Wilke, 1994; Leshner, 1995; Wilson & Anderson, 1997). Most do not incorporate an understanding of the special needs and problems of female ex-offenders or attempt to respond to the needs of their children, caregiving parents/grandparents (mostly mothers/grandmothers), and other affected family members (Women's Prison Association & Home, 1995; Morrow-Kondos, Weber, Cooper, & Hesser, 1997; Burnette, 1998; Abram, 1999; Greene, Haney, & Hurtado, 2000). There are, however, a few programs that do address such issues, and it is enlightening to look at one of these programs.

The Let's Start program has been selected for study and evaluation for three reasons. First, it serves female ex-offenders who are "predominately African American, poor, and sole heads-of-households" (Toben, 2000). Second, Let's Start is innovative. It engages women ex-offenders as support group coordinators and facilitators, self/peer/policy advocates, and community educators. It is also gender-specific, involves caregivers (mostly grandmothers) of children of incarcerated or substance abusing mothers, and infuses spirituality into its processes. Third, Let's Start has not been systematically evaluated, or even clearly specified, and few evaluations of like programs or processes exist.

THE RESEARCH PROJECT: WomenSTART

Let's Start's executive director and staff teamed up with Saint Louis University School of Social Service faculty to propose WomenSTART, a collaborative university/community agency research project funded by a grant from the School's Center for Social Justice Education and Research. This joint venture enables a more systematic examination of Let's Start than would otherwise be possible, by augmenting the limited resources of a small community-based program with faculty expertise, two paid MSW practicum students, and student research assistants. WomenSTART was created specifically to support exploration of the following research questions: What exactly is it that makes the Let's Start process unique? How do participating women ex-offenders, group coordinators, and involved caregivers see Let's Start? Will they say it has helped them and, if so, in what ways?

Multiple methods and data sources are used to describe and evaluate Let's Start. These include:

- Anonymous surveys of participants in the support group for women ex-offenders and observation of support group sessions
- Existing data sheets on participants in the support group for women ex-offenders
- In-depth interviews of Let's Start coordinators (ex-offenders who are part-time staff and paid facilitators of support group sessions)
- Field notes, audio-recordings and process analyses of caregivers group sessions

From these sources, we have collected data that are providing a clearer and better understanding of Let's Start. In November 2000, 74 of an estimated 104 women ex-offenders (71%) attending support group sessions completed a short anonymous survey at the end of a session or by mail/phone. The survey asked about their participation in Let's Start and their views about the program and program activities. Additionally, the WomenSTART research team observed more than 24 of the weekly ex-offender support group sessions and examined data sheets on 102 newcomers. A tally of attendance records for 2000 showed that 109 women (excluding volunteers) attended two or more of the support group sessions for women ex-offenders and 41 attended only one of the group sessions. All three of the ex-offenders employed as Let's Start group coordinators completed in-depth interviews. Finally, 16 of the 20 listed members on Let's Start's roster for the caregivers group (80%) participated in one or more of three audio-taped sessions. More detailed information about data collection and analysis is available from the primary author, the principal investigator for the WomenSTART project.

While the WomenSTART project seeks to include and integrate ex-offenders', coordinators', and caregivers' descriptions and assessments of Let's Start, this article focuses more narrowly on the support group for women ex-offenders and its members' participation in various social justice activities. Here we present preliminary findings regarding the Let's Start program, highlight the involvement of women ex-offenders as group facilitators, advocates, and community educators, and show how the women ex-offenders "do justice" as they perform these roles. The authors discuss why it is important to focus on citizen advocacy, provide support for it from the professional literature, and conclude with suggestions for integrating social justice activities into direct practice with support groups.

DESCRIPTION OF LET'S START

Let's Start, a support process for women ex-offenders, began in 1989 when Sr. Jackie Toben and three formerly incarcerated women began meeting informally. A weekly support group evolved and began meeting at a church in an inner-city neighborhood of St. Louis, Missouri. The group established its mission: to reduce recidivism of women offenders by providing encouragement, support, and personal development. In 1992, Let's Start incorporated its Board of Directors and became a not-for-profit public charities organization. Since its inception, Sr. Jackie Toben has served as the program's Director. In 1993, Let's Start hired a part-time person (a formerly incarcerated woman) to assist with the planning and coordination of the group activities. Other staff positions that have been added since that time are: an Administrative Assistant, Assistant Director, MSW counselor, Women's Group Coordinator, Youth Group Coordinator, and Caregivers Group Coordinator. All are part-time positions. All group coordinators are ex-offenders (Let's Start, Inc., 2000).

Working toward the accomplishment of Let's Start's mission, its staff provides the following program activities:

- Weekly support group for women ex-offenders
- Monthly support group for caregivers (mostly grandmothers) taking care of a child or children of an incarcerated or substance-abusing adult daughter or son
- Advocacy for changes in the criminal justice system, alternatives to prison, and policies responsive to the concerns of female offenders and their family members
- Community education and outreach, including "Stories of Hope," dramatic performances of composite real life stories of women who have participated in the Let's Start process
- Weekly youth support group for at-risk teenage girls (several of whom are daughters of ex-offenders attending the women's support group)
- Monthly support group for delinquent teenage girls at the St. Louis Juvenile Facility
- Special enrichment and training workshops for Let's Start coordinators and group facilitators
- Regular telephone and personal contact between coordinators and participants of support groups, as well as planned social activities (e.g., picnics, luncheons, and special celebrations)

- Information about and referrals to community services and resources
- One-on-one support and counseling, if and as needed, provided by the MSW social worker on site.

While neither Let's Start's mission nor the above program activities make explicit its commitment to support freedom from substance abuse and other addictions, the women ex-offenders interject this goal and raise this concern in *all* groups and program areas.

Support Group Sessions

The heart of the Let's Start process is the weekly support group session for women ex-offenders. According to *Let's Start Annual Report: 1999-2000*, this group averages 22-30 women in attendance each week with a total of 169 participants during that program year.

From observations of more than 24 of the weekly ex-offender support group sessions in 2000 and interviews with Let's Start coordinators, a clearer picture emerges of the Let's Start support group process. Typically, the women arrive, sign in, and take a seat in a large open circle. Usually, the director or a coordinator welcomes any newcomers and briefly explains a few basic rules of the group:

1. whatever is said in the group is to be treated as confidential information and not repeated outside of the group;
2. every woman is to have an opportunity to speak if she wishes; and
3. anyone needing or desiring professional/special help with a pressing personal problem may talk with someone (the MSW counselor) after the group session.

Almost always a Let's Start participant begins the group session with a prayer. Often this is the Serenity Prayer or the Lord's Prayer. Everyone around the circle introduces herself by simply saying, "Hello, everyone. My name is Emma and I'm an alcoholic," "Hi, I'm Betty," or "Hi, I'm Doris and a recovering addict." The group facilitator (who is most often one of the Let's Start coordinators but sometimes an unpaid member of the group) announces the topic she has chosen for the group session. For instance she might say, "The topic that I have selected for us to think and talk about today is *shame* and *blame*." A spiritual, biblical, or inspirational reading related to this topic, like the selection below, is often read aloud.

> There is a period of life when we swallow knowledge of ourselves and it becomes either good or sour (Pearl Bailey). For too many of us, feelings of shame, even self-hatred, are paramount. No one of us has a fully untar-

nished past. Every man, every woman, even every child experiences regrets over some activity. We are not perfect. Perfection is not expected in the Divine plan. But we are expected to take our experiences and to grow from them, to move beyond the shame of them, to celebrate what they have taught us. (Kasey, 1991)

After the reading, the group facilitator initiates discussion by first sharing her own personal thoughts on the topic. She then invites others, especially newcomers, to share their reflections on the topic or whatever is on their hearts and minds. Then for the next 60-90 minutes, several of the women tell their stories and talk about such matters as their struggles, problem-solving efforts, successes, and setbacks. Announcements about upcoming events such as holiday celebrations, Lobby Days, and training or public speaking opportunities often follow. The women are motivated to participate in these events by hearing others talk of their previous participation. The session ends with a closing and sometimes silent prayer, a song, or gospel hymn. The women are encouraged to contact another support group participant following the session, and to seek counseling as needed from the MSW social worker on site.

Between support sessions, Let's Start coordinators reach out and attempt to maintain regular contact with all the women who attend the group sessions, especially those who are new to the group. This is done through weekly telephone calls or visits, letters, and the monthly newsletter. Currently, Let's Start sends out 432 newsletters each month. A new feature of the newsletter this past year was a monthly article, written by Sr. Regina Siegfried, telling a Let's Start participant's story (Let's Start, Inc., 2000).

Analysis of the support group process and the facilitators' communications reveal that the facilitator typically verbalizes strong feelings related to the topic that trigger intense emotional reactions from listeners. She models self-disclosure by repeatedly making self-referent "I" statements and divulging personal information about herself. She also speaks using culturally specific colloquialisms and referents that highlight many things she has in common with other female ex-offenders in the group. The facilitator and group participants frequently call upon God or a higher power to help them to accept things beyond their control, while empowering them to act in concert with their prayers in order to change what they can–changes not only in themselves but also in their environment/circumstances (Abram, 1999). The combination of these ways of communicating through narrative, characteristic of the Let's Start process, generates experience-based knowledge that is consistent with women's ways of knowing, is accepted as credible, and is trusted (Belenky, Clinchy, Goldberger, & Tarule, 1986). This process empowers the female ex-offender who shares her story by affirming the "truth" of her reality and the value of her knowledge. At the same time, it empowers listening participants in the group by giving them an alternative to the coping model of adjusting to unjust circumstances. Sharing successful problem-solving and social change experiences with a peer support group "minimizes weaknesses and fulfills human need for emotional discharge, for affirming strengths, and for hope. It reinforces cultural values and adaptive cognitive styles, and it counteracts learned helplessness or apathy" (Pearlman & Edwards, 1982, p. 533).

The WomenSTART data show that the women are drawn to Let's Start and return to its groups because, as the coordinators explain, they feel "less vulnerable in an all female group." According to survey results, participants agree that "there is a family atmosphere at Let's Start" (86%); "it is a place where a person can be [herself] and be accepted" (88%); and "praying and talk about God, religion, and the gospel" in the group are considered positive (67%). Also, most participants agree with the statement that Let's Start has helped them "to feel less ashamed about [their] past convictions and drug use" (64%). These findings seem to support Morell's (1996) claim that "connecting treatment [or social support], spirituality, and politics can radicalize recovery . . . [and] spirituality can inspire and sustain people to move beyond external and internalized oppression" toward social justice (p. 309).

Community Outreach and Education

The community outreach and education component of Let's Start interacts with its support group process. Through speaking engagements, the performance of "Stories of Hope," and outreach efforts to youth, Let's Start participants use their past experiences in many positive ways. For example, one of the Let's Start participants performing the "Stories of Hope" acts out the following dialogue:

> I've been used before and I've been a user before. But now God is using me to help other people. I have a job now; I recruit other people into treatment, and I have to stay in recovery myself to keep my job. God has blessed me with a staff of professional people who understand chemical dependence and the power it has to devastate lives. And I try to bless others by not being ashamed to tell my story–to talk about where I came from and where I am now. I am truly a miracle.

Let's Start participants also speak to various community groups about their prison experience, about drug abuse and the causes of crime, about the need for alternatives to prison for some women, and about the harm done to children when mothers are incarcerated. Last year, Let's Start women spoke with schools and church groups, at hospitals, and in five sessions with TANF recipients in a Welfare-to-Work Program. They made panel/workshop presentations at the Criminal Justice 2000 Conference and the Annual Conference of the Missouri Association for Social Welfare. These outreach and community education activities serve not only to inform the public about women ex-offenders and their family members but also to combat the prejudices and oppression that target them.

As the female inmate population has become increasingly and disproportionately women of color, and women convicted for drug or drug-related offenses (U.S. Department of Justice, 1991; Bureau of Justice Statistics, 1999), it seems that public attitudes toward this oppressed population have hardened. Many people view women with felony drug convictions as a group of persons who are outside of or opposed to the moral community, and therefore not meriting fair treatment. This perspective has been called "moral exclusion," and it results in the viewpoint that destructive actions taken against such "outsiders" are acceptable, appropriate, or even just (Opotow, 1990). It fosters injustice in the criminal justice system (Levy, 1974). Moral exclusion enables otherwise moral people to engage in barbaric actions toward other individuals or groups (Deutsch, 1990) and to show no compassion for those outside of their circle of humanity. Moral exclusion is evident in the welfare reform provision that excludes people convicted of drug felony charges from receiving federal welfare aid and food stamps. It is also inherent in the suggestion that social workers and welfare advocates should ignore the injustice of imposing additional penalties on drug felons who have completed their sentence and paid their "debt to society." The argument given for such dispassionate political advice is that no one can risk appearing soft on criminals or crime and losing political ground by aligning himself or herself with such an unpopular out-group and cause. Consequently, more than public information, facts, or a conventional approach to community education is needed. Social workers and other social justice practitioners need to combat the harmful effects of moral exclusion, to bridge the gulf of perceived differences that separate "them" from "us" and isolate women ex-offenders from the rest of the community.

In their roles as "Stories of Hope" performers and community speakers, Let's Start participants present to diverse audiences. While sometimes they perform for other members and groups like themselves, they regularly reach out to groups that are predominately white and middle-class. They connect with people in the audience on a highly emotional and very personal level. They publicly share the pain associated with their drug use and incarceration, their joy of finding nonjudgmental acceptance in Let's Start, and their hopes for recovery and reintegration into the community. The women educate not so much by giving information to the public, as by getting people to feel and care about them as individuals and about the general plight of women ex-offenders and their family members. In this way, their outreach and community education efforts can be seen as social justice activities that serve to unravel ignorance, biases, prejudices, and racism. Correspondingly, Freeman (1997) notes that alternative stories and narratives can transform schools, families, communities, and policy makers. And Birkenmaier (1999) suggests that collecting clients' stories, views on current problems, and visions of justice related to a specific topic and submitting them to decision/policy-makers are activities that promote social justice within direct practice. However, it is important not only to collect and submit client stories but also to find and structure opportunities for clients and members of oppressed or disadvantaged groups to tell their stories in their own words.

While about a dozen women serve as Let's Start "Stories of Hope" performers, community educators, and/or public speakers, Let's Start women gave nineteen "Stories of Hope" performances that reached a combined audience of over 1,000 young people and adults during the last program year (Let's Start, Inc., 2000). The WomenSTART data indicate that more than a third (36%) of the women support group attendees completing the survey have attended a Let's Start "Stories of Hope" presentation, and 86% agree with the statement that Let's Start "gets [them] involved in community activities." It is the consensus of the women responding to the WomenSTART survey that "hearing stories of others . . . makes [them] feel less alone" (91%). The Let's Start coordinators explained that this is true not only for stories that the women exchange in the support groups but also for the "Stories of Hope" presented publicly. They shared their impressions that when the women tell and retell their stories, they change not only the way other people see them but also the way the women and other female ex-offenders see themselves. It seems that "truth telling" by female ex-offenders empowers the storytellers as it raises the consciousness of the listeners.

Advocacy

Although Let's Start publications focus on the support group process and give less attention to other program components, advocacy is a key activity that is integrated into the support process and all that Let's Start is and does. Yet advocacy is often not well understood or defined. Women ex-offenders, when they are first invited to become involved in Let's Start, think of advocacy as "something other people do for you." Similarly, Woodside and Legg (1990) describe advocacy as "the actions of individuals or groups to defend the rights of less powerful others" (p. 41), and Barker (1995) defines it as "the act of directly representing or defending others" (p. 24). Petr and Spano (1990), however, call for a redefinition of advocacy that emphasizes "helping others to speak on behalf of themselves" (p. 233).

There is a considerable amount of social work practice literature on advocacy (e.g., Pawlak & Flynn, 1990; Mickelson, 1995; Ezell, 2001; Schneider & Lester, 2001), although in this literature there are only a few studies on advocacy by clients and/or citizen groups. These include studies of client advocacy or self/peer advocacy by seniors, students, people with mental retardation, people with developmental disabilities, and other vulnerable persons (e.g., Pearlman & Edwards, 1982; Browning, Thorin, & Rhoades, 1984; Bersani, 1996). Some contributors to this literature suggest that there are therapeutic aspects of participation in advocacy. Ager (1987) reports that involvement of the elderly in such work helps to keep them within the mainstream of human activity and increase their sense of empowerment, self-esteem, and productivity. Fedorak and Griffin (1986) describe a self-advocacy program for seniors as an essential component of health promotion. Appleby (1994) examines the hypothesis that there is a positive relationship between self-advocacy and self-concept among college students with disabilities. This literature suggests that advocacy by women ex-offenders might yield important personal and therapeutic benefits.

Let's Start offers participants opportunities to effect systemic change, especially around issues of alternatives to prison for women and concerns for children of incarcerated parents. Their advocacy efforts include writing letters and obtaining signatures of other participants on letters to legislators, preparing and giving testimony at public hearings, attempting to influence policy-makers via direct communications with them (in person and by telephone), and forming alliances with other interest groups for progressive social change. Let's Start members advocate in dialogue sessions with the public defender, policy briefings of Citizens for Missouri's Children, public forums on "Issues in Women's Prisons," as well as meetings and brunches with legislators. They attend monthly meetings of the Missouri Association of Social Welfare's Criminal Justice Task Force, which reviews current legislation impacting the lives of incarcerated women and men and maintains ongoing dialogue with the Missouri Department of Corrections. Also, several Let's Start participants speak at the annual Mothers in Prison: Children in Crisis Rally, calling attention to the harm done to children when mothers are incarcerated. Last year approximately 200 people attended this rally.

In 1998, Let's Start participants' involvement in legislative advocacy led to passage of a bill that authorized the Missouri Children's Services Commission to study current policies impacting incarcerated parents and their children. Two Let's Start participants now attend the regular meetings of this Commission in order to provide information to its members. During the 2001 legislative session of the State of Missouri, advocacy efforts of Let's Start participants focused on several bills. They and their allies successfully influenced passage of a bill prohibiting the execution of offenders with profound mental retardation or sub-average intelligence that was signed into law July 2001. They worked for passage of a bill prohibiting private prisons, although unsuccessfully. And they advocated for a bill aimed at creating an office of prison/corrections ombudsman, which will be reintroduced early in the next legislative session with good prospects for passage. According to the program's advocacy coordinator, another Let's Start focus for next year's session is legislation (like California's Proposition 36) to divert nonviolent drug offenders in the state to treatment rather than incarceration. It is also noteworthy that a state congresswoman and state senator awarded one of Let's Start's coordinators an Unsung Hero Award at the 2001 Missouri Black Expo, in recognition of her legislative advocacy and fight for social justice.

Let's Start participants also are doing social justice when they advocate for themselves, other women offenders, and social reforms (e.g., affordable housing, substance abuse treatment, child welfare services, etc.). Let's Start participants learn that they have rights and to assert their rights when there is an infringement of them. They use appeal and grievance procedures when confronted with an adverse action or decision and teach other women ex-offenders to do the same when the welfare office, utility companies, and other service providers or systems prevent access to services, entitlements, benefits, and rights to which they have a legitimate claim. They speak out about injustices that offenders and their family members encounter. In 1999, for example, they called attention to MCI World Communications' high and unjust collect-long-distance rates charged for calls made by inmates at the state's 18 prisons.

> Prisoners are only allowed to call collect, which means their families or friends must pick up the tab for their long distance calls. . . . Relatives told stories of two-hour telephone calls which cost as much as $50. Others received monthly bills so high that they couldn't afford to pay them. Consequently, their telephone service was terminated. . . . What the friends and relatives of prisoners didn't know was that part of the reason for their exorbitant telephone bills was that MCI kicks back to the state 55 percent of the gross revenues it receives from inmates' calls. Officials with the Office of Administration don't call it a kickback, of course. They call it a commission. When MCI's contract expires, families and friends of the state's 25,000-plus prisoners will have paid $45 million in "commissions" to the state. ("Prisons: Calling Collect," 1999)

What is to be done when the Department of Corrections colludes with a telephone company to exploit this poor and vulnerable population? Let's Start participants and their allies have argued that this unfair policy should not continue.

They asked the state Commissioner of Administration to press MCI to lower its rates, and MCI did respond with a modest reduction.

Analysis of WomenSTART survey data revealed that many of the women ex-offenders believe advocacy can make a difference. Most agree that Let's Start has helped them "to advocate (speak out) for alternatives to prison" (57%) and "to speak out about what is wrong with the criminal justice system" (67%). Similarly, they report that Let's Start has encouraged them to try to make changes in laws that affect them (57%). Furthermore, it seems those participants involved in advocacy are more likely to say they have stopped blaming themselves or others for what's wrong in their lives compared to participants reporting no involvement in advocacy. This suggests there may be a link between involvement in advocacy and changing views about blame. Advocacy apparently moves a person away from a focus on changing her/himself, in order to adapt to environmental stress, toward actions to alleviate the stress itself. As advocacy shifts attention to environmental and systemic causes of problems, there is less personalizing of problems and less support for the assumption that failure, drug abuse, and poverty are due to personal defects and moral weaknesses (Pearlman & Edwards, 1982). The women of Let's Start assert, "Advocacy is empowering; it reinforces the support process and facilitates recovery."

THE ROLE OF SOCIAL JUSTICE PRACTITIONERS

When participants in a support process, such as the women of Let's Start, function as group facilitators, community educators and self/peer/policy advocates, then the role of professional social workers and others working with them needs to be clearly delineated–especially if we are to function as complementary social justice practitioners. From our involvement with Let's Start participants, the following are suggested as social justice activities for social workers and other professionals working in this arena:

1. Make careful and thorough assessments of the strengths of clients and members of oppressed and/or disadvantaged groups to clarify their preference for and ability to act effectively on their own behalf. If it is clear that they lack either the desire or the skills to engage in self-advocacy, then professional social worker advocacy undertaken on their behalf *may* be appropriate.
2. Provide needed training and clear away obstacles that make self-advocacy difficult. These activities are likely to be more empowering than advocacy by professionals on behalf of clients. Training may initially involve providing technical information, consultation, and guidance re-

garding strategies for influencing the policy formulation process. Clearing obstacles might mean ensuring that arrangements are made for childcare, transportation, and meals, and that expenses related to advocacy activities are covered. When such matters are taken care of, individuals who are burdened with day-to-day survival issues can more easily and effectively get involved in advocacy and other social justice actions.

3. Be attentive listeners. In support group sessions, it is important and helpful for professional social workers and other social justice practitioners to be attentive listeners. Listening involves maintenance of good eye contact, commitment to hearing what others mean to say, and suppression of one's privileged status and professional power. Listening communicates to women ex-offenders who speak that they are important, and that what they say is meaningful, valued, and accepted.

4. Model desired behavior by engaging in social action activities as a social work professional and as an informed citizen or agency/coalition representative (Birkenmaier, 1999).

5. Provide learning opportunities through speaking engagements, public presentations, and forums that serve to expand people's understanding of justice. We can, for example, educate people about the concept of "restorative justice," and invite them to work toward it by adhering to its principles.

   • Showing equal concern about and commitment to victims and offenders; involving both in the process of justice
   • Responding to the needs of victims, restoring their sense of justice, and creating ways to rectify or lessen harm done and losses incurred
   • Providing opportunities for dialogue, direct and indirect, between offenders and victims
   • Encouraging collaboration and reintegration, rather than coercion and isolation of offenders (Zehr, 1997, p. 69).

6. Promote the organization of mutual aid or support groups to take collective action on issues of concern (Swenson, 1998).

7. Capitalize on opportunities for participants to be provided with more than conventional components of support (i.e., encouragement, praise, agreement, assistance, information about community resources, etc.). Providing information and learning experiences that refute negative myths about group members, that challenge stereotypes and prejudices against them, that unravel racist thinking and interrupt racist practices, and that construct new identities in place of subordinated people's self-depreciating views: these are all ways to infuse social justice into our practice with support groups.

CONCLUSION

Let's Start is a powerful example of a support process that integrates advocacy and community education, thereby melding social support with social justice action. It challenges us all to infuse social justice into our direct and indirect practice not only with support groups, but also with individuals, other groups, families, organizations, and communities.

REFERENCES

Abram, F. Y. (1999). Grandparents parenting grandchildren of drug-abusing adult children. In C. L. Schmitz & S. S. Tebb (Eds.), *Diversity in single-parent families: Working from strength* (pp. 227-251). Milwaukee, WI: Families International, Inc.

Ager, C. L. (1987). Therapeutic aspects of volunteer and advocacy activities. *Physical and Occupational Therapy in Geriatrics, 5*(2), 3-11.

Appleby, E. T. (1994). *The relationship between self-advocacy and self-concept among college students with disabilities.* New York University: Ph.D. Dissertation.

Austin, J., Bloom, B., & Donahue, T. (1992). *Female offenders in the community: An analysis of innovative strategies and programs.* San Francisco, CA: National Council on Crime and Delinquency.

Barker, R. L. (1995). *The social work dictionary* (3rd Edition). Washington, DC: NASW Press.

Belenky, M., Clinchy, B., Goldberger, N., & Tarule, J. (1986). *Women's ways of knowing: The self, voice, and mind.* New York, NY: Basic Books.

Bersani, H., Jr. (1996). Leadership in developmental disabilities: Where we've been, where we are, and where we are going. In G. Dybwad & H. Bersani, Jr. (Eds.), *New voices: Self-advocacy and people with disabilities* (pp. 265-269). Cambridge, MA: Brookline Books.

Birkenmaier, J. M. (1999). Promoting social justice within the practicum. *The New Social Worker, 6*(2), 13-15.

Browning, P., Thorin, E., & Rhoades, C. (1984). A national profile of self-help/self-advocacy groups of people with mental retardation. *Mental Retardation, 22*(5), 226-230.

Bureau of Justice Statistics. (1999, December). *Women offenders: Special report* (Report No. NCJ 175688). Washington, DC: U.S. Government Printing Office.

Burnette, D. (1998). Grandparents rearing grandchildren: A school-based small group intervention. *Research on Social Work Practice, 8*(1), 10-27.

Deutsch, M. (1990). Psychological roots of moral exclusion. *Journal of Social Issues, 46*(1), 21-26.

Dressel, P., & Barnhill, S. K. (1994). Reframing gerontological thought and practice: The case of grandmothers with daughters in prison. *The Gerontologist, 34*(5), 685-691.

Eaton, M. (1995). *Mothers in prison, children in crisis campaign: Organizing manual.* Brooklyn, NY: Justice Works Community.

Ezell, M. (2001). *Advocacy in the human services.* Belmont, CA: Wadsworth/ Thomson Learning.

Fedorak, S. A., & Griffin, C. (1986). Developing a self-advocacy program for seniors: The essential component for health promotion. *Canadian Journal on Aging, 5*(4), 269-277.

Freeman, E. M. (1997). Alternative stories and narratives for transforming schools, families, communities, and policy-makers. *Social Work in Education, 19*(2), 67-71.

Greene, S., Haney, C., & Hurtado, A. (2000). Cycles of pain: Risk factors in the lives of incarcerated mothers and their children. *Prison Journal, 80*(1), 3-21.

Kasey, K. (Ed.). (1991). *Each day a new beginning: Daily meditations for women.* Center City, MN: Hazelden Foundation.

Leshner, A. (1995). Filling the gender gap in drug abuse research. *NIDA Notes, 10*, 1-19.

Let's Start, Inc. (2000). *Let's Start Annual Report: 1999-2000.* St. Louis, MO: Author.

Levy, C. (1974). Advocacy and the injustice of justice. *Social Service Review, 48*(1), 29-50.

Mickelson, J. S. (1995). Advocacy. In R. L. Edwards (Editor-in-Chief), *Encyclopedia of social work* (19th ed., Vol. 1, pp. 95-100). Washington, DC: NASW Press.

Morell, C. (1996). Radicalizing recovery: Addiction, spirituality, and politics. *Social Work, 41*(3), 306-312.

Morrow-Kondos, D., Weber, J. A., Cooper, K., & Hesser, J. L. (1997). Becoming parents again: Grandparents raising grandchildren. *Journal of Gerontological Social Work, 28*, 35-46.

Opotow, S. (1990). Moral exclusion and injustice: An introduction. *Journal of Social Issues, 46*(1), 1-20.

Pawlak, E. J., & Flynn, J. P. (1990). Executive directors' political activities. *Social Work, 35*(4), 307-313.

Pearlman, M. H., & Edwards, M. G. (1982). Enabling in the eighties: The client advocacy group. *Social Casework, 63*(9), 532-539.

Personal Responsibility and Work Opportunity Reconciliation Act of 1996. Public Law 104-193, 110 Stat. 2105.

Petr, C. G., & Spano, R. N. (1990). Evolution of social services for children with emotional disorders. *Social Work, 35*, 228-234.

"Prisons: Calling Collect." (1999, September 17). *St. Louis Post Dispatch,* Metro Section, p. B2.

Rawls, J. (1971). *A theory of justice.* Cambridge, MA: Harvard University Press.

Rubinstein, G. (1996). *Effects of welfare reform legislation on individuals with drug convictions.* Washington, DC: Legal Action Center.

Schneider, R. L., & Lester, L. (2001). *Social work advocacy: A new framework for action.* Belmont, CA: Brooks/Cole.

Singer, M. I., Bussey, J., Song, L., & Lunghofer, L. (1995). The psychosocial issues of women serving time in jail. *Social Work, 40*(1), 103-112.

Swenson, C. R. (1998). Clinical social work's contribution to a social justice perspective. *Social Work, 43*(6), 527-537.

Toben, J. (2000, February 13). Personal communication. St. Louis, MO: Author.

U.S. Department of Justice. (1991, March). *Women in prison.* Washington, DC: U.S. Government Printing Office.

Wilke, D. (1994). Women and alcoholism. How a male-as-norm bias affects research, assessment, and treatment. *Health & Social Work, 19*(1), 29-35.

Wilson, M. K., & Anderson, S. C. (1997). Empowering female offenders: Removing barriers to community-based practice. *Affilia, 12*(3), 342-358.

Women's Prison Association & Home, Inc. (1995). *Breaking the cycle of despair: Children of incarcerated mothers.* New York, NY: Author.

Woodside, M. R., & Legg, B. H. (1990). Patient advocacy: A mental health perspective. *Journal of Mental Health Counseling, 12*, 38-50.

Zehr, H. (1997). Restorative justice: The concept. *Corrections Today,* (December), 69.

Practicing Social Justice
with Persons with Mental Illness Residing
in Psychiatric Hospitals

Donald M. Linhorst
Anne Eckert
Gary Hamilton
Eric Young

SUMMARY. This article examines the practice of social justice with persons with mental illness residing in public psychiatric hospitals by involving them in decision making. Ten guidelines for involving clients in

Donald M. Linhorst, PhD, is Assistant Professor, School of Social Service, Saint Louis University, St. Louis, MO.

Anne Eckert, BA, RN, is a Quality Management Specialist, Quality Management Department, St. Louis Psychiatric Rehabilitation Center, 5300 Arsenal Street, St. Louis, MO 63139 (E-mail: mfEckeA@mail.dmh.state.mo.us).

Gary Hamilton, PhD, is Associate Professor, School of Social Service, Saint Louis University, 3550 Lindell Blvd., St. Louis, MO 63103 (E-mail: hamiltgr@mindspring.com).

Eric Young, MSW, was a graduate student in the School of Social Service, Saint Louis University at the time of the study (E-mail: youngeric551@aol.com).

Address correspondence to: Donald M. Linhorst, PhD, Saint Louis University, School of Social Service, 3550 Lindell Blvd., St. Louis, MO 63103 (E-mail: linhorsd@slu.edu).

The authors wish to thank the Emmett J. and Mary Martha Doerr Center for Social Justice Education and Research in the School of Social Service at Saint Louis University for their support of this research.

[Haworth co-indexing entry note]: "Practicing Social Justice with Persons with Mental Illness Residing in Psychiatric Hospitals." Linhorst, Donald M. et al. Co-published simultaneously in *Social Thought* (The Haworth Press, Inc.) Vol. 22, No. 2/3, 2003, pp. 177-189; and: *Practicing Social Justice* (ed: John J. Stretch et al.) The Haworth Press, Inc., 2003, pp. 177-189. Single or multiple copies of this article are available for a fee from The Haworth Document Delivery Service [1-800-HAWORTH, 9:00 a.m. - 5:00 p.m. (EST). E-mail address: docdelivery@haworthpress.com].

© 2003 by The Haworth Press, Inc. All rights reserved.
http://www.haworthpress.com/store/product.asp?sku=J131
10.1300/J131v22n02_12

decision making are offered, which were derived from the professional literature and a study of client decision making at a long-term public psychiatric hospital. Guidelines include making an organizational commitment to involve clients in decision making, treating the mental illness, providing clients with decision making skills, offering clients options, giving clients information to make informed choices, developing structures and processes for client participation in decision making, properly implementing decision making processes, acting upon clients' preferences, and publicizing clients' participation in decision making. The article concludes by discussing the roles played by clinical and administrative staff in promoting social justice by involving clients in decision making in public psychiatric hospitals. *[Article copies available for a fee from The Haworth Document Delivery Service: 1-800-HAWORTH. E-mail address: <docdelivery@haworthpress.com> Website: <http://www.HaworthPress.com> © 2003 by The Haworth Press, Inc. All rights reserved.]*

KEYWORDS. Decision making, social justice, psychiatric hospitals, mental illness

Although social justice goals can be pursued at the social policy level through means such as legislative and judicial advocacy, social action, and social policy analysis, we should also be cognizant of social justice issues at the agency level (Figueira-McDonough, 1993; Flynn, 1995). Some of the key justice issues at this level concern decision making arrangements including the establishment of effective modes of client participation. In this paper we examine client involvement in decision making in public psychiatric hospitals.

It is useful to recall that public psychiatric hospitals historically have been viewed as total institutions in which patients had no decision making power even in the smallest areas of their lives (Goffman, 1961; Chamberlin, 1978). The realities and possibilities for client involvement in decision making in today's psychiatric hospitals, however, present a more complex picture. One reason that these realities and possibilities are not clearly understood is that there has not been sufficient research on client participation in psychiatric hospitals. Much of the research has instead focused on community-based psychiatric services in which client involvement has been promoted through such means as self-help groups, client-run organizations, and membership on advisory groups and boards of directors (Carling, 1995; Chamberlin, 1978; Davidson et al., 1999; Pratt, Gill, Barrett, & Roberts, 1999; Vandergang, 1996).

Reasons other than social justice exist for involving persons with mental illness in decision making. Those who participate in decision making are more likely to meet their treatment goals and to be satisfied with their services (Bassman, 1997; McCarthy & Nelson, 1991). In addition, organizations that solicit client participation in decision making develop services that are more responsive to client needs (Croft & Beresford, 1992; Katan & Prager, 1986). Finally, client participation in decision making facilitates the recovery process (Pratt et al., 1999).

This paper promotes the practice of social justice by providing guidelines for involving clients in decision making in public psychiatric hospitals. For this, we draw upon the professional literature and present the experiences of one hospital to illustrate their application. We conclude with a discussion of the roles played by clinical and administrative staff in promoting client participation in decision making in public psychiatric hospitals.

The site of the study was St. Louis Psychiatric Rehabilitation Center (SLPRC), one of four long-term public psychiatric hospitals operated by the Missouri Department of Mental Health (DMH). The Joint Commission on the Accreditation of Healthcare Organizations (JCAHO) accredits SLPRC, which includes 212 beds distributed over four 25-bed wards and fourteen 8-bed cottages located on hospital grounds. The hospital is divided into four treatment programs. Three programs are ward-based, including a program for persons with the most severe mental illness who have been unresponsive to treatment, a forensic program to restore competency to stand trial, and a program for persons whose major mental illness has stabilized but behaviors associated with personality disorders prevent their release. The fourth program is cottage-based and is for persons whose major mental illness has been stabilized but who require skill training before discharge will occur. The average length of hospitalization is about six years. Schizophrenia is the most common major mental illness, with about half of the clients also having personality disorders and substance abuse diagnoses. Mean age is about 44 years, 60% are African American, and 80% are male. Almost 80% are forensic clients who enter SLPRC under court order from state criminal courts. Most of these clients have been committed as not guilty by reason of insanity and require a court order to be discharged. The remaining clients have legal guardians who have signed them into the hospital.

We used multiple methods to examine clients' role in decision making at SLPRC. First, since decision making can occur at various levels (Harp, 1994; Hasenfeld, 1987), we examined it at three levels within SLPRC: treatment planning, residential unit operation (a cottage or ward), and hospital-wide policies and practices. Second, we reviewed documents to determine expectations for client involvement in decision making and to seek examples of such involvement. Documents included DMH and SLPRC mission, vision, and value statements, hospital and program policy manuals, committee meeting minutes, and Missouri statutes. Third, we held focus groups with 17 client groups and 15 staff groups to obtain their views on actual client involvement in decision making and the barriers to that participation. In total 35% of clients participated in the focus groups with at least two groups held in each of the four programs. All executive staff participated, as did 75% of middle managers, 50% of professional staff, and 13% of paraprofessional staff. More detailed information about data collection and analysis is provided elsewhere (Linhorst, Young, Eckert, & Hamilton, 1999).

GUIDELINES FOR PRACTICING SOCIAL JUSTICE BY INVOLVING CLIENTS IN DECISION MAKING

Make an Organizational Commitment to Client Participation

Clients will not be able to meaningfully participate in decision making unless there is a strong organizational commitment to do so. The involvement of clients in decision making can be a complex, long-term undertaking and will not succeed unless clients, clinical staff, and middle and upper managers are supportive of the process (Carling, 1995). In particular, strong administrative support is required to develop an organizational culture supportive of client participation and a nonhierarchical management style that can accept such participation (Carling, 1995; Dillón, 1994; Gutierrez, GlenMaye, & DeLois, 1995).

Four forces were in action at SLRPC to create an organizational culture supportive of client participation in decision making. First, value statements of both DMH and SLPRC supported client participation in treatment planning. Second, the SLPRC vision statement emphasized client decision making, which read: "Rehabilitation through choices: People with mental illness will make meaningful choices about how they socialize, live, learn, and work." Third, JCAHO standards required client participation in making decisions about their care and in improving organizational effectiveness. Fourth, during the early 1990s, SLPRC and the other three long-term DMH facilities adopted psychosocial rehabilitation as their primary service model (Linhorst, 1995). A key element of this approach is that clients should participate in decision making in all areas of their lives, including the organizations from which they receive services (Cook & Hoffschmidt, 1993; Pratt et al., 1999).

Provide Staff Training

Mission statements, accreditation standards, and program models do not automatically translate into practices that meaningfully involve clients in decision making. Extensive training of staff is needed to facilitate acceptance of client participation and to provide all levels of staff with the skills needed to interact with clients in ways that promote a meaningful and respectful exchange of ideas (Fisher, 1994; Freund, 1993; Gutierrez, GlenMaye, & DeLois, 1995; Starkey & Leadholm, 1997).

At SLPRC, clinical, administrative, and support staff received training in the DMH and SLPRC mission, vision, and values. In addition, all clinical staff received training in the principles of psychosocial rehabilitation, and clinical staff in the cottage-based program received extensive training on promoting client participation in treatment planning. Considerably less training was directed specifically at working with clients in organizational decision making. Such training, if provided at all, typically was on-the-job training when clients and staff were working together on improvement projects.

Treat Clients' Mental Illness

Even if an organization supports client involvement in decision making, considerable evidence exists that the severity of mental illness makes it unfeasible and inappropriate for some clients at certain times to participate in decision making (Chinman et al., 1999; Davidson et al., 1999; Gutierrez, GlenMaye, & DeLois, 1995; Hoge & Feucht-Haviar, 1995; Husted, 1999; Torrey, 1994). Thus, one important task of practicing social justice is to treat clients' mental illness to allow them to meaningfully participate in decision making. Torrey (1994) reminds us, however, that decision making ability related to mental illness is not an all-or-none phenomenon. Even clients with the most severe mental illness may have some logical ability to participate in some types of decisions during certain times.

Both SLPRC staff and clients cited the presence of an active mental illness as a factor that limited the involvement of many clients in decision making at the treatment planning, residential, and hospital-wide levels. These opinions were supported by actual practice. The program that worked with the most psychiatrically stable clients (the cottage program) had the most client participation at all levels of decision making, while the program that worked with clients with the most severe, active mental illness had the lowest level of client participation in decision making. However, some SLPRC clients from each of the four programs made contributions to decision making at all three levels.

Provide Clients with Decision-Making Skills

Even if clients' mental illness is stabilized, many clients lack the skills and experience to meaningfully participate in decision making (Chinman et al.,

1999; Patterson & Marks, 1992; Starkey & Leadholm, 1997). Penney (1994) is highly critical of mental health organizations for expecting clients to participate in decision making while not providing them with the necessary skills or experience. To address this at the treatment planning level, one public psychiatric hospital provided clients with information about the function of treatment planning and how to formulate goals (Starkey & Leadholm, 1997). In addition, clients may need assistance in learning how to run client meetings on their residential units and how to work with staff in joint problem solving groups. To facilitate learning, clients need opportunities to practice their new skills. Even small decisions, such as selecting leisure activities, can be practice opportunities (Dillon, 1994).

Each of the four SLPRC programs taught basic decision making skills, and varied that instruction according to the program model and the disabilities of the clients it served. In addition to this general training, SLPRC clients needed specific skills training in working with other clients and staff in work groups, the setting in which many decisions were made. Efforts to provide this latter type of training were unsystematic, and as a result many clients received little or no special training on how to participate effectively in meetings and work groups.

Provide Clients with Choices

Even if clients are psychiatrically stable and possess decision making skills, participation in decision making is not meaningful unless clients have a range of options from which to choose (Bassman, 1997; Carling, 1995). At the treatment planning level, this would include options for treatment goals and treatment activities to meet those goals. At the residential level, this could include options for food, furniture, personal items, wake-up and sleep times, and many other areas. At the hospital-wide level, this could include options for recreation activities, visiting hours, and handling personal funds, to name a few. When considering the choices clients can make, caution is urged to not provide clients with options they do not have the capability to meaningfully consider (Ferleger, 1994; Sundram, 1994; Surles, 1994). In fact, Ferleger (1994) argues that providing choices to those clients who do not have the capacity to rationally make them is neglectful and can put clients at risk.

At SLPRC, treatment planning options were limited in those programs for clients with the most severe illness, and were greatest in the cottage-based program, which worked with the most psychiatrically stable clients. Having said that, there was strong support among clients and staff to increase options for all clients in the following areas: client outings, leisure activities, educational/vocational activities, and unstructured time for clients. In the residential areas, there was some variation in the choices available to clients that were unrelated to clients' ability or program guidelines. Clients had consideration choice in clothing selection, room decoration, and chore assignments. In hospital-wide decision making, clients had options for providing input and they were able to suggest policy and practice options that staff had not considered.

Provide Clients with Information

Clients need information to participate in decision making and for their choices to be informed ones (Hagner & Marrone, 1995; Means & Smith, 1994). This includes information about meeting times, the topics being discussed, and the process through which decisions are being made. Information is also needed that describes each option and its consequences.

Some SLPRC clients and staff identified the need for clients to have more information on the following topics: what treatment services were available, how clients can move from one program to another, how clients can participate in their residential units (e.g., clients in one cottage were unaware that clients in another cottage planned the weekly menu), the major policies being discussed at the hospital level, and options available for clients to become involved in decision making at the hospital level.

Develop Formal Structures and Processes for Decision Making

The development of formal structures and processes for client participation in decision making is essential for such participation to be comprehensive and ongoing (Flynn, 1995). Structures and processes identified in the literature included client councils; having clients serve with staff on task forces, study groups, planning meetings, advisory boards and similar meetings; administrators holding monthly meetings with clients; and others (Barnes & Wistow, 1994; Beeforth et al., 1990; Carling, 1995; Linhorst, Eckert, Hamilton, & Young, 2001; Starkey & Leadholm, 1997). To maximize client participation, some facilities have appointed advocates to work with individual clients or to serve as a liaison between client groups and staff (Ishiyama, 1970; Kieffer, 1984). In addition to these special positions, most clinical and administrative staff will have to devote more of their time to the decision making process in order to include clients (Chinman et al., 1999; Gutierrez, GlenMaye, & DeLois, 1995; Starkey & Leadholm, 1997).

At SLPRC, treatment planning on the three ward-based programs did not, by design, emphasize client participation (Linhorst, Hamilton, Young, & Eckert, 2002). The typical process was for staff to write the plan and, when completed, to explain the plan to the client. The majority of clients and staff in these programs agreed that clients could negotiate with staff to make changes, although changes did not always result. This lack of involvement appeared to be associated with two factors. The severity of mental illness prevented some clients from meaningfully participating. Also, by program design, most treatment activities were required. With the exception of leisure and recreational activities, clients had few choices of treatment activities. Contrary to the ward-based programs, the treatment planning process in the cottage program called for clients to be present at and to actively participate in the development of treatment plans (Linhorst, Hamilton et al., 2002). This was more feasible in the cottage program because clients' mental illness tended to be stabilized. In addition, the cottage program offered a range of treatment activities from which clients could select to match their individual goals when they were discharged (e.g., live in an apartment, obtain a job).

Considerable variation existed both within and across SLPRC programs in the structures and processes for decision making in the residential units. All units had some type of weekly or monthly meeting of clients and staff, but the involvement of clients in those meetings and the decisions made in them varied greatly. In some instances clients, with staff assistance, made decisions about meal selection, sleep times, television programming, chore rotation, and others. At the other extreme, staff in some residential units used these meetings to inform clients about decisions that staff already had made. The manner in which clients sought to change the ward or cottage rules also varied. The most frequent staff and client responses included meeting with the treatment team, filing an official grievance, and discussing the issue at the residential meeting. Eight other means were offered with less frequency to influence change.

Based upon a review of SLPRC documents, four structures or processes were identified through which clients could potentially influence hospital-wide policy (Linhorst, Hamilton, & Eckert, in press). These included the Consumer Council, a 10-member council comprised of current SLPRC clients facilitated by a staff member (Linhorst et al., 2001); the hospital's formal policy review process, through which all hospital policies are regularly reviewed; participation in the hospital's performance improvement system, which involves staff and clients working together on time-limited performance improvement teams to address a particular problem; and filing a formal grievance, which can possibly lead to policy change if the grievance is related to a systems issue rather than an individual issue. In addition, clients and staff indicated that clients could influence hospital-wide policy through informal requests made directly to SLPRC executive staff.

We found substantial evidence that clients influenced hospital-wide policies and procedures through all of the above means (Linhorst, Hamilton, & Eckert, in press). A partial list of changes in which clients played substantial direct roles included an increase in the client spending budget, an expansion of visiting hours, the offering of more diverse pastoral services, more choices of personal care products, and many more. However, none were major policy changes, although all improved the quality of clients' lives.

Implement the Developed Processes

Even if seemingly sound structures and processes are developed through which clients can engage in decision making at the treatment, residential, and hospital-wide levels, these means still must be properly implemented, which can be difficult to achieve. For example, Holland et al. (1981) found wide variation in the participation of staff and clients in decision making on a public hospital ward, while Beeforth et al. (1990) found variance in the success of patient councils, which was associated with the degree of administrative support they received.

Implementation of decision making processes at SLPRC was inconsistent in a number of areas. In the cottage program where clients were supposed to be present during treatment planning, residents typically were not present in one of the cottages. Even in those cottages in which clients were present during treatment planning, some staff and clients indicated that actual client input varied by the case manager who led the treatment planning meeting. Inconsistent implementation also occurred in the residential units, particularly in clients' participation in decision making during residential meetings and in specific decision areas such as food selection in the cottages and television program selection. At the hospital-wide level, implementation varied in the expedient handling of client grievances, the sharing of information about the Consumer Council on the residential units, and the involvement of clients in performance improvement teams. In the two-year period since the completion of this study, implementation has improved through additional staff training, staff oversight, and an increased awareness on the part of both clients and staff to involve clients in decision making.

Act on Clients' Preferences

To promote social justice by meaningfully involving clients in decision making, organizations must commit to acting on the decision preferences expressed by clients. The first step in this process is being honest and clear with clients about their level of decision making authority. This can range from clients having final decision making authority to clients expressing only their preference with staff making final decisions (Means & Smith, 1994). To be ambiguous about the clients' role and not to act on their preferences can be more damaging to clients than not seeking their preferences at all (Barnes & Wistow, 1994). In one public psychiatric hospital, an explicit written agreement was signed between the patient council and management that outlined the areas in which the hospital was obligated to accept the decisions of the council and those areas in which they were required to solicit client input but not necessarily required to act on it (Glasman, 1991).

At SLPRC, most of the clients in the cottage program stated that their preferences for services were incorporated into the treatment plan, although this was not universal. In the three ward-based programs, staff typically wrote the treatment plan and then brought the client in to discuss it. In these instances, about half of the clients indicated they could negotiate with staff if they had disagreements. The degree to which clients' preferences were acted upon in the wards or cottages varied considerably across residential units. Regarding client involvement in hospital-wide decisions, it was clear to both staff and clients that the executive staff members were the final decision maker. The executive staff members stated they respected the decision preferences of clients, acted upon them in many cases, and explained their reasons to clients when they did not act on their preferences. Considerable evidence existed to support that they indeed did act in this manner.

Publicize Clients' Participation in Decision Making

A final guideline for practicing social justice by involving clients in decision making is to publicize clients' participation in decision making when it occurs. While we found no references to this in the professional literature, we identified many instances in which both SLPRC clients and staff were unaware of the positive contribution to decision making made by clients. When clients were asked in the focus group by what means they could influence hospital-wide policy, half cited the Consumer Council and the other half indicated that clients could not influence policy. Some clients in each focus group had not even heard of the Consumer Council, and those who had could list only a few of its accomplishments. In addition, they were unaware of the positive changes that had resulted from clients' participation in the policy review process, the performance improvement system, and the client grievance process. Staff had more knowledge than did clients of the avenues through which clients had participated in decision making, but they could offer few specific examples. Publicizing clients' successes provides clients with confidence and increases clients' credibility with staff that clients can indeed participate in decision making.

CONCLUSION

The practice of social justice with persons with mental illness residing in psychiatric hospitals by involving them in decision making requires the efforts of both clinical and administrative staff. Clinical staff promote social justice when they treat clients' mental illness and provide clients with decision making skills. In addition, clinical staff can facilitate client decision making when treatment plans are written, when decisions are made in the residential unit, and when clients and clinical staff participate together on performance improvement projects. The practice of social justice for administrators involves making an organizational commitment to client participation that is reflected in the program's mission, supporting staff training, providing staff with the time to meaningfully involve clients in decision making, and offering clients a range of options at each decision making level. Administrators also promote social justice by respecting and acting on the decisions made by clients. For persons with mental illness, who traditionally have been powerless, the practice of social justice through their participation in decision making facilitates the recovery process and helps them to gain greater control of their lives.

REFERENCES

Barnes, M., & Wistow, G. (1994). Learning to hear voices: Listening to users of mental health services. *Journal of Mental Health, 3*, 525-540.

Bassman, R. (1997). The mental health system: Experiences from both sides of the locked doors. *Professional Psychology: Research and Practice, 28*, 238-242.

Beeforth, M., Conlan, E., Field, V., Hoser, B., & Sayce, L. (Eds.). (1990). *Whose service is it anyway? Users' views on co-ordinating community care.* London, England: Research Development for Psychiatry.

Carling, P. J. (1995). *Return to community: Building support systems for people with psychiatric disabilities.* New York: Guilford Press.

Chamberlin, J. (1978). *On our own: Patient-controlled alternatives to the mental health system.* New York: Hawthorn Books.

Chinman, M. J., Allende, M., Weingarten, R., Steiner, J., Tworkowski, S., & Davidson, L. (1999). On the road to collaborative treatment planning: Consumer and provider perspectives. *The Journal of Behavioral Health Services and Research, 26*, 211-218.

Cook, J. A., & Hoffschmidt, S. J. (1993). Comprehensive models of psychosocial rehabilitation. In R. W. Flexer & P. I. Solomon (Eds.), *Psychiatric rehabilitation in practice* (pp. 81-97). Boston, MA: Andover Medical Publishers.

Croft, S., & Beresford, P. (1992). The politics of participation. *Critical Social Policy, 35*, 20-44.

Davidson, L., Chinman, M., Kloos, B., Weingarten, R., Stayner, D., & Tebes, J. K. (1999). Peer support among individuals with severe mental illness: A review of the evidence. *Clinical Psychology: Science and Practice, 6*, 165-187.

Dillon, M. R. (1994). Consumer choice is the American way. In C. J. Sundram (Ed.), *Choice and responsibility: Legal and ethical dilemmas in services for persons with mental disabilities* (pp. 117-125). New York: New York State Commission on Quality Care.

Ferleger, D. (1994). The place of "choice." In C. J. Sundram (Ed.), *Choice and responsibility: Legal and ethical dilemmas in services for persons with mental disabilities* (pp. 69-97). New York: New York State Commission on Quality Care.

Figueira-McDonough, J. (1993). Policy practice: The neglected side of social work intervention. *Social Work, 38*, 179-188.

Fisher, D. B. (1994). Health care reform based on an empowerment model of recovery by people with psychiatric disabilities. *Hospital and Community Psychiatry, 45*, 913-915.

Flynn, J. P. (1995). Social justice in social agencies. In R. L. Edwards (Ed.), *Encyclopedia of social work* (19th ed.) (pp. 2173-2179). Washington, D.C.: NASW Press.

Freund, P. D. (1993). Professional role(s) in the empowerment process: "Working with" mental health consumers. *Psychosocial Rehabilitation Journal, 16*, 65-73.

Glasman, D. (1991, September 5). The challenge of patient power. *The Health Service Journal, 101*, 16-17.

Goffman, E. (1961). *Asylums: Essays on the social situation of mental patients and other inmates.* Chicago: Aldine Publishing.

Gutierrez, L., GlenMaye, L., & DeLois, K. (1995). The organizational context of empowerment practice: Implications for social work administration. *Social Work, 40*, 249-258.

Hagner, D., & Marrone, J. (1995). Empowerment issues in services to individuals with disabilities. *Journal of Disability Policy Studies, 6*, 18-37.

Harp, H. T. (1994). Empowerment of mental health consumers in vocational rehabilitation. *Psychosocial Rehabilitation Journal, 17*, 83-89.

Hasenfeld, Y. (1987). Power in social work practice. *Social Service Review, 63*, 469-483.

Hoge, S. K., & Feucht-Haviar, T. C. (1995). Long-term, assenting psychiatric patients: Decisional capacity and the quality of care. *Bulletin of the American Academy of Psychiatry and the Law, 23*, 343-352.

Holland, T., Knoick, A., Buffum, W., Smith, M. K., & Petchers, M. (1981). Institutional structure and resident outcomes. *Journal of Health and Social Behavior, 22*, 433-444.

Husted, J. R. (1999). Insight in severe mental illness: Implications for treatment decisions. *Journal of the American Academy of Psychiatry and the Law, 27*, 33-49.

Ishiyama, T. (1970). The mental hospital patient-consumer as a determinant of services. *Mental Hygiene, 54*, 221-229.

Katan, J., & Prager, E. (1986). Consumer and worker participation in agency-level decision-making: Some considerations of their linkage. *Administration in Social Work, 10*, 79-88.

Kieffer, C. H. (1984). Citizen empowerment: A developmental perspective. In J. Rappaport, C. Swift, & R. Hess (Eds.), *Studies in empowerment: Steps toward understanding and action* (pp. 9-36). New York: Haworth Press.

Linhorst, D. M. (1995). Implementing psychosocial rehabilitation in long-term inpatient psychiatric facilities. *Journal of Mental Health Administration, 22*(1), 58-67.

Linhorst, D. M., Eckert, A., Hamilton, G., & Young, E. (2001). The involvement of a consumer council in organizational decision making in a public psychiatric hospital. *The Journal of Behavioral Health Services and Research, 28*(4), 427-438.

Linhorst, D. M., Hamilton, G., & Eckert, A. (in press). Promoting client participation in organizational decision making. *Social Work.*

Linhorst, D. M., Hamilton, G., Young, E., & Eckert, A. (2002). Opportunities and limitations to empowering persons with severe mental illness through treatment planning. *Social Work, 47*(4), 425-434.

Linhorst D. M., Young E., Eckert A., & Hamilton, G. (1999). *An evaluation of client empowerment at St. Louis Psychiatric Rehabilitation Center* (Unpublished report). St. Louis, MO: Saint Louis University, School of Social Service, Center for Social Justice Education and Research.

McCarthy, J., & Nelson, G. (1991). An evaluation of supportive housing for current and former psychiatric patients. *Hospital and Community Psychiatry, 42*, 1254-1256.

Means, R., & Smith, R. (1994). *Community care: Policy and practice.* London: MacMillan Press.

Patterson, J. B., & Marks, C. (1992). The client as customer: Achieving service quality and customer satisfaction in rehabilitation. *Journal of Rehabilitation, 58*, 16-21.

Penney, D. J. (1994). Choice, common sense, and responsibility: The system's obligations to recipients. In C. J. Sundram (Ed.), *Choice and responsibility: Legal and ethical dilemmas in services for persons with mental disabilities* (pp. 29-32). New York: New York State Commission on Quality Care.

Pratt, C. W., Gill, K., Barrett, N. M., & Roberts, M. M. (1999). *Psychiatric rehabilitation.* New York: Academic Press.

Starkey, D., & Leadholm, B. A. (1997). PRISM: The psychiatric rehabilitation integrated service model–A public psychiatric hospital for the 1990's. *Administration and Policy in Mental Health, 24*, 497-508.

Sundram, C. J. (1994). A framework for thinking about choice and responsibility. In C. J. Sundram (Ed.), *Choice and responsibility: Legal and ethical dilemmas in services for persons with mental disabilities* (pp. 3-16). New York: New York State Commission on Quality Care.

Surles, R. C. (1994). Free choice, informed choice, and dangerous choices. In C. J. Sundram (Ed.), *Choice and responsibility: Legal and ethical dilemmas in services for persons with mental disabilities* (pp. 17-23). New York: New York State Commission on Quality Care.

Torrey, E. F. (1994). Protecting the rights, the person, and the public: A biological basis for responsible action. In C. J. Sundram (Ed.), *Choice and responsibility: Legal and ethical dilemmas in services for persons with mental disabilities* (pp. 37-44). New York: New York State Commission on Quality Care.

Vandergang, A. J. (1996). Consumer/survivor participation in the operation of community mental health agencies and programs in metro Toronto: Input or impact? *Canadian Journal of Community Mental Health, 15*, 153-170.

Youth Who Murder
and Societal Responsibility:
An Issue of Social Justice

Larry G. Morton II
Cynthia A. Loveland Cook

SUMMARY. Society's punitive response to criminal youth has led to the virtual elimination of rehabilitation services for youth who commit homicide. This paper offers an overview of etiological factors contributing to youth homicide. Using Brickman's model of helping and coping, insight is offered into why American society has taken such a punitive stance toward youth homicide. Proposed changes that support social justice for these youths are presented at individual, family, community, and societal levels with a focus on prevention and intervention. *[Article copies available for a fee from The Haworth Document Delivery Service: 1-800-HAWORTH. E-mail address: <docdelivery@haworthpress.com> Website: <http://www.HaworthPress.com> © 2003 by The Haworth Press, Inc. All rights reserved.]*

Larry G. Morton II, MSW, is a doctoral student in Political Science at the University of Missouri–St. Louis.

Cynthia A. Loveland Cook, PhD, is Associate Professor in the School of Social Service at St. Louis University.

Address correspondence to: Larry G. Morton II, 6048 Clemens Avenue, St. Louis, MO 63112.

This article is dedicated to Vincent R. Greer, who was sentenced to life imprisonment without parole for a crime committed at the age of fifteen.

[Haworth co-indexing entry note]: "Youth Who Murder and Societal Responsibility: An Issue of Social Justice." Morton II, Larry G., and Cynthia A. Loveland Cook. Co-published simultaneously in *Social Thought* (The Haworth Press, Inc.) Vol. 22, No. 2/3, 2003, pp. 191-204; and: *Practicing Social Justice* (ed: John J. Stretch et al.) The Haworth Press, Inc., 2003, pp. 191-204. Single or multiple copies of this article are available for a fee from The Haworth Document Delivery Service [1-800-HAWORTH, 9:00 a.m. - 5:00 p.m. (EST). E-mail address: docdelivery@haworthpress.com].

© 2003 by The Haworth Press, Inc. All rights reserved.
http://www.haworthpress.com/store/product.asp?sku=J131
10.1300/J131v22n02_13

KEYWORDS. Youth homicide, attribution of responsibility, risk factors, social justice, intervention, prevention

INTRODUCTION

In 1999, 9% of all murders in the United States were committed by children under the age of 18 (Snyder, 2000). A large proportion of these crimes coincide with an increase in the use of weapons, especially firearms (Jenson & Howard, 1998; Kelleher, 1998; Zimring, 1998). Snyder (2000) reported a doubling of arrests between 1987 and 1993 in both weapons law violations and youth arrest rates for murders. Between 1993 and 1999, youths arrested for both murder and weapons law violations have declined, with murder rates dropping 68% and weapons arrest rates falling 39% (Snyder, 2000). Although many juvenile murders occur in large cities, no part of this country is immune (Jenson & Howard, 1998). Besides the obvious victims of youth homicide (the deceased and their families), there are other victims as well. One of the most neglected is the offending youth who is likely to receive no rehabilitation, particularly when incarcerated with adults.

Our country's response to juvenile homicide is to adopt "get tough" policies, rather than promote social reform or rehabilitation (Niehoff, 1999). Between 1985 and 1999, in response to real and imagined youth involvement in gang activities, policy changes were enacted that limited treatment options in favor of more punitive and controlling measures, such as the transfer of youths to the adult courts at younger and younger ages (Jenson & Howard, 1998). Youth involvement in tragic school shootings, including those in Jonesboro, Arkansas, and Columbine, Colorado, have increased the demand for even more stringent and punitive policies by both legislators and the general public alike. At the same time, the costs of incarcerating one youth are estimated to cost $35,000 to $64,000 annually (Kelleher, 1998). Youths released from adult incarceration are more likely to reoffend compared to those who received rehabilitation services through the juvenile justice system, even when they committed the same type of crime (Krisberg & Howell, 1998).

This article examines the assumptions underlying this country's punitive ("get tough") approach to juvenile justice using the classic attributional model developed by Brickman, Rabinowitz, Karuza, Coates, Cohn and Kidder (1982). Their model provides important insight into why the United States has taken an especially punitive approach to juvenile homicide. First, an overview of the etiologic factors contributing to juvenile homicide is presented. Second, attribution models will be described that focus on both the ultimate cause of youth violence and the ultimate responsibility for its solution. Lastly, proposed changes at individual, family, community, and societal levels will be discussed that support the socially just treatment of these youths.

ETIOLOGIC FACTORS CONTRIBUTING TO JUVENILE HOMICIDE

Biological Factors

Hotly debated since its inception, Lorenz's (1966) biological theory views aggression as instinctual to the human species. He posits that people have a natural build-up of aggressive energy, which is independent of external stimuli. This pent-up energy builds within an individual until it is finally released. Unlike lower animal species, human beings do not have an innate inhibition against harming their own species, so it is more likely they will aggress against their own kind.

Biologically derived factors have been clearly associated with youth homicide. For example, Lewis, Pincus, Bard, Richardson, Prichep, Feldman and Yeager (1988) found that youths sentenced to death for murder showed high rates of head trauma, abnormal neurological signs, and mentally ill family members. Raine and Jones (1987) also discovered that lower heart rates characterized youth with aggressive conduct disorders, a finding consistent with adult criminals. Furthermore, attention deficit disorder, whose origins are neurological in nature, is closely linked with the diagnosis of conduct disorder, which can be manifested by aggressive behaviors (Wasserman & Miller, 1998). These problems are often associated with impulsivity and act as a catalyst for the development, continuation, and escalation of behavior problems, including violent behavior (Loeber, 1990).

Temperament and impulsivity are other biological factors associated with aggression. Youth who are temperamental and impulsive may be difficult to socialize due to their poor response to positive parenting, including reinforcement and appropriate punishment for inappropriate behaviors (Pepler & Slaby, 1994). Another contributing factor is high testosterone levels in male youths (Dabbs, 2000). The effects of high testosterone appear to lessen if the youth is more integrated with positive social influences (Booth & Osgood, 1993; Dabbs, 2000). However, Mattaini, Twyman, Chin and Lee (1996) argue that testosterone increases after aggressive physical encounters; thus, increased levels of testosterone are not the cause of aggression but the outcome.

Psychological Factors

The frustration-aggression hypothesis, originally developed by Dollard, Dobb, Miller, Mowrer and Sears (1939), theorizes that violent aggression is a response to frustration caused by an inability to achieve desired goals. Berkowitz (1978) later suggested that mental and physical pain, rather than frustration, is the primary cause of aggression.

Psychotic symptomology can precede youth homicide (Cornell, Benedek & Benedek, 1987). Menninger and Mayman (1956) coined the term "episodic dyscontrol" to explain how severe developmental deficits could cause inability to control violent aggression. Psychotic symptomology is not a common etiologic factor in youth homicide, but it requires the most intense treatment and intervention when it does occur (Cornell et al., 1987).

Antisocial personality disorder is a common psychiatric disorder often used to explain youth homicide. These youths are often called "superpredators," a popular term used by politicians and the general public to dehumanize violent and homicidal youths (Elikann, 2000). However, the American Psychiatric Association states that youths cannot be diagnosed with this disorder until the age of 18 and only after they have exhibited sufficient evidence of conduct disorder after the age of 15 (Kelleher, 1998). Many youths are, thus, misdiagnosed.

Post Traumatic Stress Disorder is a serious risk factor for youths who have experienced violence in their homes and communities (Byer, 1999; Heide, 1999; Jenkins & Bell, 1994; Smith & Thornberry, 1995). Witnessing violence can affect the formation of a child's personality and can result in overidentification with the victim (internalization) or with the perpetrator (externalization) (Eth, 1989). Thus, youths who witness violence are at higher risk for engaging in the same behavior.

Social Factors

Bandura's (1963) theory of social learning posits that aggression is acquired through social reinforcement. He maintains that aggression does not originate internally, so its causes can be altered. Social factors have been the most commonly studied causes for youth homicide. The most common social risk factors include substance and alcohol abuse, disorganized and abusive families, minority background, poverty and violent communities with lack of support, and poor educational achievements (Block & Block, 1991; Huizinga & Jakob-Chien, 1998; Jenkins & Bell, 1994; Jenson & Howard, 1998; Lewis et al., 1988; Smith, & Thornberry, 1995). One of the most prevalent risk factors for serious and violent youth behavior, including murder, is previous delinquency and first arrest at an early age (Farrington & Loeber, 1998; Loeber, Farrington, & Waschbusch, 1998; Snyder, 1998).

The "violence-prone trajectory" established by Becker, Barham, Eron and Chen (1994) describes a child's developmental pathway that can lead to violence. For example, poverty and social disorganization contribute to a lack of structure in the family system. Weak bonding of children to their caretakers is a known predictor of poor peer relations and increased aggressiveness. In turn, these behaviors often promote rejection by conforming peers. It is not uncommon for these children to perform poorly in school with sporadic school attendance, numerous suspensions, and finally expulsions. These youths often begin to gravitate to others like themselves and enter into deviant peer group relationships. At the same time, they are also likely to be exposed to violence in their communities and homes, which increases their risk for aggressive and violent behaviors (Becker et al., 1994; Byer, 1999; Eth, 1989). In the most extreme case, this developmental pathway can contribute to some children becoming homicidal.

Another social contribution to youth homicide is easy access to firearms with ownership tripling since 1983 (Jenson & Howard, 1998; Kelleher, 1998; Snyder & Sickmund, 1999; Zimring, 1998). The increase of firearm use and juvenile homicide are highly correlated (Blumstein, 1995; Kelleher, 1998; Zimring, 1998). The 400% increase in gang-related murders from 1980 to 1992 also makes gang activity a strong predictor of youth homicide (Kelleher, 1998).

The social, biological and psychological factors known to contribute to youth homicide help society understand how these tragedies occur. At the same time, they also set the stage for the determination of who is responsible for preventing them and who is responsible for the solution when they do occur. The next section describes society's attribution of responsibility for the cause and solution for youth homicide in this country with special emphasis on Brickman's Model of Helping and Coping (1982).

ATTRIBUTIONAL RESPONSIBILITY FOR YOUTH HOMICIDE

Theories of attribution have long been used to understand people's actions and how they view their own behavior (Aronson, 1988; Heider, 1944; Hewstone, 1983; Kelly, 1973). Brickman et al. (1982) extended this theory to include attribution of responsibility for both problems and their solutions (see Figure 1). The following four attributional models were developed:

1. *Moral Model* in which people are seen as responsible for both their problems and solutions;
2. *Enlightenment Model* when people are responsible for their problems, but not for the solutions;
3. *Medical Model* in which people are neither responsible for their problems nor their solutions; and
4. *Compensatory Model* when people are not responsible for their problems, but are responsible for solutions.

Society's current view of youths who commit homicide consistently fits Brickman's Moral Model. When youths are tried as adults and receive adult sentences, they are clearly seen as responsible for their actions. Moreover, when youth are sentenced to adult correctional facilities, usually there are few, if any, rehabilitation services. Society is saying, in effect, that these youths are responsible for rehabilitating themselves in an environment where essentially no services are provided. To compound the social injustice of this situation, these youths are more likely to be sexually assaulted, to become more criminally sophisticated, and, if ever released, are more likely to recidivate (Elikann, 2000; Joiner, 2000).

The juvenile justice system was established during the Progressive Era in 1899 by Jane Addams and Julia Lathrop (Roberts & Brownell, 1999). Since then, the attributional model has fluctuated between the Medical Model (society responsible for the problem and for the solution) and the Enlightenment Model (the child is responsible for the problem, while society is responsible for the solution). One consistent viewpoint throughout the history, however, is belief in the effectiveness of parental "authoritarian" punishment or "authoritative" rehabilitation for juveniles. Although the Medical Model, which was the original model for the juvenile justice system, attributes youth criminal history to societal oppression, the model fails to involve youths in rehabilitation plans and, thus, does not foster their accountability.

During much of the 20th century, the United States maintained an Enlightenment Model approach to juvenile justice. Youths were given more treatment-oriented services based on the premise that although they were responsible for their crimes, they could become productive, law-abiding citizens with rehabilitation. This model assumed that the cause of the problem was solely attributed to defects in the character of youths, thereby freeing society from any responsibility. Although youths received treatment, they had little or no input into their treatment, decreasing the likelihood of long-term success (Loeber & Farrington, 1998).

Since 1985, highly publicized gang activity and crack cocaine distribution, along with an increased prevalence of violence, led the general public to

FIGURE 1. Brickman's Attribution Theory: Responsibility for Helping and Caring

		Who Is Responsible for the Problem?	
Who Is Responsible for the Solution?		**Child**	**Society**
	Child	Moral Model	Compensatory Model
	Society	Enlightenment Model	Medical Model

quickly adopt a "lock them up and throw away the key" attitude. Politicians jumped on the bandwagon, and legislation was passed supporting stricter punishment for youths, particularly their transfer into the adult criminal court system. The Moral Model was implemented and remains ensconced today.

The implementation of this model, particularly the increased imprisonment of youth offenders, the cutbacks in funding for rehabilitative treatment, and the war on drugs, was initiated primarily by the Reagan Administration in response to the general public's demand to eliminate the violence they felt was overtaking their communities (Smiley, 1996). The unfortunate result of these criminal justice policies has been their disproportionate focus on the most vulnerable among us: the poor, minorities, and youths (Smiley, 1996, p. 158; Tonry, 1995). With punishment and public safety as the primary goal, the ultimate outcome is a "quick fix" rather than long-term gains that focus on rehabilitation and accountability for the youth involved in homicide.

Clear (1991) offers insight into why the Moral Model has become the acceptable intervention of choice in our society today:

> The reasoning would be something like this: "Just because the kid's attitude is bad doesn't mean that he can avoid paying back the victim or the community. He has to pay that price because his actions deserve it." The underlying rationale is clearly punitive although we are pleased in many instances the imposition of such punishments seems to have a remarkably ameliorative effect on juvenile attitudes. Yet even without the ameliorative effect, we would feel justified in imposing these sanctions because they demonstrate the unacceptableness of the behavior. (p. 39)

The point stressed is that punishment of youths has become acceptable when taken only at face value, without further justification or demonstrated success. Punishment for punishment's sake has become an acceptable form of social justice in this country. American society is less worried about rehabilitation that elicits positive changes in the behaviors that are likely the source of the criminal action (Altschuler, 1998). As Tonry (1995) points out:

> Americans have a remarkable ability to endure suffering by others. We lock up our citizens at rates of five to fifteen times higher than those in other Western countries (p. 197). . . . As long as our crime control policies treat symptoms and not ailments, they are doomed to failure. (p. 208)

Current punitive juvenile corrections policies are largely determined by "anecdotes, flawed research, and media-popular fads" (Krisberg & Howell, 1998). This situation contributes to the lack of structure that has become inherent in juvenile corrections, and which contributes to its overall ineffectiveness. The Moral Model of juvenile justice is problematic in that morals and values are illusive. Legislation is supposed to be based on the perceived morals and values of the general public. However, the perceptions of public opinions by policy makers may be biased, misinformed, or distorted by legislators to fit their own viewpoints.

Punitive juvenile correction policies based on the Moral Model lead to the temporary suppression of criminal behavior (Altschuler, 1998). However due to prison overcrowding and the astronomical costs for confinement, prison sentences are often reduced. Too often youths are released back into their communities with the same risk factors that contributed to their original incarceration, but now they are hardened and sophisticated criminals through their exposure to adult criminals. Although imprisonment may be considered an effective deterrent for youth homicide, without rehabilitative treatment these youths are more likely to return to their communities to commit more serious and violent crimes.

Although Brickman's model of helping and coping offers insight into the punitive nature of our current criminal justice system for youths who murder, it also offers insight into needed change. The next section of the paper describes the compensatory model as an avenue of change in offering socially just services to this special population.

The Compensatory Model as an Avenue for Change

Research scientists from various fields have made major strides toward understanding the many social, psychological, environmental and biological factors that contribute to youth homicide. Despite this information, the United States has chosen a reactive, rather than a proactive, approach to managing these tragic situations. This line of attack has lasting negative implications, not only for the youths involved, but also for the future safety of our society as a whole, and for social justice in America.

Brickman's Compensatory Model offers an important perspective on helping youths who commit homicide. From a preventive perspective, the model holds society responsible for the inadequacy of its efforts to prevent youth homicide. Society is also held accountable for not implementing intervention programs known to be effective in the reduction of violent crime (Elikann, 2000). Thus, family courts would be responsible for *not* intervening when delinquency occurs at early ages. Schools would be held accountable for *not* intervening when risk factors are recognized, but ignored, or when their only intervention strategy is suspension or expulsion.

Prevention at early points in the violence-prone trajectory of children who commit homicide can redirect them away from violent behaviors (Becker et al., 1994; Byer, 1999; Jenson, & Howard, 1998; Mattaini et al., 1996). During these critical times, parent-child bonding can be improved. Preventive educational strategies can be used to help children strengthen their social skills, develop their cognitive skills in problem solving, change their ideas about the appropriateness of violence, and improve their self-esteem. Children can also learn how to make more accurate assessments of the intentions of others, while acquiring a better understanding of the ambiguity of many interpersonal interactions. Preventive education on conflict resolution, impulse control, and anger/behavior management can also increase the likelihood that these children will refrain from violence. School-based programs are ideal for high-risk students, particularly those who demonstrate aggressive behavior with peers, drop out of school and/or are close to being suspended. Successful program components could include violence prevention, academic tutoring, sports/recreation, aesthetic art activities, and parenting education.

Societal responsibility does not end with preventive programs geared toward the behavior of children, however. A society whose core values support social justice understands its responsibility for helping fellow citizens improve their living situations, strengthen their communities, and correct the deplorable conditions of some schools, all factors that contribute to youth violence. For example, community-based prevention programs can help generate public support for societal and environmental changes that help children who are prone to committing violent acts. They can help the public become aware that the root causes of youth violence are likely to be injustice, racism, inequality, low income, and despair. With these root causes in mind, concentrated efforts can be placed on coalition building between the public and private sectors to help these children. Furthermore, it is critically important that these programs lobby for increased dollars from state and federal legislators so that preventive efforts will continue and improve. For community-based prevention programs to be successful, they need to address the multisystemic factors that contribute to youth violence, rather than focus on one narrow area of specialization. With these kinds of efforts, it is estimated that prevention and early intervention programs would reduce crime by 50%, while costing the public one-sixth the cost of incarceration (Elikann, 2000).

Once youth homicide has occurred, the Compensatory Model would hold youths responsible for their rehabilitation. Our society's current "lock them up and throw away the key" attitude has left many youths incarcerated in adult prisons with few resources to help them rehabilitate themselves. Youths destined for an adult correctional facility need intervention programs in place to help insure the likelihood that they can live a healthier life in prison, or in society should they be released. Intervention must be meaningful to youths and demonstrate evidence of its effectiveness. An important start is for professionals to give youths a say about what intervention strategies would be most effective for them. Listening to these youths and fostering open communication will facilitate a better understanding of their rehabilitation needs and a more individualized approach to helping them. Staff needs to learn how to be effectual advocates for those youth who accept responsibility for their crime and want to rehabilitate themselves. Through these approaches, youths are more likely to become invested in their successful rehabilitation.

Without rehabilitation services geared to help young offenders, it is more likely they will return to their communities to commit even more serious and violent crimes. To remedy this situation, it is imperative that the juvenile justice system rethinks its treatment of youth offenders and reallocates its resources accordingly. Housing juvenile offenders in quarters separate from adult criminals is one step, thereby making youth less available as targets of sexual abuse and less likely to assimilate the culture of adult criminality. The provision of rehabilitation programs for youth offenders is needed, along with staff that is trained to work with this special population.

As noted earlier by Tonry (1995), the only way to effectively control crime is through treatment of the root causes of criminal behavior. In so doing, rehabilitation tackles the issues that will remain untreated if punitive measures are the only services offered to juvenile offenders. It is through this process that the youths will become accountable for their crimes and society will become aware of the injustices that contributed to the youth homicide. Rehabilitation services may offer hope to youth offenders, but ultimately the expectation would be that those professionals working with youth offenders would come together to advocate for the massive systemic changes that must occur. In order for social justice to occur, these changes must take place at clinical, programmatic and policy levels that target poverty, family dysfunction, school conditions, dangerous neighborhoods, disorganized communities, a fragmented juvenile justice system, and new legislation.

At the same time, they need to rectify the plight of the juvenile justice system, which has been lost in a sea of dysfunction for over a century. This country needs to take responsibility for its children in a fashion that is productive and caring; otherwise, it could be argued that we are a neglectful and abusive nation. The implementation of Brickman's Compensatory Model would allow society to take their rightful responsibility for the oppression and victimization of children.

Faith-based human services organizations appear to be at the forefront for future implementation of the Compensatory Model when dealing with homicidal youth. There must be a willingness to analyze the complexity of this issue without ascribing root causes to single, illusive factors, such as spiritual impoverishment. Faith-based organizations must be willing to form collaborative partnerships with other community-based agencies that affect the child involved in homicide, as well as continuing to work on innovative rehabilitative programs for these youths.

CONCLUSION

Richard Rhodes (1999) states in his biography of Criminologist Lonnie Athens:

> Criminal violence emerges from . . . brutal social experiences visited upon vulnerable children, who suffer for our neglect of their welfare. . . . If violence is a choice they make, and therefore their personal responsibility, as Athens demonstrates it is, our failure to protect to them from having to confront such a choice is a choice *we* make, just as a disease epidemic would be implicitly our choice if we failed to provide vaccines and antibiotics. Such a choice–to tolerate the brutalization of children as we continue to do–is equally violent and equally evil, and we reap what we sow. (p. 322)

Social justice would dictate that society must protect its children from the social experiences that lead to their opting to commit homicide. For a youth to be accountable for that fatal decision, there must be a society responsible for their developmental well-being. Accountability on the part of society for the proper care of its children yields children who are accountable for their actions, rather than children who are held accountable by a society that has been abusive and neglectful towards them before and after the commission of homicide.

Using Brickman's model of attributional responsibility, this article addressed the underlying reasons society has adopted its "get tough" policies in determining the proper interventions for homicidal youths. Since mid-1980 the Moral Model of holding youths responsible for their crime and for their own solutions is what lives in the heart of our society. This punitive stance leads to a false sense of safety and security on the part of the general public. Legislators feed into the public's need for safety by implementing Moral Model policies that alienate these youths from society, while offering them little chance for successful rehabilitation.

The Compensatory Model, on the other hand, would hold society and youths accountable for acts of youth homicide. Youths who commit this most serious and violent of crimes usually have multiple social risk factors, such as poor school performance and attendance, prior arrests, family dysfunction, mental health issues, disorganized communities, gang activity, and drug use. A society that recognizes its contribution to youth homicide is more likely to initiate prevention or intervention strategies, before a serious crime has occurred. Furthermore, rehabilitative action would be initiated early with youths actively involved in treatment planning. Through this approach, youths are more likely to be invested in their rehabilitation and open to accountability for their crime.

REFERENCES

Altschuler, D.M. (1998). Intermediate sanctions and community treatment for serious and violent juvenile offenders. In R. Loeber & D.F. Farrington (Eds.), *Serious and violent juvenile offenders: Risk factors and successful intervention* (pp. 367-385). Thousand Oaks: Sage.

Aronson, E. (1988). *The social animal (5th edition).* New York: W.H. Freeman and Company.

Bandura, A. & Walters, R.H. (1963). *Social learning and personality development.* New York: Holt, Rinehart & Winston.

Becker, J.V., Barham, J., Eron, L.D. & Chen, S.A. (1994). The present status and future directions for psychological research and youth violence. In L.D. Eron, J.H. Gentry, & P. Schlegel (Eds.), *Reason to hope: A psychosocial perspective on violence and youth* (pp. 435-445). Washington, DC: American Psychological Association.

Berkowitz, L. (1978). *Aggression: A learning analysis.* Englewood Cliffs, NJ: Prentice-Hall.

Block, C.R. & Block, R.B. (1991). Beginning with Wolfgang: An agenda for homicide research. *Journal of Crime and Justice, 14,* 31-70.

Blumstein, A. (1995). Youth violence, guns, and the illicit-drug industry. *Journal of Criminal Law and Criminology, 86,* 10-36.

Booth, A. & Osgood, D.W. (1993). The influence of testosterone on deviance in adulthood: Assessing and explaining the relationship. *Criminology, 31,* 93-117.

Brickman, P., Rabinowitz, V.C., Karuza, Jr., J., Coates, D., Cohn, E. & Kidder, L. (1982). Models of helping and coping. *American Psychologist, 37,* 368-384.

Byer, M. (1999). Recognizing the child in the delinquent. *Kentucky Children's Rights Journal, 7,* 16-26.

Clear, T.R. (1991). Juvenile intensive probation supervision: Theory and rationale. In T.L. Armstrong (Ed.), *Intensive interventions with high-risk youths: Promising approaches in juvenile probation and parole* (pp. 29-44). Monsey, NY: Criminal Justice Press.

Cornell, D.G., Benedek, E.P. & Benedek, D.M. (1987). Juvenile homicide: Prior adjustment and a proposed typology. *American Journal of Orthopsychiatry, 57,* 383-393.

Dabbs, J.M. (2000). *Heroes, rogues, and lovers: Testosterone and behavior.* New York: McGraw-Hill.

Dollard, J., Dobb, L., Miller, N., Mowrer, O. & Sears, R. (1939). *Frustration and aggression.* New Haven: Yale University Press.

Elikann, P. (2000). The solution to youth crime in America. *The Champion,* 18-24.

Eth, S. (1989). The adolescent witness to homicide. In E.P. Benedek & D.G. Cornell (Eds.), *Juvenile homicide* (pp. 85-113). Washington, DC: American Psychiatric Press, Inc.

Farrington, D.P. & Loeber, R. (1998). Major aims of this book. In R. Loeber & D.F. Farrington (Eds.), *Serious and violent juvenile offenders: Risk factors and successful intervention* (pp. 1-10). Thousand Oaks: Sage.

Heide, K.M. (1999). *Young killers: The challenge of juvenile homicide.* Thousand Oaks, CA: Sage.

Heider, F. (1944). Social perception and phenomenal causality. *Psychological Review, 51,* 358-374.

Hewstone, M. (1983). Attribution theory and common-sense explanations: An introductory overview. In M. Hewstone (Ed.), *Attribution theory: Social and functional extensions* (pp. 1-26). Oxford: Basil Blackwell.

Huizinga, D. & Jakob-Chien, C. (1998). The contemporaneous co-occurrence of serious and violent juvenile offending and other problem behaviors. In R. Loeber & D.F. Farrington (Eds.), *Serious and violent juvenile offenders: Risk factors and successful interventions* (pp. 47-67). Thousand Oaks: Sage.

Jenkins, E. & Bell, C. (1994). Violence among inner-city high school students and post-traumatic stress disorder. In S. Friedman (Ed.), *Anxiety disorders in African Americans* (pp. 76-88). New York: Springer.

Jenson, J.M. & Howard, M.O. (1998). Youth crime, public policy, and practice in the juvenile justice system: Recent trends and needed reforms. *Social Work, 43,* 324-334.

Joiner, L.L. (2000). Time for juveniles. *Emerge, 11*(5), 28-31.

Kelleher, M.D. (1998). *When good kids kill.* Westport, CT: Praeger.

Kelly, H.H. (1973). The process of causal attribution. *American Psychologist, 28,* 107-128.

Krisberg, B. & Howell, J.C. (1998). The impact of the juvenile justice system and prospects for graduated sanctions in a comprehensive strategy. In R. Loeber & D.P. Farrington (Eds.), *Serious and violent juvenile offenders: Risk factors and successful interventions* (pp. 346-366). Thousand Oaks: Sage.

Lewis, D.O., Pincus, J.H., Bard, B., Richardson, E., Prichep, L.S., Feldman, M. & Yeager, C. (1988). Neuropsychiatric, psychoeducational, and family characteristics of 14 juveniles condemned to death in the United States. *American Journal of Psychiatry, 145,* 584-589.

Loeber, R. (1990). Developmental and risk factors of juvenile antisocial behavior and delinquency. *Child Psychology Review, 10,* 1-41.

Loeber, R. & Farrington, D.P. (1998). *Serious and violent juvenile offenders: Risk factors and successful interventions.* Thousand Oaks: Sage.

Loeber, R., Farrington, D.P. & Waschbusch, D.A. (1998). Serious and violent juvenile offenders. In R. Loeber & D.P. Farrington (Eds.), *Serious and violent juvenile offenders: Risk factors and successful interventions* (pp. 13-29). Thousand Oaks: Sage.

Lorenz, K. (1966). *On aggression.* New York: Harcourt Brace Jovanovich.

Mattaini, M.A., Twyman, J.S., Chin, W. & Lee, K.N. (1996). Youth violence. In M.A. Mattaini & B.A. Thyer (Eds.), *Finding solutions to social problems: Behavioral strategies for change* (pp. 75-111). Washington, DC: American Psychological Association.

Menninger, K. & Mayman, M. (1956). Episodic dyscontrol: A third order of stress adaptation. *Bulletin of the Menninger Clinic, 20,* 153-165.

Niehoff, D. (1999). *The biology of violence.* New York: The Free Press.

Pepler, D.J. & Slaby, R.G. (1994). Theoretical and development perspectives on youth and violence. In L.D. Eron, J.H. Gentry, & P. Schlegel (Eds.), *Reason to hope: A psychosocial perspective on violence and youth* (pp. 27-58). Washington, DC: American Psychological Association.

Raine, A. & Jones, F. (1987). Attention, autonomic arousal, and personality in behaviorally disturbed children. *Journal of Abnormal Child Psychology, 15,* 583-599.

Rhodes, R. (1999). *Why they kill: The discoveries of a maverick criminologist.* New York: Vintage.

Roberts, A.R. & Brownell, P. (1999). A century of forensic social work: Bridging the past to the present. *Social Work, 44,* 359-369.

Smiley, T. (1996). *Hard left: Straight talk about the wrongs of the right.* New York: Doubleday.

Smith, C. & Thornberry, T.P. (1995). The relationship between childhood maltreatment and adolescent involvement in delinquency. *Criminology, 33,* 451-481.

Snyder, H.N. (1998). Appendix: Serious, violent, and chronic juvenile offenders–An assessment of the extent of the trends in officially recognized serious criminal behavior in a delinquent population. In R. Loeber & D.P. Farrington (Eds.), *Serious and violent juvenile offenders: Risk factors and successful interventions* (pp. 428-444). Thousand Oaks: Sage.

Snyder, N.H. (2000). *Juvenile arrests 1999.* Washington, DC: U.S. Department of Justice, Office of Juvenile Justice and Delinquency Prevention.

Snyder, H.N. & Sickmund, M. (1999). *Juvenile offenders and victims: A national report.* Washington, DC: U.S. Department of Justice, Office of Juvenile Justice and Delinquency Prevention.

Tonry, M. (1995). *Malign neglect: Race, class, and punishment in America.* New York: Oxford University Press.

Wasserman, G.A. & Miller, L.S. (1998). The prevention of serious and violent juvenile offending. In R. Loeber & D.P. Farrington (Eds.), *Serious and violent juvenile offenders: Risk factors and successful interventions* (pp. 197-247). Thousand Oaks: Sage.

Zimring, F.E. (1998). *American youth violence.* New York: Oxford University Press.

Children of High-Conflict Custody Disputes: Striving for Social Justice in Adult-Focused Litigation

Barbara E. Flory

Marla Berg-Weger

SUMMARY. Children whose parents experience a divorce or separation frequently do not have a voice during the legal proceedings that determine custody and visitation. This paper describes one program that serves to give a voice to the children in these situations. Heritage House, a supervised visitation and custody exchange program, was established as a way to improve the quality of parents' and children's interactions and decrease the potential for violence while maintaining parent/child ties. The initial evaluation of this program is discussed along with the implications of the program's design and operationalization for other programs. *[Article copies available for a fee from The Haworth Document Delivery Service: 1-800-HAWORTH. E-mail address: <docdelivery@haworthpress.com> Website: <http://www.HaworthPress.com> © 2003 by The Haworth Press, Inc. All rights reserved.]*

Barbara E. Flory is Program Coordinator at Heritage House, Provident Counseling, 2650 Olive Street, St. Louis, MO 63103 (E-mail: bf@providentc.org).

Marla Berg-Weger is Associate Professor and Director of Field Education in the School of Social Service at St. Louis University.

The authors wish to thank the Emmett J. and Mary Martha Doerr Center for Social Justice Education and Research in the School of Social Service at the St. Louis University for their support of this research. The authors additionally wish to thank Julie Birkenmaier and Sarah Boeker for their assistance on this manuscript.

[Haworth co-indexing entry note]: "Children of High-Conflict Custody Disputes: Striving for Social Justice in Adult-Focused Litigation." Flory, Barbara E., and Marla Berg-Weger. Co-published simultaneously in *Social Thought* (The Haworth Press, Inc.) Vol. 22, No. 2/3, 2003, pp. 205-219; and: *Practicing Social Justice* (ed: John J. Stretch et al.) The Haworth Press, Inc., 2003, pp. 205-219. Single or multiple copies of this article are available for a fee from The Haworth Document Delivery Service [1-800-HAWORTH, 9:00 a.m. - 5:00 p.m. (EST). E-mail address: docdelivery@haworthpress.com].

© 2003 by The Haworth Press, Inc. All rights reserved.
http://www.haworthpress.com/store/product.asp?sku=J131

10.1300/J131v22n02_14

KEYWORDS. Collaboration, social services, law, high-conflict divorce, supervised access/custody exchange

INTRODUCTION

During the last half of the twentieth century, the changing social fabric of our lives has dramatically affected families. The feminist movement brought greater equality to women and mutuality in marriage and altered gender roles as fathers began participating more fully in child-rearing responsibilities. These events created shifts and altered societal views on marital breakup that eventually led to the inception of no-fault divorce laws. The father's rights movement raised issues about sex discrimination in custody decision-making that demanded equal protection issues be addressed (Kelly, 1997; Mason, 1994). Books such as *Surviving the Breakup* (Wallerstein & Kelly, 1980) and *Dividing the Child* (Maccoby & Mnooken, 1992) appeared on bookshelves and became overnight bestsellers. In the end, the playing field for mothers and fathers with respect to child custody determination is being leveled (Kelly, 1997). Mason (1999), however, asserts, "It is in this quarter century that the child's needs have been eclipsed by the needs of their parents" (p. 2).

At the turn of the twenty-first century, forty-five percent of all first marriages end in divorce and sixty percent of second marriages meet with the same fate (Wallerstein, Lewis & Blakeslee, 2000). These "facts of life" challenge many long-standing social norms and create compromises to social justice that impact children's well-being, because the leveled playing field on which child custody determination is resolved is governed by rules of entitlement. Mason (1999) notes, "Many children are exchanged like chattel between parents who insist on their right to them" (p. 1). Many other children are the focus of high-conflict child custody disputes that place child and adult safety at risk when violence erupts as ex-partners meet face-to-face to transfer children for visitation purposes. For precisely these reasons, family courts across the country are re-evaluating service delivery methods.

As The Honorable Thomas J. Frawley (1999) observed, "The days we do business within the confines of the courthouse are over." Propelled by that belief, one community addressed these issues by forming a public/private partnership between family court and a private not-for-profit mental health agency. The program, Heritage House, has dramatically altered service delivery in the community. This paper frames the issues that contribute to high conflict child custody disputes; describes Heritage House, a supervised access and custody exchange center; outlines the program objectives; and, finally, discusses the implications for social justice practice.

FRAMING THE ISSUES

Each year in America, approximately one million children are affected by the aftermath of parental separation and divorce (Mason, 1999; Maccoby & Mnooken, 1992). Although most families will amicably separate and transform into cooperative co-parenting roles approximately one year after divorce, a small percentage (30-40%) will continue to disagree about child custody arrangements three to five years post-divorce (Garrity & Baris, 1994; Johnston, 1994; Maccoby & Mnooken, 1992; Pearson & Anhalt, 1993). The longer the duration of the dispute, the more intractable the issues become. In an effort to seize control of the spiraling conflict, an estimated ten percent of these families enter and exit the court system as if through a revolving door (Ahrons, 1994; Maccoby & Mnooken, 1992).

At the turn of the twenty-first century, approximately one-third of our children are born outside the bounds of marriage (Mason, 1999). Current custody laws dictate that biology alone entitles parents to participate in children's lives, even those who have chosen to be uninvolved for one, five, or more years after birth (Mason, 1994). Family courts have commingled visitation issues of never-married parents with visitation issues of divorced parents by ruling alike in applying *the best interest of the child* standard (the standard that guides all child-focused judicial decisions concerning custodial arrangements) (Mason, 1994).

As a culture, Americans often question what motivates these "dysfunctional" parents to engage in such escalations, assuming parents who love their children would put aside their differences in the best interest of the child. Parental love for children is not usually the issue in custody cases. If anything, these parents may love their children too intensely, often becoming overly and dysfunctionally attached. After the divorce, children may be the parent's primary companion and link to the community. As such, rearing children helps the parent maintain important emotional and social ties (Mason, 1999).

While fear of social isolation may be one force driving parents' concern about "losing" the children, it is likely the least toxic reason why parents withdraw into polarized positions seeking to maintain care and control of their children. Issues falling on the low to mid-range of the toxic continuum include parenting skills, transition times, details of visits and disparaging comments (the five most frequently cited reasons in the literature) (Garrity & Baris, 1994). On the mid- to high end of the continuum is the court's ability to thrust an uninvolved parent into a child's life without so much as a formal introduction. On the high end of the continuum is parental fear that the child is at risk for emotional and/or physical harm due to poor parenting skills resulting in the use of inappropriate discipline. On the extreme high end of the continuum is domestic violence, the most toxic reason for parents' retreats into polarized positions. Unless proper safeguards to help ensure children's safety can be instituted, some custodial parents will continue to interfere with the noncustodial parent/child relationship, defying court orders and risking sanctions as severe as incarceration.

In the last twenty years, the legal system's response to domestic violence has evolved to include more frequent arrest, victimless prosecution, civil protection including 24-hour availability to adult abuse protection orders, shelters for battered women, court-based victim advocate programs and community policing by specially trained police officers. "In that time society has moved from virtual denial of the existence of domestic violence to a somewhat grudging acknowledgment that it is a pervasive and serious problem with legal, sociological, and psychological dimensions" (Cahn & Meier, 1995, p. 339). A growing body of literature suggests that the tightened laws addressing battering have resulted in perpetrators using the legal system to continue the cycle of abuse via probate and civil courts (Stone & Fialk, 1997). This misuse of the system has added a new dimension to child custody determination. The batterer's attempts to gain custody and control are often mistakenly viewed as a sincere desire to maintain, establish or reestablish a healthy parent/child relationship. Field (1998) notes, "Visitation, in the context of a domestic violence case, becomes one more means of the batterer controlling the victim, and maintaining power over her. It gives the batterer opportunities to interact with her, directly or through the use of the children" (p. 289). In such cases, the safety of the victim and children becomes paramount. Exposing the facts in a court of law is the only way to impose legal remedies and safeguards.

Regardless of the point of the continuum on which the issues fall, these highly entrenched disputes are complex and do not lend themselves to easy resolution. Children caught in the middle of parental escalations live with feelings of fear and intimidation that create constant tension and uneasy alliances (Garrity & Baris, 1994).

> Being caught in their parents' pain and anger has detrimental effects on children's happiness and human relationships. Moreover, we are becoming more aware of the long-term dangers that interparental hostility

poses for children of divorce. Nothing matters–not custody decisions, visiting arrangements, nor whether the child is a boy or girl–as much as whether parents can minimize fighting. Over time, parental wars take a greater toll on a child's development than any other single factor in divorce. (Garrity & Baris, 1994, p. 35)

When parents cannot or should not decide how each will spend time with their children, adversarial litigation is necessary to resolve the dispute (Rotman, 2000). Court involvement ensures that ex-partners' rights will be protected (i.e., noncustodial parental right to visitation and custodial parental right to receive child support) (Maccoby & Mnooken, 1992). These legal protections contribute to the likelihood of escalated conflict because frequent visitation means increased contact, therefore, increased opportunity for violence to erupt. In fact, research suggests that most conflict occurs at the time when children are transferred from one parent to another as this is the point ex-partners have contact with each other (Garrity & Baris, 1994). Unfortunately, children have no rights under the law; they are the silent parties in litigation (Mason, 1999; Wallerstein et al., 2000).

PROGRAM DESCRIPTION

In the mid-1990s, two events occurred in the St. Louis community that emphasized the need to protect parents and children involved in high-conflict child custody disputes, particularly when domestic violence was a known issue. In a 1996 Report to the Community, the Domestic Violence Council identified the availability of supervised visitation between noncustodial parents and their children as a gap in service delivery. Independent of that finding, The Honorable Thomas J. Frawley (1999) identified the "need for a safe place where families could go when there were allegations of abuse and neglect. It needs to be a family friendly place. And the children need to know they will be safe when visiting their parent." That vision became the catalyst that forged the formation of a public/private partnership between St. Louis City Family Court and Provident Counseling, a private not-for-profit mental health agency. This vision led to the founding of Heritage House, a supervised visitation and custody exchange center. The project was intended to fill the gap between law and social services by establishing a needed resource for all families, married or unmarried, who are entrenched in litigation over child custody.

Historically, supervised visitation between noncustodial parent and child is judicially ordered when the court determines that a child's safety is at risk. As defined by program collaborators, supervised visitation is third-party guided contact between the noncustodial parent and child for the purpose of maintaining or forming a relationship. Service delivery occurs on three levels to:

1. ensure the safety of children when abuse is alleged;
2. reintroduce parent and child after a prolonged separation; and
3. introduce parent and child when no prior relationship exists.

Custody exchange is the transfer of children from custodial to noncustodial parent for the purpose of temporary custody. In the context of child abuse and neglect, supervised visitation services have a well-established history as a means to facilitate family reunification. However, supervised visitation is a relatively new service within the domestic relations arena with origins emanating largely from grassroots organizing. Over time, the judiciary has slowly embraced the practice of ordering supervised visitation on domestic relations cases to ensure the safety of children and minimize their risk of exposure to interparental conflict (Flory, Dunn, Berg-Weger & Milstead, 2001).

The goal of the Heritage House project is to improve and augment current services and ensure the safety of children who are the focus of high-conflict child custody disputes by providing a caring environment in which supervised access and custody exchange occurs. The intent of the program is to fill identified gaps in services; hence, the center operates during nonbusiness hours, evenings, weekends and holidays, employs off-duty police officers to ensure the same level of safety at the center that families experience at family court and provides guided supervised visitation and custody exchange services. Paid professional clinicians who possess a range of therapeutic, conflict management, psychoeducational and advocacy skills respond to clients' needs as they transcend the difficult process of separation and divorce provide services. This attention to education and experience ensures that staff is properly trained to handle the issues surrounding this highly conflicted, often violent population. Moreover, clinicians are qualified diagnosticians, able to assess emotional stressors placed on children. Once diagnosed, staff intervenes with parents to help them focus on children's best interests (in actuality, parents' mutual interests) rather than adult self interests.

At Heritage House, interaction between ex-partners is prevented by a program structure designed to provide maximum safety for all family members. Entry into the center is monitored by two off-duty police officers that are present during all hours of operation. Upon entry into the building, every person is scanned with a handheld metal detector. Entry is limited to only those people who are directly involved in a case. Persons other than parents who transport children to and from visitation must be preapproved to enter the building *before* arriving at the center. Supervised access and custody exchange appointments are scheduled in permanent time slots with ex-partners' arrival and departure times staggered to ensure ex-partners do not meet one another. Strict adherence to scheduled times promotes the safety of all parties (Flory et al., 2001).

In order to establish a baseline for service delivery and plan for future expansion, access to services is limited to court-ordered referrals. Heritage House is a fee-for-service program with fees reinvested into the program and dedicated to program expansion. Fees are court-ordered; thus, every family is expected to pay a fee, even a minimal one. As part of a United Way funded agency, Heritage House bases fees on ability to pay and no one is denied service. Agency policy permits the Project Coordinator to reduce, or even waive fees as indicated.

The creation of Heritage House is a unique concept nationwide that introduces a collaborative element between social sciences and the law that allows for a more balanced view of the family system. The center operates as an adjunct service of the court during interim court processes. Staff is charged with obtaining vital information through direct observation about parents' ability and readiness to co-parent their children. Therefore, the program structure serves to complement the law by providing a needed social service. Heritage House staff maintain a balanced role, factually documenting ex-partners' participation as ordered, and parent and child behavior at the anxiety-provoking time of transfer of children (Flory et al., 2001).

However, factual documentation alone is insufficient. When parents are unable to determine the way in which each will spend time with their children and place decision-making in the hands of a judge who is sworn to uphold justice, full disclosure of the facts surrounding the dispute is essential. Recognizing that effective communication lies at the heart of sound decision-making, a primary program objective is to open channels of communication that facilitates disclosure of factual information. Informed decision-making translates into sound parenting plans, but implementing parenting plans presents a near insurmountable challenge for high-conflict families that cannot communicate with each other with civility. Hence, third-party assistance with implementation of temporary and final court orders is the second program objective, and the third objective is program evaluation. A literature review of supervised visitation services reveals a sparse body of information and no literature was found on custody exchange services. Therefore, any new information about families who use such services will be a valuable resource for the court, professional and educational communities.

Communication

Social services and the law often find themselves on opposites sides of the table when discussions about child welfare and families take place. Much of the reason for conflict is attributable to the inability of each group to "hear" the other. This failure to "hear" is largely due to discipline-specific language that often precludes meaningful understanding. "Although the languages of our various human service systems use many of the same words–risk, consequences, need, capacity, causation, supervision, discipline and the like–their meanings, and most importantly, the contexts and values they represent, will vary dramatically" (Franz, 1997, p. 1). A primary objective of Heritage House programming is to break down communication barriers by eliminating discipline-specific jargon, seek clarification and engage in a common-language that all professionals can understand. To complete the metaphor, the objective of the program is to join hands around the table, forming mutually beneficial relationships that address the needs of court, community and families (Flory, 2000).

Heretofore, the incorporation of social science into child custody proceedings has largely occurred through the use of custody evaluators (most often clinical psychologists) to determine which parent is more "fit" (Mason, 1994). Communication between evaluator and judge is limited to expert testimony at the time of the trial. Such testimony often serves to further escalate the dispute by pathologizing parents' behaviors (Pfeffer, 1999). The strengths-based intervention philosophy of Heritage House differs from this traditional deficit-based approach in two ways. First, when subpoenaed to testify, Heritage House staff serves as fact-based witnesses, avoiding making recommendations about custodial arrangements. Second, Heritage House rejects the notion that divorce is a pathological, even deviant, occurrence; thus, it does not characterize personal behaviors in terms of "fitness" (Ahrons, 1994; Pfeffer, 1999). Rather, each parent is assumed to share in the responsibility for the emotional and physical well-being of the children (Mandel & Went, 2000).

The provision of understandable, factual documentation avoids "two important problems with the application of social science to custody issues:

1. utilizing an expert witness 'selectively to promote arrangements,' and
2. the inherent risk of 'taking away the court's ultimate decision-making power' " (Mason, 1994, p. 192).

When domestic violence is an issue, a third, and perhaps even more important unidentified problem emerges that inhibits justice from being served, namely, male batterers often function well during evaluation while their partners appear pathological (Field, 1998). Heritage House views behavior as choice; each person is held responsible and accountable for personal behavior. Over time, a more balanced perspective of ex-partners behavior is achieved.

Regardless of the marital status of separating couples, three essential elements are necessary to develop a successful visitation plan. The plan must:

1. minimize conflict;
2. maximize the time spent with both parents as long as both parents know and love the children, can keep the children safe and are willing to parent; and
3. address the developmental needs of the children (Garrity & Baris, 1994).

To endure, visitation plans must address *the best interest of the child*. Heritage House programming eliminates contact, thus minimizing conflict between ex-partners, maximizing time spent with both parents by enforcing court-ordered visitation and helping parents understand the developmental needs of children. The factual information provided by Heritage House staff informs judicial decision-making and helps ensure visitation plans appropriately reflect the needs of individual families.

While effective communication is an important aspect of informed decision-making and subsequent development of any plan, communication is only the first step. When parties maintain polarized positions regarding child custody, legal judgements do not necessarily end the dispute and the disputing parties often access the system numerous times, hence the phrase "revolving door" use of the system. To end, or at a minimum, to slow the turning of the door, lending assistance to families with the implementation of court-ordered parenting plans–something that has not occurred in the past–is needed and recommended (Mason, 1994).

Implementation

Heritage House staff are charged with implementing court orders exactly as written. The process begins when a temporary order is entered at the time of the first court hearing and service continues so long as subsequent review hearings require, extending beyond issuance of a final order, as needed. This unique approach "ensure[s] a method of progression from most restrictive visitation (supervised visits) to least restrictive visitation (facilitated custody exchange)" during active court involvement (Flory et al., 2001, p. 473). During the implementation process, ongoing communication keeps the court informed about parents' ability to safely co-parent their children. In short, the implementation phase of the process provides a safety net for children when most needed. This safety net is particularly important when a history of alleged child abuse and/or domestic violence is an issue.

Domestic violence presents a particular challenge in the domestic relations arena because theoretical models often cause the untrained/unskilled person to believe the cycle of violence ends when separation happens. In actuality, more women victims are killed in the process of leaving than at any other time (Missouri Coalition Against Domestic Violence, 1998). "The greatest risk to abused parents and their children is associated with case outcomes," because "the abuser is forced to acknowledge his loss of control over his partner and his loss of the relationship itself, on which he may be profoundly dependent" (Dalton, 1999, p. 289). For example, after a child visitation hearing, a father shot and killed his ex-partner and her mother outside a courthouse in a southern city ("Man kills 2," 2001). The foregoing illustrates the importance of protection for victims and children and emphasizes the need for implementation of parenting plans in safe surroundings where ex-partners' behavior can be closely monitored and parent/child bonds maintained. In that way, if imminent safety concerns arise, swift remedies are achieved.

Early anecdotal evidence and Heritage House program statistics indicated the program was reaching the intended goal of ensuring safety and enabling increased noncustodial parent/child contact. However, the collaborative partners acknowledged that anecdotal evidence alone was insufficient to expand programming or seek major funding sources. Given the cutting-edge nature of Heritage House programming aimed at systemic change, the partners deemed evaluation that is more formal a priority.

Evaluation

As a part of the initial conceptualization process in developing new programming, the collaborative partners wanted to enhance program integrity by maintaining ethical practice. Securing a research grant from the Emmett J. and Mary Martha Doerr Center for Social Justice Education and Research helped realize the goal. The exploratory evaluation effort examines Heritage House's ability to achieve the mission of improving the overall well-being of children who are the focus of high-conflict child custody disputes.

Forty-five adults court-ordered to participate in Heritage House programming took part in the study. Participating families are racially diverse, relatively well-educated and gainfully employed, with mothers and fathers earning a mean income of $23,829 and $29,205 respectively (range: $5,200-$72,000). Approximately half of the participants are divorced from their ex-partner (46.7%); more than a third have never married their ex-partner (35.6%) and the remainder is newly divorcing parents (11.1%) (Flory et al., 2001). The effort creates a profile of the families who participate in supervised access/custody exchange programs, providing information on high-conflict families than was previously known.

The objective of this exploratory study was to determine if visitation frequency increased, if inter-parental conflict decreased and the subsequent effects, if any, increased visitation had on child well-being during the six-month duration of the study. Pre- and post-test instruments measure frequency of visitation, interparental conflict and changes in children's behaviors and emotional and physical health (Flory et al., 2001).

Findings reveal that visitation frequency significantly increased (M = 8.16, sd = 6.27; t(44) = −3.967, p = .000), and interparental conflict significantly decreased (M = 11.71, sd = 11.44; t(30) = 3.02, p = .005) over the six-month period (Flory et al., 2001). These findings document that Heritage House intervention serves as an effective resource to help ex-partners maintain safe contact.

In spite of this dramatic increase in visitation between noncustodial parent and child, child well-being remained stable with no significant differences found between entry and completion of the study. Participating parents maintained similar attitudes about parenting, and their attitudes are similar to those found in the general population. However, a subscale analysis indicate parents hold significantly more appropriate attitudes toward corporal punishment (t (27) = 2.882, p = .008) after participation in the program (Dunn, 2000). This portion of the study suggests that Heritage House intervention helps protect vulnerable children from the adverse effects of interparental conflict by helping parents to grasp the importance of not using physical force as a means of control over their children.

IMPLICATIONS FOR SOCIAL JUSTICE PRACTICE

The mere fact that parental disputes involving children must be litigated raises questions regarding social justice, because the laws governing dissolution of marriage and child custody are aimed at the legal termination of marriage and the division of marital property, not the well-being of children. The issue of equity becomes critical for the often unrepresented children. Remarkably, although the issues before the court involve children, society neglects to acknowledge the sheer numbers of children processed through the Domestic Relations Divisions of Family Courts. In the City of St. Louis, Missouri, alone, an average of 8,049 domestic filings were entered between 1991-96, and 7,212 were judicially disposed (City of St. Louis Annual Report to the Community, 1996). The number of children involved in such proceedings is not reflected in any existing data (Miller, 1998). Thus, this vulnerable child population remains invisible and the emotional implications of court-ordered visitation for divorced and never-married parents are unclear. Mason (1994) offers, "We must consider whether we are serving our children's best interest, or treating them as commodities to be fought over" (p. xii).

At face-value, the "best interest" standard sounds child-centered; however, the concept is an illusive standard with no agreed upon definition; rather, judges in many locales are given general guidelines only (Mason, 1994). The Uniform Marriage and Divorce Code (1970) defines the standard as a composite of the following contingencies:

1. the wishes of the child's parents as to custody;
2. the needs of the child for a continuing relationship with both parents;
3. the interaction and interrelationship of the child with parents, siblings, and other person who may significantly affect the child's best interests;
4. the child's adjustment to his home, school and community; and
5. the mental and physical health of all individuals involved. The court shall not consider conduct of a present or proposed custodian that does not affect his relationship to the child (UMDC§ 402).

In 1999, Mason suggests that the UMDC does not define child's interests and creates vagaries in judicial decision-making. Clearly, the nebulousness of the standard renders its application inequitable. Over time, observation and factual documentation concerning children's age and developmental stage reaction to visitation indirectly helps children gain a voice in court proceedings and serves to promote treatment that is more equitable. The words of a two-year old, "Thank you for bringing my daddy," or a seven-year old, "I'm not afraid anymore," serve as powerful reminders to the court about children's essential need to have two parents safely involved in their lives (Heritage House child clients).

While the highly structured programming of Heritage House may appear punitive, it serves to address social justice issues concerning safety for all family members and the community. There is perhaps no greater social injustice than perpetrating violence on innocent bystanders, particularly children. Every citizen has the right to safety whether in their home or in a public space. Participation in programming provides protection from life-threatening contact that may result when violent partners meet face-to-face when transferring children. As an example, in one urban area a custody exchange transfer occurring at a busy subway station tragically ended when a father slashed his ex-spouse repeatedly in the face and neck as their children and horrified rush-hour commuters looked on (Daley & Rowdy, 1998). This example illustrates a need for centers like Heritage House, yet Heritage House is one of a few programs of this kind operating nationwide that offers a broad scope of services to maximize safety.

Moreover, a secure and supportive environment aids abused women in developing a greater sense of agency (Buel, 1994; Weitzman, 2000). The safe surroundings at Heritage House help women regain self-confidence, and, thus, the revictimization often experienced by the victim is lessened when they meet face-to-face with the batterer in the courtroom. Consequently, when required to tell their story of abuse, the lowered levels of anxiety result in more coherent testimony, and, thereby, help to ensure justice is served.

Heritage House addresses the social justice issue of access to needed services in two ways:

1. the reduction or waiving of fees as necessary; and
2. the provision of services during nontraditional hours (evenings, weekends, and major holidays) (Flory, 1998).

Services offered during nonbusiness hours preclude removing children from school and parents from work so that the noncustodial parent and child can maintain frequent and consistent contact.

Brill (1989) found that most social workers do not discuss injustices with those in positions of authority, and approximately forty percent have never taken action on social justice issues. Of those who have, few report success when they have done so. Perhaps more telling is that Brill (1989) purports only five percent or less of social workers receive training in justice issues. If this finding is accurate, it represents an indictment against the social work education community that delivers a mandate to university officials to initiate curriculum review to ensure Council on Social Work Education guidelines are being met.

As professional social workers, we are bound ethically to uphold social justice (NASW *Code of Ethics*, 1996). Therefore, the authors propose that the first imperative for social work professionals is to consider their role in ensuring social justice on the micro level, taking action as needed. The second imperative is to take on the challenge of educating and enlightening other service professionals to bring about social change on the macro level. The Heritage House program suggests that program development can encompass and address social justice issues when focused on long-term systemic change and can do so with successful outcomes.

CONCLUSION

Complex issues such as high-conflict divorce demand that social services and the law join hands around the table to embrace families for the good of society at large. If *the best interest of children* is to be served, communication barriers between social services and the law must be broken down, implementation of parenting plans must become commonplace, and program evaluation must be standard practice to ensure efficacy of program services. Perhaps then the balance between children's needs and those of their parents will be restored.

REFERENCES

Ahrons, C. (1994). *The good divorce.* New York: Harper-Collins.

Brill, C. K. (1989). The Impact of Social Work Practice on the Social Injustice Content in the NASW *Code of Ethics.* Doctoral Dissertation. Brandeis University.

Buel, S. (1994). The Dynamics of Family Violence. National Council of Juvenile and Family Court Judges, Conference Highlights. Courts and Communities: Confronting Violence in the Family. San Francisco, CA.

Cahn, N. & Meier, J. (1995). Domestic violence and feminist jurisprudence: Toward a new agency. *The Boston University Public Interest Journal, 4*(2), 339-361.

City of St. Louis Annual Report to the Community. (1996). St. Louis, Missouri.

Daley, B. & Rowdy, Z. R. (October 20, 1998). T-stop attack hurts 4: Rush-hour crowd views bloody melee. *Boston Globe,* p. B1.

Dalton, C. (1999). When paradigms collide: Protecting battered parents and their children in the family court system. *Family and Conciliation Courts Review, 37*(3), 273-296.

Dunn, J. (2000). Heritage House Stakeholder Survey. Unpublished data.

Field, J. K. (1998). Visits in cases marked by violence: Judicial actions that can help keep children and victims safe. *Court Review,* Fall, 23-31.

Flory, B. E. (1998). Heritage House: A Step Beyond the Best Interest of the Child. Paper presented at the 12th National Conference on Child Abuse and Neglect, Cincinnati, Ohio.

Flory, B. E. (2000). The Future of Supervised Visitation. Paper Presented at the 3rd Annual Interdisciplinary Conference: Domestic Violence & Children, Kansas City, MO.

Flory, B. E., Dunn, J., Berg-Weger, M., & Milstead, M. (2001) An exploratory study of supervised access and custody exchange services: The parental experience. *Family and Conciliation Court Review, 39*(4), 469-482.

Franz, J. (1997). The sixth paradigm: Finding a common language to link our divergent human services perspectives. *www//calliope@paperboat.com/calliope/paradigm. html.*

Frawley, T. J. (1999). Administrative Judge, Twenty-second Judicial Circuit of Missouri, St. Louis City Family Court. Personal communication.

Garrity, C. B. & Baris, M.A. (1994). *Caught in the middle: Protecting the children of high-conflict divorce.* San Francisco: Jossey-Bass Publishers.

Johnston, J. R. (1994). High-conflict divorce. *The Future of Children: Children and Divorce.* Center for the Future of Children, David and Lucille Packard Foundation, *4*(1), 165-182.

Kelly, J. (1997). The Determination of Child Custody in the USA. *www.wwlia.org/us-cus.htm.*

Maccoby, E. E. & Mnooken, R. H. (1992). *Dividing the child: Social and legal dilemmas of custody.* Cambridge, Massachusetts: Harvard University Press.

Man kills 2, then himself, after child visitation hearing. (2001, March 10) *St. Louis Post Dispatch,* p. NATION/WORLD 23.

Mandel, D. & Went, J. (2000). Using batterer accountability strategies to increase safety for children. Unpublished manuscript.

Mason, M. A. (1994). *From father's property to children's rights: The history of child custody in the United States.* New York: Columbia University Press.

Mason, M. A. (1999). *The custody wars: Why children are losing the legal battle and what we can do about it.* New York: Basic Books.

Miller, K. (1998). Personal communication.

Missouri Coalition Against Domestic Violence (MCADV). (1998). *Services statistics.*

National Association of Social Workers. (1996). *Code of Ethics.* Washington, D.C.: NASW Press.

Pearson, J. & Anhalt, J. (1993). When parents complain about visitation. *Mediation Quarterly, 11*(2), 139-156.

Pfeffer, J. G. (1999). A narrative-collaborative approach to custody evaluation. *Journal of Systemic Therapies, 18*(4), 1-17.

Rotman, A. (2000). President's Letter. *Association of Family and Conciliation Courts Newsletter, 19*(4), 2.

Stone, A. E. & Fialk, R. J. (1997). Recent development: Criminalizing the exposure of children to family violence: Breaking the cycle of abuse. *Harvard Women's Law Journal, 20. http://web.lexis-nexis.com/universe/document.*

Uniform Marriage and Divorce Code. (1970). § 402.

Wallerstein, J. S. & Kelly, J. B. (1980). *Surviving the breakup: How children and parents cope with divorce.* New York: Basic Books.

Wallerstein, J. S., Lewis, J. M., & Blakeslee, S. (2000). *The unexpected legacy of divorce: A 25 year landmark study.* New York: Hyperion.

Weitzman, S. (2000). *Not to people like us: Hidden abuse in upscale marriages.* New York: Basic Books.

Practicing Social Justice with Persons with Developmental Disabilities Who Enter the Criminal Justice System

Donald M. Linhorst
Leslie Bennett
Tami McCutchen

SUMMARY. Persons with developmental disabilities who enter the criminal justice system face injustices throughout the process. For example, their disability often goes undetected, they are more likely to incriminate themselves because they do not understand their Miranda rights, they are more likely to be imprisoned rather than receive probation, and they typically serve longer prison sentences. Based upon a review of the literature and the experiences of one program, this article provides strategies for practicing social justice with this population, which require intervention at the individual, organizational, and social policy levels. *[Article copies available for a fee from The Haworth Document Delivery Service: 1-800-HAWORTH. E-mail address: <docdelivery@haworthpress.com> Website: <http://www.HaworthPress.com> © 2003 by The Haworth Press, Inc. All rights reserved.]*

Donald M. Linhorst, PhD, is Assistant Professor in the School of Social Service, Saint Louis University.

Leslie Bennett, MSW, and Tami McCutchen, MSW, were students in the School at the time of the study.

Address correspondence to: Donald M. Linhorst, Saint Louis University, School of Social Service, 3550 Lindell Blvd., St. Louis, MO 63103 (E-mail: linhorsd@slu.edu).

The authors wish to thank the Emmett J. and Mary Martha Doerr Center for Social Justice Education and Research in the School of Social Service at Saint Louis University for their support of this research.

[Haworth co-indexing entry note]: "Practicing Social Justice with Persons with Developmental Disabilities Who Enter the Criminal Justice System." Linhorst, Donald M., Leslie Bennett, and Tami McCutchen. Co-published simultaneously in *Social Thought* (The Haworth Press, Inc.) Vol. 22, No. 2/3, 2003, pp. 221-235; and: *Practicing Social Justice* (ed: John J. Stretch et al.) The Haworth Press, Inc. 2003, pp. 221-235. Single or multiple copies of this article are available for a fee from The Haworth Document Delivery Service [1-800-HAWORTH, 9:00 a.m. - 5:00 p.m. (EST). E-mail address: docdelivery@haworthpress.com].

© 2003 by The Haworth Press, Inc. All rights reserved.
http://www.haworthpress.com/store/product.asp?sku=J131
10.1300/J131v22n02_15

KEYWORDS. Social justice, developmental disabilities, mental retardation, criminal justice

Persons with developmental disabilities are at risk of encountering social injustices at each stage of the criminal justice process. In response, a small number of communities have developed special programs for this population. One such program is Options For Justice, Inc. (OFJ), a private nonprofit organization serving residents of St. Louis City and St. Louis County, Missouri. OFJ provides training to criminal justice and social service personnel, and advocacy and case management services to offenders with developmental disabilities during the pretrial and post-disposition phases of the criminal justice process. Created in 1990, OFJ has trained over 1,500 personnel from the criminal justice system and provided direct services to over 600 clients. In 1998, the Center for Social Justice Education and Research at Saint Louis University funded an evaluation of OFJ. Two publications already have emerged from that study, one detailing the development and implementation of OFJ to guide other communities that wish to start similar programs (Linhorst, Bennett, & McCutchen, in press), and a second providing the results of an evaluation of rearrests among OFJ clients who participated in the case management program (Linhorst, McCutchen, & Bennett, 2001).

The purpose of this article is to raise awareness of the social injustices faced by offenders with developmental disabilities and to provide strategies to challenge these injustices. To accomplish this, we draw upon the professional literature and the experiences of OFJ. We first identify the social injustices faced by offenders with developmental disabilities. Then we discuss five practice interventions to promote social justice for this population including training of criminal justice and social service personnel, advocating for offenders during the pretrial phase, creating jail and prison-based programs for those who are incarcerated, establishing programs for offenders in the post-disposition phase who reside in the community, and advocating for social policies that promote justice for offenders with developmental disabilities. To provide a context for this discussion, we begin by defining developmental disabilities and describing the characteristics of this offender population.

AN OVERVIEW OF OFFENDERS
WITH DEVELOPMENTAL DISABILITIES

The two most common developmental disabilities of offenders are mental retardation and learning disabilities. Mental retardation is generally defined as a significant limitation in general intellectual functioning with concurrent limitations in adaptive functioning, with onset occurring before the age of 22 years (Jacobson & Mulick, 1996). Persons with learning disabilities typically have average or above average intelligence, but they have significant academic and perceptual language deficits and no other primary handicapping condition (Grande, 1991). Offenders with mental retardation have been the primary focus of most programs and research, although some programs, including OFJ, serve offenders with all types of developmental disabilities. At OFJ, the primary disability was mental retardation for 66% of clients, a learning disability for 30% of clients, and other developmental disabilities for the remaining 4%. The learning disabilities of OFJ clients are those that have resulted in significant functional problems.

Noble and Conley (1992) reviewed the literature and found that offenders with developmental disabilities were mostly males, tended to be relatively young, and a substantial percentage was nonwhite. At OFJ, 92% of clients were males, mean age was 26.7 years (median = 25, range = 16-59), and 80% were Black. Noble and Conley also reported that the vast majority of crimes committed by persons with developmental disabilities were misdemeanors and less serious felonies. This is consistent with the OFJ population, of which 34% had committed misdemeanors, 40% nonviolent felonies, and 26% felonies against persons. Noble and Conley also found that the number of jail and prison inmates with mental retardation ranged from 2% to 10%. Based upon a 1995 census of 1.1 million inmates in state and federal prisons (Bureau of Justice Statistics, 1997), an estimate of the number of inmates with mental retardation would then range from 22,000 to 110,000 inmates. Applying the same range of 2% to 10% to the St. Louis area, between 800 and 4,000 inmates in the St. Louis City and St. Louis County jails would be expected to have mental retardation. Estimates at the national and local levels would be considerably higher if learning disabilities were included.

SOCIAL INJUSTICES FACED BY OFFENDERS WITH DEVELOPMENTAL DISABILITIES

A number of authors have presented the injustices experienced by offenders with developmental disabilities, particularly those with mental retardation (Biklen, 1997; Bonnie, 1990; Denkowski & Denkowski, 1985; Ellis & Luckasson, 1985; Gardner, Graeber, & Machkovitz, 1998; McAfee & Gural, 1988; Perske, 1990; Petersilia, 1997; Santamour, 1986). These injustices can assume three forms. The first is the increased likelihood of a person with mental retardation being convicted of a crime that he or she did not commit. Persons with mental retardation are more likely to confess to a crime they did not commit because of perceived intimidation by the actual offenders, by police, or by prosecuting attorneys, or because of wanting to please the interrogator. This possibility is increased because mental retardation often goes undetected throughout the criminal justice process. Haggerty, Kane, and Udall (1972, p. 66) summarize the impact of this when it occurs, for example, at the pretrial phase: "Simply put (in almost all cases), a mentally retarded suspect who has been charged with a crime cannot understand the charge, cannot tell his side of the story, and cannot help his lawyer defend him. If no one realizes he is retarded, this gravely hinders his chances for a fair trial."

The second form of injustice is associated with defendants during the pretrial phase of the criminal justice process. Although persons with mental retardation are no more likely to commit criminal acts than the general population, they are more likely to be arrested because they are less able to hide their crimes and avoid detection. They are more likely to incriminate themselves because of a lack of understanding of their Miranda rights. Also, many defendants with mental retardation are never referred for pretrial evaluations unless they present behaviors that are perceived to be bizarre. This lack of referral increases the chances that some defendants who were actually incompetent to stand trial were instead convicted. Defendants with mental retardation are more likely to be jailed rather than receive bail during the pretrial phase because they often cannot afford bail, or they are perceived to pose too high of a risk as a result of their lower intelligence and their often being unemployed or not having a stable residence. Finally, they are less likely to receive plea bargains, which results in longer sentences.

The third form of injustice occurs during the post-disposition phase. Once convicted, offenders with mental retardation are more likely to be incarcerated and less likely to receive probation for the same perceived reasons cited above for not receiving bail. Once imprisoned, offenders with mental retardation typically fare poorly in jails and prisons. They are more likely to be victims of assault, to be sexually exploited, and to be incited into rule violations by other inmates. In addition, they have more difficulty adjusting to routines, which also can lead to rule violations. Next, few participate in habilitation programs in prisons because of the lack of programs appropriate to their condition. Even if prison programs are available, some people choose not to participate in order to prevent being identified to other inmates as having mental retardation. Finally, persons with mental retardation tend to have longer prison terms because of the commission of rule violations and perceptions of being poor risks for parole.

THE PRACTICE OF SOCIAL JUSTICE

To overcome these injustices, the practice of social justice with offenders with developmental disabilities requires a comprehensive strategy that includes multiple methods directed to persons within the criminal justice and social service systems and to persons with developmental disabilities who enter the criminal justice system. Five are described below.

Train Criminal Justice and Social Service Personnel

Most personnel within the criminal justice system have limited, if any, knowledge of developmental disabilities and their potential impact on the ability of persons to maneuver through the criminal justice system. One judge summarized the need for training from the judicial perspective: "Judges, by and large, don't know much about mental retardation. . . . The judiciary has a need for more information, more knowledge, and more understanding. We need more lawyers who understand the difficulties and can present rich, meaningful, and detailed evidence" (Exum, Turnbull, Martin, & Finn, 1992, pp. 1, 4). Among criminal justice personnel, training should be directed to police officers, public defenders and other defense attorneys, prosecuting attorneys, judges, jail and prison personnel, and probation and parole officers.

A number of training programs have been developed to address the training needs of criminal justice personnel (e.g., The Arc, 2001a; Kennedy, Goodman, Day, & Griffin, 1982; Messinger & Davidson, 1992; Montgomery, 1982; Santamour, 1989). The National Association for Retarded Citizens (The Arc, 2001a) has developed extensive training materials about offenders with developmental disabilities as part of its "Access to Justice Initiative." These include separate training aids specifically for police officers, for attorneys, judges, and other court personnel, and for persons with developmental disabilities. In addition, to promote the sharing of training materials, the Arc has assembled a listing of programs across the country that are involved in training and other activities that benefit offenders with developmental disabilities.

The OFJ Executive Director provides training to police officers at two time points. He trains police recruits at the St. Louis City and St. Louis County police academies and police officers in both jurisdictions as part of their required continuing education. Although not done on an ongoing basis, the OFJ Executive Director also has provided training to jail personnel, attorneys, judges, and probation and parole officers. While the training content varies by the participants' role in the criminal justice system, it typically includes a description of various developmental disabilities, how to identify persons with such disabilities, how to communicate with them, limitations to participation in the criminal justice process as a result of the disability, and facts to overcome misconceptions that could impact the placement of defendants on bond, probation, or parole. These content areas are similar to those found in the previously referenced training materials.

Members of the social service community who work with persons with developmental disabilities also can benefit from training. Typically, such training educates social service professionals about the criminal justice process, the problems defendants with developmental disabilities may encounter throughout this process, and how they may assist their clients in working through the process. For some professionals, training can address the pretrial evaluation of offenders with developmental disabilities and the provision of court testimony. The American Association on Mental Retardation, the oldest and largest interdisciplinary organization of professionals that works with persons with mental retardation, has provided leadership in the education of professionals about the needs of offenders with mental retardation (DeMoll, 1992). At the local level, the OFJ Executive Director has provided training in the above content areas to staff in both public and private social service agencies.

Advocate for Clients During the Pretrial Phase

The presence of mental retardation and other developmental disabilities can make it exceedingly difficult to navigate through each step of the pretrial phase of the criminal justice process. An uninformed decision or action at any point in the pretrial phase can have a lasting consequence (e.g., confessing without understanding the Miranda rights, agreeing to a plea bargain without really understanding the consequence of the decision). The essential first step in providing advocacy services during the pretrial process is to identify persons with developmental disabilities as they enter the criminal justice system. As previously indicated, developmental disabilities often go undetected when persons are arrested and proceed through the system. The provision of training to criminal justice personnel facilitates their identification. Other means also can identify offenders with developmental disabilities. For example, one advocacy program was successful in adding the following questions to the standardized interview that occurred during the jail booking process: "Have you ever been in special classes in school? Have you ever been told you are retarded? Have you ever been in a workshop? Have you ever been in a state hospital?" (Beilin, 1982, p. 467). OFJ, too, was able to add questions to the St. Louis County booking process, including "Have you ever been in special education?" and "Do you receive SSI or a monthly check?" Such questions should reflect current practice within a community and be sensitive to persons with developmental disabilities. It would not be prudent in most instances, for example, to use questions about state hospitals since most persons with developmental disabilities are no longer institutionalized, or to use terms such as "retarded" that may alienate the person.

Once offenders with developmental disabilities have been identified, at least three types of advocacy services are needed to assist them through the pretrial process. One is to advocate for a pretrial evaluation if there is any question as to the defendant's competency to stand trial or criminal responsibility at the time of the offense (Bonnie, 1990). A second is to facilitate effective communication between attorneys and defendants to ensure they can meaningfully participate in their own defense. A third is to assess clients' eligibility for social services, assist clients in obtaining services, and serve as a case manager. Among other things, this may increase the willingness of courts to grant bail or probation if they know that defendants are going to be receiving services.

Various models exist for the provision of pretrial services to offenders with developmental disabilities (The Arc, 2001a). In one community, the seven developmental disability regional centers that received funds from the state mental health department created the position of law enforcement liaison officer, and supplemented that position with psychological and medical services on an as-needed basis (Beilin, 1982). That liaison officer, whose office was located in the jail, assessed defendants believed to have had a developmental disability, served as a liaison between the jail and regional center programs, and trained law enforcement personnel. Another community created an advocacy program that included a manager, a psychologist, a rehabilitation specialist, one advocate for each of the four courts, an attorney, and a paralegal (Moschella, 1986). In addition, selected state chapters of the National Association of Protection and Advocacy Services have identified defendants with mental retardation as a priority population (DeMoll, 1992). Protection and Advocacy Services are federally funded organizations that exist in each state that are mandated to protect the rights of persons with disabilities, including mental retardation and other developmental disabilities.

OFJ has four case coordinators who provide direct service to clients at both the pretrial and post-disposition phases of the criminal justice process. During the pretrial stage, OFJ case coordinators typically educate clients about the pretrial process, and when appropriate provide information to family or close friends. Case coordinators do not give legal advice; they seek to ensure that clients understand the legal process, their dispositional options, and the ramifications of each option. They also may educate the court about the client's disability and sentencing alternatives, and initiated collaboration among community providers.

Provide Prison-Based Services

As previously stated, many offenders with developmental disabilities adjust poorly to prison life. They may commit rule violations because they do not understand the expected routine, which can lead to a loss of privileges and extend the length of incarceration. In addition, they are more likely to be victims of assault and sexual exploitation than the general inmate population. To contend with this, a limited number of states have reported the development of specialized programs within their prisons for inmates with developmental disabilities, particularly mental retardation (Conine & Maclachlan, 1982; Grande, 1991; Hall, 1985, 1992; Pugh, 1986). These programs typically have the dual goals of assisting the inmate to adjust to prison life and facilitating community inclusion upon the inmate's release. To achieve these goals, prison-based programs usually contain multiple components. For example, one program had a three-week assessment period when inmates entered the program, and then offered academic training, life skills training, recreational training, vocational training, and medical and social services including counseling and case management to meet the inmate's individual needs (Conine & Maclachlan, 1982). Another program offered habilitation, social support, security, and continuity of care to assist with the transition to community life (Pugh, 1986). OFJ does not provide advocacy services within prisons during the post-disposition phase of the criminal justice process, although they develop service plans with those inmates who will participate in the OFJ case management program when released.

Provide Community-Based Services

Offenders with developmental disabilities who have been sentenced and are residing in the community on probation and parole are at a high risk of reoffending (Day, 1993). As such, programs that work with these clients typically have one or more of the following goals: to promote community inclusion, to reduce recidivism, and to successfully complete probation or parole (Gardner & Krauss, 1982; Lustig, 1998; Morton, Hughes, & Evans, 1986; Schnapp, Nguyen, & Johnson, 1996; Wood & White, 1992). Programs usually offer case management services to assist with achieving these goals. These services can be operated by probation/parole departments as special programs (e.g., DeSilva, 1980) or as freestanding private nonprofit agencies (e.g., Wood &

White, 1992). Regardless of the program type, case managers and their clients usually complete treatment plans, often referred to as individual justice plans, to guide the attainment of client and program goals. Areas commonly addressed in these plans include living arrangements, vocational or educational needs, leisure and recreation activities, family relationships, medical or psychological treatment, transportation, and finances.

OFJ shares the goals of promoting community inclusion and reducing recidivism. During the post-disposition phase of service delivery, the OFJ case coordinator typically assesses the client's needs, makes referrals to community services, educates the social service agencies about the client's legal status and how they could support the client, assists the client in meeting community appointments, initiates a collaboration among community providers involved with the client, and provides other services as needed. OFJ staff give priority to assisting clients to meet their conditions of probation or parole as determined by the judge during sentencing.

Advocate for Just Social Policies

Another means to address injustices faced by offenders with developmental disabilities is to seek change at the social policy level. The first step in this process is to get on the legislative agenda. Unfortunately, little attention has been paid to the plight of offenders with developmental disabilities. Petersilia (1997, p. 368) describes this: "The MR [mentally retarded] offender has never attracted the attention that other specialized populations have or that their numbers alone should warrant. For example, we spend inordinate amounts of time and energy debating programs and policies for elderly inmates, child molesters, spouse assaulters, and offenders with AIDS." Thus, first steps in the advocacy process are to create awareness among legislators and the general public about the injustices faced by offenders with developmental disabilities and to forge relationships with key members of the executive and legislative branches of government.

Complicating the agenda setting process is that under the United States' system of federalism, social policies affecting offenders with developmental disabilities are made at the federal, state, and local levels of government. This federal system has both disadvantages and advantages for promoting social justice (Linhorst, in press). Comprehensive change necessitates work at all three levels of government, which requires large amounts of time and financial resources. However, the federal system does allow progress to be made at the local level more rapidly and with fewer resources then at the federal or state levels. For example, while it may not be possible in the foreseeable future to obtain federal legislation requiring and funding the development of special community-based programs for all offenders with developmental disabilities, it is possible to work with local or state officials to create such programs in communities within a particular region of the state, such as was done in creating OFJ (Linhorst, Bennett, & McCutchen, in press).

Seven areas for social policy advocacy are suggested. The first is to assign responsibility for offenders with developmental disabilities. Considerable evidence exists that neither the developmental disability system nor the criminal justice system wants to work with this population, which intersects both policy areas (DeMoll, 1992; DeSilva, 1980; Forget, 1980; Rockowitz, 1986; Schapp, Nguyen, & Johnson, 1996). Schapp, Nguyen, and Johnson (1996) provide an example of a state effort to ensure that offenders with developmental disabilities were properly served by both systems. A state council was created in Texas that was comprised of 19 members from the developmental disability and criminal justice systems that had as its goal the promotion of "close, effective coordination and collaboration" between both systems (p. 362). McGee and Menolascino (1992) believe that such cooperation also is needed at the local level.

Second, a large gap exists in research and evaluation related to offenders with developmental disabilities (McGee & Menolascino, 1992; Moschella, 1986; Noble & Conley, 1992). The Arc (2001c), for example, is lobbying the federal government, and particularly the Department of Justice, to guide and fund systematic research in this area, including the development of models of best practice for working with offenders with developmental disabilities. Research is needed that describes their involvement in each stage of the criminal justice process, identifies the risk factors for persons with developmental disabilities committing crimes, and evaluates the effectiveness of programs that work with this population (Conley, Luckasson, & Bouthilet, 1992).

Third, social policy is needed to ensure comprehensive training of all personnel in the criminal justice system (The Arc, 2001b, 2001c; Biklen, 1977; Conley, Luckasson, & Bouthilet, 1992). Once again, The Arc (2001b, 2001c) is advocating for the Department of Justice to take a leadership role in promoting such training to ensure fair treatment of offenders with developmental disabilities. Currently, wide variation exists in the amount and quality of training provided to criminal justice personnel. In addition, as previously discussed, training is needed by professionals who work in the developmental disability field to assist their clients to maneuver through the criminal justice system, should they be arrested.

Fourth, social policy could promote defendants' access to legal services that incorporate the impact of the disability on the legal proceedings. This includes access to knowledgeable defense attorneys, particularly public defenders, special advocates, and professionals to provide pretrial evaluations and expect testimony (The Arc, 2001b; Biklen, 1977; Conley, Luckasson, &

Bouthilet, 1992). Without this special expertise, defendants with developmental disabilities are unlikely to receive just treatment during the pretrial phase.

Fifth, several policy changes could facilitate justice during sentencing. Of foremost importance is requiring that courts take the presence of the developmental disability into consideration during sentencing (The Arc, 2001b; Conley, Luckasson, & Bouthilet, 1992; Laski, 1992). Sentencing should focus on habilitative goals, as well as public safety goals, and defendants with developmental disabilities should not be incarcerated in jails or prisons that do not have habilitation programs appropriate to their needs (Conley, Luckasson, & Bouthilet, 1992). In addition, courts should have the option to use intermediate sanctions to avoid imprisonment whenever possible. Intermediate sanctions are community-based programs that provide greater supervision than regular probation, which have been used successfully with other criminal justice populations (Laski, 1992; Petersilia, 1997). Federal sentencing guidelines would have to be modified in order to incorporate some of these changes (Conley, Luckasson, & Bouthilet, 1992). Finally, mental health courts are emerging as another alternative for working with developmentally disabled offenders. These courts have specially trained judges and other court personnel who typically work with defendants with mental illness or developmental disabilities who have been arrested for nonviolent crimes, usually misdemeanors (Baker, 1998; Watson et al., 2000). It seeks to balance public safety with the needs of defendants and, when possible, to divert defendants to treatment or habilitation programs.

Sixth, following sentencing, programs are needed in prisons and in the community to work with offenders with developmental disabilities. Funding is perhaps the greatest obstacle to the creation of such programs (Morton, Hughes, & Evans, 1986). It is unlikely that programs will be funded on a large scale nationwide until awareness of the problem is increased, until the role of each level of government is set, and until responsibility for this population is assigned to the criminal justice system, the developmental disability system, or a combination of the two.

A final social policy issue is whether offenders with mental retardation should be subject to the death penalty. The Arc (2001b) and many others (e.g., Conley, Luckasson, & Bouthilet, 1992) oppose the execution of such offenders. The Arc argues against the death penalty because of the injustices that can occur throughout the criminal justice process as a result of the presence of mental retardation. Currently, 12 states do not have the death penalty, and an additional 16 states and the federal government that have the death penalty have banned the execution of offenders with mental retardation. Twenty-two states still allow offenders with mental retardation to be executed. Advocates continue to lobby in those states that allow executions, with mixed success.

Lobbying efforts were successful in Missouri and Florida, as those states recently banned such executions, while the Governor of Texas vetoed a bill in June 2001 that would have banned executions of persons with mental retardation in that state (Ganey, 2001).

CONCLUSION

The practice of social justice with persons with mental retardation and other developmental disabilities who enter the criminal justice system requires intervention at multiple levels. First, the practice of social justice should include one-on-one work with offenders with developmental disabilities to ensure that their rights are protected during the pretrial process, that they receive habilitation if imprisoned, and that they receive those community-based support and social services needed to reduce the risk of reentering the system. Second, the practice of social justice should be targeted at the organizational level, including the training of criminal justice personnel, the provision of advocates to work with offenders with developmental disabilities, and the development of habilitation programs in prisons and communities that can address the special needs of this population. Third, the practice of social justice requires advocating for social policies that assign responsibility for this population, that support research and evaluation activities that can improve services, that require comprehensive training of criminal justice personnel, and that require and fund prison- and community-based programs for this population. Thus, the practice of social justice for offenders with developmental disabilities requires the concerted efforts of direct service staff, administrators in the criminal justice and social services systems, and social policy advocates.

REFERENCES

The Arc (The National Association for Retarded Citizens). (2001a, August 8). The Arc's Access to Justice Initiative [On-line]. Available: http://www.thearc.org/ada/crim.html

The Arc (The National Association for Retarded Citizens). (2001b, August 8). Position Statement: Access to Justice and Fair Treatment Under the Criminal Law [On-line]. Available: http://www.thearc.org/posits/justice.html

The Arc (The National Association for Retarded Citizens). (2001c, March 5). 2000 Legislative Goals [On-line]. Available: http://www.thearc.org/ga/2000goals.html

Baker, D. (1998). Special treatment: A one-of-a-kind court may offer the best hope for steering nonviolent mentally ill defendants into care instead of jail. *ABA Journal, 84*, 20-22.

Beilin, B. (1982). The mentally retarded offender in an urban jail setting: From identification to advocacy and legal intervention. In M. B. Santamour & P. S. Watson (Eds.), *The retarded offender* (pp. 464-476). New York: Praeger.

Biklen, D. (1977). Myths, mistreatment, and pitfalls: Mental retardation and criminal justice. *Mental Retardation, 15,* 51-57.

Bonnie, R. J. (1990). The competence of criminal defendants with mental retardation to participate in their own defense. *The Journal of Criminal Law and Criminology, 81,* 419-446.

Bureau of Justice Statistics. (1997, May). *Correctional populations in the United States, 1995* (Publication No. NCJ-163916). Washington, DC: U.S. Department of Justice, Office of Justice Programs, Bureau of Justice Statistics.

Conine, A. D., & Maclachlan, M. B. (1982). The special learning unit for developmentally disabled offenders. In M. B. Santamour & P. S. Watson (Eds.), *The retarded offender* (pp. 450-463). New York: Praeger.

Conley, R. W., Luckasson, R., & Bouthilet, G. N. (1992). Introduction. In R. W. Conley, R. Luckasson, & G. N. Bouthilet (Eds.), *The criminal justice system and mental retardation: Defendants and victims* (pp. xix-xxvi). Baltimore: Paul H. Brookes.

Day, K. (1993). Crime and mental retardation: A review. In K. Howells & C. R. Hollin (Eds.), *Clinical approaches to the mentally disordered offender* (pp. 111-144). New York: John Wiley and Sons.

DeMoll, C. (1992). Advocacy service systems for defendants with mental retardation. In R. W. Conley, R. Luckasson, & G. N. Bouthilet (Eds.), *The criminal justice system and mental retardation: Defendants and victims* (pp. 191-207). Baltimore: Paul H. Brookes.

Denkowski, G. C., & Denkowski, K. M. (1985). The mentally retarded offender in the state prison system: Identification, prevalence, adjustment, and rehabilitation. *Criminal Justice and Behavior, 12,* 55-70.

DeSilva, B. (1980). The retarded offender: A problem without a program. *Corrections Magazine, 6,* 24-33.

Ellis, J. W., & Luckasson, R. A. (1985). Mentally retarded criminal defendants. *The George Washington Law Review, 53,* 414-493.

Exum, J. G., Turnbull, H. R., Martin, R., & Finn, J. W. (1992). Points of view: Perspectives on the judicial, mental retardation services, law enforcement, and corrections systems. In R. W. Conley, R. Luckasson, & G. N. Bouthilet (Eds.), *The criminal justice system and mental retardation: Defendants and victims* (pp. 1-16). Baltimore: Paul H. Brookes.

Forget, C. A. (1980). The mentally retarded person in the criminal justice system. *Journal of Offender Counseling, Services and Rehabilitation, 4,* 285-295.

Ganey, T. (2001, July 3). Holden bars death penalty for mentally retarded; Texas governor rejected a similar ban in that state. *St. Louis Post-Dispatch,* p. B4.

Gardner, J., & Krauss, M. W. (1982). The Shriver-MassCAPP Project: A residential community program for mentally retarded adult parolees. In M. B. Santamour & P. S. Watson (Eds.), *The retarded offender* (pp. 358-370). New York: Praeger.

Gardner, W. I., Graeber, J. L., & Machkovitz, S. J. (1998). Treatment of offenders with mental retardation. In R. W. Wettstein (Ed.), *Treatment of offenders with mental disorders* (pp. 329-364). New York: Guilford Press.

Grande, C. G. (1991). Corrections and the learning disabled offender. In R. S. Greene (Ed.), *Mainstreaming retardation delinquency* (pp. 43-62). Lancaster, PA: Technomic.

Haggerty, D. E., Kane, L. A., Jr., & Udall, D. K. (1972). An essay on the legal rights of the mentally retarded. *Family Law Quarterly, 6,* 59-71.

Hall, J. N. (1985). Identifying and serving mentally retarded inmates. *Journal of Prison and Jail Health, 5,* 29-38.

Hall, J. N. (1992). Correctional services for inmates with mental retardation: Challenge or catastrophe? In R. W. Conley, R. Luckasson, & G. N. Bouthilet (Eds.), *The criminal justice system and mental retardation: Defendants and victims* (pp. 167-190). Baltimore: Paul H. Brookes.

Jacobson, J. W., & Mulick, J. A. (1996). Definition of mental retardation. In J. W. Jacobson & J. A. Mulick (Eds.), *Manual of diagnosis and professional practice in mental retardation* (pp. 13-53). Washington, DC: American Psychological Association.

Kennedy, M., Goodman, M., Day, E., & Griffin, B. W. (1982). *Mentally retarded offenders: A handbook for criminal justice personnel.* Cuyahoga County, Ohio.

Laski, F. J. (1992). Sentencing the offender with mental retardation: Honoring the imperative for intermediate punishments and probation. In R. W. Conley, R. Luckasson, & G. N. Bouthilet (Eds.), *The criminal justice system and mental retardation: Defendants and victims* (pp. 137-152). Baltimore: Paul H. Brookes.

Linhorst, D. M. (in press). Federalism and social justice: Implications for social work. *Social Work.*

Linhorst, D. M., Bennett, L., & McCutchen, T. (in press). The development and implementation of a program for offenders with developmental disabilities. *Mental Retardation.*

Linhorst, D. M., McCutchen, T., & Bennett, L. (2001). Recidivism among offenders with developmental disabilities participating in a case management program. Manuscript submitted for publication.

Lustig, S. (1998, August). The hidden population in the criminal system: Providing successful advocacy services to defendants with mental retardation. Presentation to the President's Committee on Mental Retardation for the Next Generation Leadership Symposium, Criminal Justice Issues, Washington, DC.

McAfee, J. K., & Gural, M. (1988). Individuals with mental retardation and the criminal justice system: The view from States' Attorneys General. *Mental Retardation, 26,* 5-12.

McGee, J. J., & Menolascino, F. J. (1992). The evaluation of defendants with mental retardation in the criminal justice system. In R. W. Conley, R. Luckasson, & G. N. Bouthilet (Eds.), *The criminal justice system and mental retardation: Defendants and victims* (pp. 55-77). Baltimore: Paul H. Brookes.

Messinger, R., & Davidson, P. W. (1992). Training programs and defendants with mental retardation: History and future directions. In R. W. Conley, R. Luckasson, & G. N. Bouthilet, *The criminal justice system and mental retardation: Defendants and victims* (pp. 221-235). Baltimore: Paul H. Brookes.

Montgomery, R. H., Jr. (1982). Curriculum for use in training criminal justice personnel. In M. B. Santamour & P. S. Watson (Eds.), *The retarded offender* (pp. 260-271). New York: Praeger.

Morton, J., Hughes, D., & Evans, E. (1986). Individualizing justice for offenders with developmental disabilities: A descriptive account of Nebraska's IJP model. *The Prison Journal, 66,* 52-66.

Moschella, A. L. (1986). In search of the mentally retarded offender: The Massachusetts Bar Association's Specialized Training and Advocacy Program (1974-1978). *The Prison Journal, 66,* 67-76.

Noble, J. H., Jr., & Conley, R. W. (1992). Toward an epidemiology of relevant attributes. In R. W. Conley, R. Luckasson, & G. N. Bouthilet (Eds.), *The criminal justice system and mental retardation: Defendants and victims* (pp. 17-53). Baltimore: Paul H. Brookes.

Perske, R. (1990). *Unequal justice? What can happen when persons with retardation or other developmental disabilities encounter the criminal justice system.* Nashville: Abingdon.

Petersilia, J. (1997). Justice for all? Offenders with mental retardation and the California corrections system. *The Prison Journal, 77,* 358-380.

Pugh, M. (1986). The mentally retarded offenders program of the Texas Department of Corrections. *The Prison Journal, 66,* 39-51.

Rockowitz, R. J. (1986). Developmentally disabled offenders: Issues in developing and maintaining services. *The Prison Journal, 66,* 19-23.

Santamour, M. B. (1986). The offender with mental retardation. *The Prison Journal, 66,* 3-18.

Santamour, M. B. (1989). *The mentally retarded offender and corrections: An updated prescriptive package.* Laurel, MD: American Correctional Association.

Schnapp, W. B., Nguyen, T., & Johnson, J. (1996). Services for offenders with mental impairments: A Texas model. *Administration and Policy in Mental Health, 23,* 361-365.

Watson, A., Luchins, D., Harahan, P., Heyrman, M. J., & Lurigio, A. (2001). Mental health court: Promises and limitation. *The Journal of the American Academy of Psychiatry and the Law, 28,* 476-482.

Wood, H. R., & White, D. L. (1992). A model for habilitation and prevention for offenders with mental retardation; the Lancaster County (PA) Office of Special Offenders Services. In R. W. Conley, R. Luckasson, & G. N. Bouthilet (Eds.), *The criminal justice system and mental retardation: Defendants and victims* (pp. 153-165). Baltimore: Paul H. Brookes.

Index

© 2003 by The Haworth Press, Inc. All rights reserved.

SPECIAL 25%-OFF DISCOUNT!

Order a copy of this book with this form or online at:
http://www.haworthpress.com/store/product.asp?sku=4930
Use Sale Code BOF25 in the online bookshop to receive 25% off!

Practicing Social Justice

_____ in softbound at $22.46 (regularly $29.95) (ISBN: 0-7890-2107-2)
_____ in hardbound at $37.46 (regularly $49.95) (ISBN: 0-7890-2106-4)

COST OF BOOKS _____	❏ **BILL ME LATER:** ($5 service charge will be added)
Outside USA/ Canada/	(Bill-me option is good on US/Canada/
Mexico: Add 20% _____	Mexico orders only; not good to jobbers,
POSTAGE & HANDLING _____	wholesalers, or subscription agencies.)
(US: $4.00 for first book & $1.50	
for each additional book)	❏ **Signature** _____
Outside US: $5.00 for first book	
& $2.00 for each additional book)	❏ **Payment Enclosed: $** _____
SUBTOTAL _____	❏ **PLEASE CHARGE TO MY CREDIT CARD:**
in Canada: add 7% GST _____	❏ Visa ❏ MasterCard ❏ AmEx ❏ Discover
	❏ Diner's Club ❏ Eurocard ❏ JCB
STATE TAX _____	**Account #**_____
(NY, OH, & MIN residents please	
add appropriate local sales tax	**Exp Date** _____
FINAL TOTAL _____	
(if paying in Canadian funds, convert	**Signature**_____
using the current exchange rate,	_(Prices in US dollars and subject to_
UNESCO coupons welcome)	_change without notice.)_

PLEASE PRINT ALL INFORMATION OR ATTACH YOUR BUSINESS CARD
Name
Address
City   State/Province   Zip/Postal Code
Country
Tel   Fax
E-Mail

May we use your e-mail address for confirmations and other types of information? ❏Yes❏ No
We appreciate receiving your e-mail address. Haworth would like to e-mail special discount
offers to you, as a preferred customer. **We will never share, rent, or exchange your e-mail
address.** We regard such actions as an invasion of your privacy.

Order From Your Local Bookstore or Directly From
The Haworth Press, Inc.
10 Alice Street, Binghamton, New York 13904-1580 • USA
Call Our toll-free number (1-800-429-6784) / Outside US/Canada: (607) 722-5857
Fax: 1-800-895-0582 / Outside US/Canada: (607) 771-0012
E-Mail your order to us: Orders@haworthpress.com

Please Photocopy this form for your personal use.
www.HaworthPress.com

BOF03

DATE DUE

NOV 2 6 2005

SEP 1 2 2007

APR 2 8 2008

OCT 2 4 2010

GAYLORD   PRINTED IN U.S.A.